Michael Stephenson
John Weal

Nuclear
Dictionary

Longman

Longman Group Limited,
Longman House, Burnt Mill, Harlow,
Essex CM20 2JE, England
and Associated Companies thoughout the world.

First published 1985

British Library Cataloguing in Publication Data

Stephenson, Michael
  The nuclear dictionary.
  1. Atomic power
  I. Title   II. Weal, John
  621.48   TK9145

ISBN 0-582-89212-0

Set in 8½/9½pt AM Plantin with Megaron Bold
Printed in Great Britain by Butler & Tanner Ltd.,
London & Frome

Introduction

The *Nuclear Dictionary* has been written for those who feel bombarded, and perhaps defeated, by the mass of information available on the 'nuclear debate'. Drawing data from a wide variety of sources, we have attempted to organize it in an accessible way, and explain it with as little jargon as possible. The basic alphabetical sequence has been reinforced with appropriate cross-references (denoted either by terms in small capitals within each entry, or at the end of entries). Further reading is listed in the bibliography at the end of the book.

In an area that is changing daily, even hourly, we recognize the inevitable impermanence of 'facts'; and in a subject so riven with special pleading, the difficulty of establishing objective opinion. However, we have striven to ensure that the information in this book is as accurate as possible at the time of going to press. Any errors are, of course, ours alone, but without the considerable assistance of Malcolm Dando, Senior Lecturer, and Andrew Kelly, Research Assistant, both of the School of Peace Studies at Bradford University; William Hendry; Owen Greene of the Open University; David Guinness, Hilary Embling and the staff of CND's Information Room, this book would have been much the poorer.

Personal thanks are also due to Denise Riley, for her unfailing encouragement, and to Sarah for her understanding during the hectic months the book was being written.

Accidents Measures Agreement, 1971 The 'Agreement on Measures to Reduce the Risk of Outbreak of Nuclear War between the United States of America and the Union of the Soviet Socialist Republics' has three main elements:

1 Each side pledged to maintain and improve their safeguards against the accidental or unauthorized use of nuclear weapons.

2 Each party agreed to notify the other immediately in the case of an accident involving the possible detonation of a nuclear weapon.

3 Each party agreed to supply advance information on any planned missile launch that could be interpreted as threatening by the other party.

The agreement also stated that 'in situations requiring prompt clarification', the 'Hot Line' link (see the 'HOT LINE' AGREEMENT) would be used.

The agreement was the first official recognition of the inherent danger with nuclear-weapons systems – that, despite the complex command-and-control procedures, a nuclear war could be triggered by technical malfunction or human error.

accuracy
see CIRCULAR ERROR PROBABLE, MISSILE ACCURACY

Acheson-Lilienthal Plan
see OPPENHEIMER, J ROBERT

advanced cruise missile
see ADVANCED CRUISE MISSILE PROGRAM

advanced cruise missile program The program began in 1977 as the response of the US Department of Defense to a perceived weakness in existing cruise missiles. It set out to investigate:

1 Modifications to existing cruise missiles.

2 An Advanced Cruise.

3 An Intercontinental-Range Cruise.

4 A new bomber-launched weapon to replace existing short-range attack missiles.

The work on an Advanced Cruise is intended to increase range to approximately 4,800 km, increase survivability through stealth features, increase mission-planning flexibility, improve the altimeter, reduce the radar cross-section, upgrade the guidance software, add icing sensors, reduce fuel consumption and achieve higher performance through a new engine design, reduce the radar signature and improve mobility through improvements to airframe design. By 1986 approximately 2,000 advanced air-launched cruise missiles will have been procured to replace the existing Boeing ALCM (AGM-86B) but whether the new Advanced Cruise technology will be applied to existing ground- and sea-launched cruise is not clear.

In 1982 the Vought Corporation received a research grant for work on an intercontinental-range cruise. A 'regenerative' engine would re-cycle some of the exhaust emission and, in combination with high-energy jellied fuels, would achieve ranges between 6,000 and 8,000 km.

advanced gas-cooled reactor (AGR) The type of nuclear reactor chosen by the British Central Electricity Generating Board (CEGB) as a second-generation follow-up to the Magnox Reactor. Heat extraction is by carbon dioxide gas under pressure (40 atmospheres, 634°C), giving an efficiency of 41.6 per cent. The fuel is uranium dioxide pellets 2 per cent enriched and clad in thin stainless steel.

Though theoretically more efficient than the Magnox, in practice, problems have been encountered in construction. Not a single AGR has been exported and the ones that have been built have been out of commission for long periods. Unquestionably the CEGB's decision to go for AGRs instead of light-water reactors or the Canadian heavy-water design was an expensive mistake, made under pressure from the Atomic Energy Authority. In 1973 British nuclear reactors actually generated less electricity than in 1968.

advanced inertial reference sphere
see MISSILE ACCURACY

advanced strategic air-launched missile (ASALM)
The objective of this program – sometimes referred to as the Lethal Neutralization Program, ie designed to knock out Soviet defences (AWACS) – is to equip US bombers with supersonic air-to-ground and air-to-air cruise missiles in place of short-range attack missiles (SRAMs – air-to-surface weapons). ASALMs will be more accurate and faster, with high-speed manoeuvring and, critically, terminal high-speed penetration of air defences than either the SRAMs or the air-launched cruise missile (ALCMs).

It was originally planned to have 1,200 ASALMs deployed by 1983. It is a one-stage missile, with an integral rocket-ramjet engine delivering a W80 200 kt warhead.
Specifications
Range: 320+ km
Speed: Mach 4
Accuracy: CEP 100 m
Yield: 1×200 kt
see also CRUISE MISSILE, ADVANCED CRUISE MISSILE PROGRAM

Advanced Technology Bomber (ATB, 'Stealth')
In August 1980 the US Department of Defense announced its intention to develop a bomber with a radically reduced radar and infra-red

detectability. The US Air Force plans to deploy 100–150 ATBs by the early 1990s to replace the B1-B and remaining B-52 bombers.

The ATB will achieve its stealth characteristics by reducing the aircraft's weight and the size of its tail, modifying shapes and angles to streamline its profile, adding non-metallic and radar-absorbing materials, reducing exhaust temperatures and modifying fuels to reduce infra-red emissions.

Northrop Corporation and General Electric are the main contractors, and the cost of 100–150 ATBs is estimated at $22–40 million.

Aegis ship-to-air missile

A US air defence system based on the Standard-2 (SM2) surface-to-air and surface-to-surface missiles. It is mounted on US Navy CG-16 and CG-28 class cruisers and CGN and DDG-37 class destroyers. Its function is to defend ships against enemy aircraft, cruise missiles and surface ships. The cost of the defence system to date is somewhere in the region of $1.5 billion.

Specifications
Range: 104 km
Speed: Mach 2–5
Yield: $1 \times$ W81 'low kt' nuclear warhead or can be conventionally armed
CEP: na

Airborne Warning and Control (AWACS)

see NORTH AMERICAN AEROSPACE DEFENSE COMMAND

air burst

The effects of nuclear explosion – in terms of blast, heat and radiation – vary not only with the size of the weapon, the weather conditions and the geography of the target, but also – and most importantly – with the height at which the explosion occurs. Nuclear devices can be set to explode either at ground level (see GROUND BURST) or at any height above it, up to tens of thousands of feet. In air-burst explosions the fireball does not touch the ground and the blast, heat and initial radiation are spread over a wide area. As the explosion occurs well clear of the ground, little solid matter is sucked up from the surface to become fallout, compared with a ground-burst explosion, though the debris of the weapon itself could cause a significant fallout threat. Air-burst explosions would be particularly effective if used against cities and large industrial installations where the aim would be to create the maximum damage over the widest area.

Immediate effects of a 150 kt air-burst explosion:

Ground zero to 1 mile
dead: 98%; injured: 2%
● *Blast:* all buildings destroyed except reinforced structures and they would be severely damaged; 420 mph winds would batter people to

death, so anyone caught in the open would probably die; most people inside buildings would die as the buildings collapsed on them

● *Heat:* all combustible matter would ignite and flesh would melt; strong likelihood of a firestorm which, by consuming all oxygen locally, would kill by suffocation even those people who were in blast-proof shelters

● *Radiation:* lethal but academic, as blast, heat or fire would almost certainly kill first

1 mile to 2 miles from ground zero
dead: 50%; injured: 40%

● *Blast:* 190 mph winds would toss people like feathers – most people caught in the open would immediately be killed or fatally injured; domestic buildings destroyed, almost all buildings severely damaged, all windows blown out; many people would die crushed under buildings, many more would be torn to pieces by flying glass

● *Heat:* anyone caught in the open would be charred beyond repair; numerous random fires might link up with the central firestorm if one occurred

● *Radiation:* anyone not in a shelter and not killed by other means could expect to receive a very serious initial dose; perhaps 50% of those so affected could recover, though without proper treatment secondary infections might account for a greater percentage loss

2 miles to 5 miles from ground zero
dead: 15%; injured: 40%

● *Blast:* huge damage to buildings nearer the 2-mile radius; even at 5 miles roof tiles and chimney pots would be blown off and trees uprooted; all windows blown out, with danger from flying glass; winds at the outer perimeter still gale force

● *Heat:* up to 3–3½ miles skin would be charred; at about 5 miles the effect would be like instant, severe sunburn; occasional fires to about 4 miles from ground zero

● *Radiation:* near the inner perimeter some people would receive a high initial dose and might die of complications in the course of a few months for want of proper medical attention; everyone exposed within the outer perimeter could expect to suffer radiation sickness but, barring secondary infections, should survive

5 miles to 10 miles from ground zero
injured: 25%

● *Blast:* all windows blown out up to about 7 miles, so many injuries from flying glass; other incidental damage causing danger to life; trivial blast damage at 10 miles where winds would be down to about 35 mph

● *Heat:* whereas past 5 miles exposed skin would be reddened as with sunburn, at 10 miles only a hot wind would be felt; the incidence of fires should be minimal

● *Radiation:* varying from survivable radiation sickness at the inner edge of the band to nothing more than light discomfort towards the 10 mile radius

Air Force Satellite Communications System
see COMMAND, CONTROL, COMMUNICATIONS AND INTELLIGENCE

airland battle
see DEEP STRIKE

air-launched cruise missile (ALCM)
The subsonic air-to-ground cruise missile represents one of the main areas of US nuclear expansion. The future of strategic bombers – B-52s and the B-1B – is seen in terms of flying launch-pads for ALCMs. Of the 1,499 ALCMs planned, 200–350 are presently deployed (the information varies depending on the source). Originally, 4,348 had been ordered, but advances in Soviet defences against low-flying cruise lead to the abbreviation of the ALCM programme in favour of the development of the advanced strategic air-launched missile (ASALM).

In structure, performance and lethality, ALCMs are very similar to ground-launched and sea-launched cruise missiles.

The B-52G has 12 ALCMs externally mounted on wing pylons, the B-52H has 12 externally and eight in an internal bomb bay, and the B-1B bomber, when operational, will carry up to 22 ALCMs.

Specifications
Range: 2,500 km
Speed: 550 mph
Accuracy: CEP 30 m
Yield : 1×200 kt
Number planned: 1,499
Number deployed: 200–350
For Soviet ALCMs, see AS-2 KIPPER, AS-3 KANGAROO, AS-4 KITCHEN, AS-6 KINGFISH

all-up round (AUR)
On each ground-launched cruise missile transporter there will be four all-up rounds, consisting of the missile, the canister from which it is fired and its booster.
see also TRANSPORTER-ERECTOR-LAUNCHER, GROUND-LAUNCHED CRUISE MISSILE

Alternate National Military Command Center (US)
see COMMAND, CONTROL, COMMUNICATIONS AND INTELLIGENCE

Antarctic Treaty, 1959
This was the first of the post World War II arms limitations agreements. It not only banned nuclear weapons from the Antarctic continent, but also demilitarized the entire area, stating that the Antarctic should be used for peaceful purposes only. It also set up guidelines for co-operative exploration.

Seen as the first true example of international co-operation and restraint over arms limitation, the treaty served as a model for 'nonarmament' treaties, such as those banning nuclear weapons from outer space (Outer Space Treaty, 1967), from Latin America (Treaty of Tlatelolco, 1967) and from the seabed (Seabed Treaty, 1971). No such restrictions have been agreed for the Arctic.

Anti-Ballistic Missile (ABM) Treaty, 1972
Signed by President Nixon and General Secretary Brezhnev on 26 May 1972, the treaty restricts both sides to only two anti-ballistic missile areas each (one to protect the capital, the other to protect an ICBM site), so restricted and located that they do not have the capacity to provide a nationwide ABM defence system. At each site, there are to be no more than 100 interceptor missiles and 100 launchers. Complex technical provisions govern the nature of the permitted radar cover.

The Treaty also prohibits the development of surface-to-air missiles (SAMs) which, if improved, might be capable of intercepting ICBMs and SLBMs. While further deployment of radars intended to warn of an ICBM attack are not prohibited, they must be located only along the territorial boundaries of each country and outward facing, so as to proscribe a role as internal ABM defence. Both sides also agreed to prohibit the testing or deployment of mobile land-based, sea-, air-, or space-based ABM systems.

The treaty is reviewed every five years and is renewable. Article XV of the Treaty states that the treaty shall be of 'limited duration'.

In the event, the USA abandoned attempts to establish a land-based ABM system under the terms of the Treaty, while the USSR developed, and continues to up-grade, the GALOSH complex around Moscow.

see STAR WARS

anti-ballistic missiles (ABMs)
SALT I attempted to limit the superpowers' ability to neutralize an ICBM attack, on the grounds that an efficient ABM system would give one power a war-fighting ascendancy. With the dismantling of the nuclear NIKE-HERCULES air-to-air system, the USA has only one ABM network – the GENIE air-to-air missile – presently deployed for the defence of the US homeland.

The US Army is carrying out research into ABMs, but the development of a system capable of defending the mobile basing currently envisaged for future US ICBMs would necessitate the revision of SALT I agreements. As Secretary of Defense, Caspar Weinberger, said in evidence to the US House Armed Services Committee on 6 October 1981: 'If we find at the conclusion of the study that there is a far more effective system that would require revision of the treaty, I think it's fair to say we wouldn't hesitate to seek those revisions.' In 1981, President Reagan put it another way: 'No nation that placed its faith in parchment or paper while at the same time it gave up its protective hardware ever lasted long enough to write many pages in history ... The argument, if there is any, will be over which weapons, and not whether we should forsake weaponry for treaties and agreements.'

Under the terms of SALT I, the USSR and the USA were allowed one fixed ABM system. The USSR retained the GALOSH network around Moscow. There are eight sites, armed with ABM-IB ground-to-air missiles with a nuclear yield in the megaton range, 32 in all (according to *Military Balance, 1983/84*). A new Soviet ABM is currently being deployed.

anti-submarine rocket
see SUBROC

arms control and arms limitation
Arms limitation and control should not be confused with DISARMAMENT. Since 1945 only the Biological Warfare Convention (1972) has destroyed existing weapons – and even this treaty looks less and less likely to hold (and has been broken in 'local' wars such as Indochina, the Gulf war, and possibly Afghanistan). The achievements of the talks and treaties have been more modest:

1   To remove certain geographical areas from the nuclear arms race: ANTARCTIC TREATY (1959); Latin America through the TREATY OF TLATELOLCO (1967), which was not ratified by Argentina.

2   To exclude nuclear weapons from being sited on the seabed (1971) or outer space (1967), including the moon. Submarines were of course not included in the former treaty which, curiously, was not signed by France or China. In fact, the USA is researching into 'pop-up' missiles which would be stationed on the sea-bed. As for outer space, the USA did explode a nuclear device there in 1962 and discovered that many satellites were severely damaged by the electromagnetic pulse effect. So the treaty only codified what no state is likely to do. Laser beams, etc, were included in the treaty but in a loose way: high-energy beams for stationing in space may be developed but not deployed.

3   To prohibit atmospheric nuclear tests or tests with a yield of more than 150 kt. The Partial Test Ban Treaty (1963) was a significant gain ecologically (see RADIATION). However, more tests have been conducted underground since its signature than took place in the atmosphere before it was signed. China and France refused to sign it, not least because it was partially aimed at their programmes: they still needed to conduct atmospheric tests while the USA and USSR did not. Similarly with the Threshold Test Ban Treaty (1974) limiting kiloton yields, the US, Soviet and British programmes no longer required tests of such magnitude so were unaffected – not so the Indian, Chinese or French programmes.

4   To obtain the signatures of over 100 states to the Non-Proliferation

Treaty (1968). Although symbolically important, it was not signed by precisely those states with nuclear weapons research programmes nearing completion (eg South Africa, Israel, India, Pakistan, Argentina, amongst others). It also permitted nuclear weapons still 'owned' by an existing nuclear power to be sited within countries that were not nuclear-armed and who may have signed the Non-Proliferation Treaty. It permitted 'peaceful nuclear applications' to be carried on by signatories. Lastly, the continued adherence of non-nuclear states to the terms of the treaty was (and is still) conditional on the nuclear powers reaching agreement on the cessation of the nuclear arms race 'at an early date'.

Given the importance of the 'German question' in previous arms negotiations, and Soviet fear of a West Germany armed with independent nuclear weapons, this treaty can usefully be seen as the resolution of the 'German question' at the nuclear level (see PROLIFERATION).

Chronology
1 *1945–49: US monopoly*
The March 1946 Acheson-Lilienthal Report proposed giving US nuclear technology to an international authority. The Baruch Plan (June 1946) specified that agreement on sanctions would be a precondition for joining (nullifying the USSR's veto power in the UN Security Council). Control thus preceded prohibition, as would be expected in a proposal coming from a nation in sole possession of the bomb. The USSR rejected this and countered with a proposal to destroy all weapons in existence and to cease all production. Prohibition here precedes control, as could be expected from a nation with nuclear inferiority, a bureaucratic obsession with secrecy and a not unjustified fear of espionage.

This deadly game of pat-ball characterized most future arms talks. The US did not want to part with its monopoly until it had restructured the post-war world order. The USSR feared that it would not be safe until it, too, had nuclear arms. Thus did national egotism and mistrust foreclose on the greatest opportunity for nuclear disarmament, with results on the world economy and world arms levels that no one could then conceive.

2 *1949–54: Primitive arms race and Cold War*
In 1949 the USSR exploded an A-bomb. In 1950 the USA decided to develop the H-bomb. The arms race was under way in the context of the Korean War. There were no arms limitation talks.

3 *1954–57: a second chance*
Various plans emanating from Britain, France, the USA and USSR juggled with banning/reducing the number of atomic weapons, troop withdrawals in Europe, a denuclearized zone in both parts of Germany (Soviet and Polish proposal), a nuclear test ban, and, of course, verification and inspection. The two sides moved closer until the

Stassen Memorandum (May 1957) was torpedoed by a wing of the Eisenhower Administration and the USA's European allies. The talks dried up for six years.

4 *1963–68: the years of second best*

These were the years of the 1963 Hot Line Agreement, the Outer Space Treaty, Tlatelolco and the Non-Proliferation Treaty. The Partial Test Ban Treaty was an extension of this period. Discussion on the key arsenals virtually dried up. Thus in 1964 the USSR proposed the elimination of all long-range nuclear bombers. The US had marked superiority here so the Johnson Administration would not talk. Instead, it proposed a 'verified freeze' on strategic missiles. As the USSR had only a quarter of US missile strength the Politbureau rejected this, characterizing it 'control without disarmament'. Thus were the opportunities lost on both sides.

5 *1968–79: the bitter years of SALT*

see STRATEGIC ARMS LIMITATION TALKS

6 *1979–?: the new Cold War*

While the main talks have centred around intermediate-range nuclear forces (INF) and Strategic Arms Reduction Talks (START) the period has seen a two-fold process: the development of one missile system after another and the simultaneous attempt to blame their development on the supposed strength and intentions of 'the other side' in an ideological war to hegemonize public opinion 'at home'. Currently START is at a stop while the INF talks have been abandoned.

Meanwhile the Mutual and Balanced Force Reductions (MBFR) talks, which, since 1973, have been a forum for the two sides to agree tank, troop and tactical nuclear warhead reductions in Europe, have not progressed. The only significant reduction was a unilateral gesture by the Warsaw Treaty Organization (WTO) which pulled out 20,000 Soviet troops and 1,000 tanks from East Germany in 1980.

Arms limitation talks tend to be a distillation of the current state and direction of the arms race. Agreements are either about matters that pose no problems to either side because they never contemplated them anyway, or about matters that are not technically achievable at the time of signing, or which have become unnecessary to the development of the superpowers' own programmes. Talks are often a public relations exercise to convince populations and other states that 'efforts are being made'. Sufficient time is allowed for both sides to develop fully the armaments likely to be limited by a treaty before it is signed, while huge loopholes are left in the treaty itself for the development of newer and more dangerous weapons after its signature. In this sense, arms talks serve as a spur to the arms race they are meant to control and reverse. Secondary questions, such as verification, can always be wheeled out if talks look like achieving something. (The COMPRE-HENSIVE NUCLEAR TEST BAN TREATY of 1963 foundered because the US and UK demanded seven on-site checks each year while the

USSR agreed to only three. In point of fact verification by satellite and seismograph was arguably even then accurate enough for the treaty to be policed with very little on-site inspection at all.) Lastly, the very nature of treaties dealing in arms limitation instead of the actual destruction of particular categories of weapon breeds both suspicion and the danger that the treaty will be breached on the assumption that the other side is doing the same.

Arms Control and Disarmament Agency (ACDA) Set

up by the USA in 1961, the Agency's aims were:

1 'The conduct, support and co-ordination of research for arms control and disarmament policy formulation.'

2 'The preparations for and management of US participation in international negotiations in the arms and disarmament field.'

3 'The dissemination and co-ordination of public information concerning arms control and disarmament.'

4 'The preparation for, operation of, or, as appropriate, direction of US participation in such control systems as may become part of US arms control and disarmament activities.'

Two years of the Reagan Administration produced the following assessment of the ACDA from B. M. Blechman and J. E. Nolan in 'Reorganising for more Effective Negotiations', *Foreign Affairs,* summer 1983:

> 'after cuts of nearly one-fourth in the agency's staff and one-half in its research budget, the firing of Eugene Rostow ... delays of two years or more in appointments to most of its executive positions, and the present director's inauspicious beginning, there is little question that the ACDA is in no position to fulfil its responsibilities effectively.'

The Agency's Research Council has been abolished, as also the Operations Analysis Division. Its library, the largest arms-control library in the USA, which had been in existence for over 21 years, has been transferred to the special books section of George Washington University, and the Agency is reduced to using the computer facilities of the US Railway Association.

artillery fired atomic projectile see ARTILLERY, NUCLEAR

artillery, nuclear Cannon and self-propelled guns make up the

largest category of nuclear weapons. Although the USSR's total of nuclear artillery is not known, the USA and NATO combined have 2,327 pieces firing shells in the 1–2 kt range (*Military Balance,* 1983–84.) Other sources state that the US Army alone has 'over 3,500 nuclear-capable artillery guns deployed,' for which there are 5,000 nuclear shells (*Nuclear Weapons Databook,* Vol. 1, 1984).

The newest guns have a range of about 30 km and the shells (AFAP, artillery fired atomic projectiles) are also becoming more sophisticated, incorporating electronic programmers and memories, target sensors and rocket motors. Shells are also of the 'neutron' or enhanced radiation type. A long-range cannon artillery with a range of 80 km is being developed by the US Nuclear Defense Agency for deployment in the mid-1980s.

AS-2 Kipper cruise missile
Code-named Kipper by NATO, this is a Soviet short-range (about 200 km) air-launched cruise missile. The missile flies to its target area controlled by a programmed autopilot, to which there are command override options. It is probably deployed on TU-16 Badger-C bomber aircraft, and carries a nuclear warhead in the 1 kt range. It is seen principally as an anti-shipping missile. About 90 are currently in service.

AS-3 Kangaroo cruise missile
This is the largest of the Soviet air-launched cruise missiles. It has a range of approximately 650 km, and carries a nuclear warhead of about 800 kt at speeds of Mach 2. It is deployed on TU-95 Bear bombers. Its main role is as a medium- to long-range stand-off strategic missile for use against area targets – a country's principal ports or major cities, for example.

AS-4 Kitchen cruise missile
This is one of the most advanced of the Soviet air-launched cruise missiles. Estimates of its range vary from 300–800 km, and it is probably equipped with INERTIAL GUIDANCE plus active radar homing for terminal guidance to the target. There appear to be two versions in service, one for strategic use and one for naval operations. The strategic missile has a nuclear warhead of approximately 200 kt. The naval missile is equipped with a conventional high explosive payload for anti-ship or tactical targets.

The AS-4 is thought to arm the TU-95 Bear and the TU-26 Backfire B aircraft, and about 600 are currently deployed.

AS-5 Kelt
Carried on the TU-16 Badger aircraft, this is the most widely deployed of the Soviet air-launched missiles – about 1,000 have been produced. Estimates of their range vary from 160 km to 320 km. Liquid fuelled, they are equipped with INERTIAL GUIDANCE and active radar homing for the terminal phase. They are in service with the Soviet Naval Air Force as an anti-ship weapon and for other tactical roles.

AS-6 Kingfish cruise missile
Code-named Kingfish by NATO, this high performance air-launched cruise missile is in service with the Soviet Naval Air Force, deployed on their TU-16 Badger aircraft. The missile has a range of about 200 km, and travels at speeds of up to Mach 3. It carries either one nuclear warhead of 350 kt yield, or a conventional warhead. It is estimated that about 850 are now in service.

AS-7 Kerry Little is known about this new Soviet air-to-surface missile. It is probably deployed on the SU-24 Fencer variable geometry fighter-bombers and is believed to have a range of about 10 km.

ASMP missile Similar to a SHORT-RANGE ATTACK MISSILE (SRAM), the French air-launched jet-powered ASMP (Air Sol à Moyenne Portée) has a range of 100 km and carries a 150 kt warhead. By the late 1980s, 100 will be deployed on Mirage IVA, Mirage 2000N and Super Etendard aircraft.

ASROC An American anti-submarine rocket launched from surface ships, as opposed to the submarine-launched SUBROCs. Whereas SUBROC is nuclear only, ASROC has a dual capability. A new vertical launch system (VLA) is being developed which, apart from increasing the reaction time, will increase the range of ASROC and thus enable launch ships to attack and destroy enemy submarines while remaining out of range of enemy torpedoes. The VLA system should be fully operational by 1987.

At present there are approximately 850 1 kt ASROC warheads deployed on 170 US ships.

assured destruction component The warheads, delivery systems and accompanying computer-based guidance and control systems that give a state the capacity to respond to a surprise attack and to inflict an 'unacceptable' degree of damage upon an aggressor's society and military structure. Until recent improvements in anti-submarine warfare, submarines were regarded as the key assured destruction components of a strategic triad because they were virtually undetectable.
see MUTUAL ASSURED DESTRUCTION

atomic bomb

Definition

An atomic bomb achieves its vastly increased blast over any conventional bomb by the fission process. Certain substances are unstable in that nuclear binding forces cannot easily hold together the neutrons and protons which make up their atomic structure. They emit radiation splitting into two – fission – as they decay. This is either a natural process or induced if the substance is bombarded with a neutron. Uranium, one such substance, occurs naturally in two forms: U-238 (ie 92 protons plus 146 neutrons), which can absorb low energy neutrons, and U-235 (92 protons plus 143 neutrons), which is far less stable. The latter makes up only 0.7 per cent of mined uranium but U-238 can be enriched to make U-235. About 15 kg of U-235 is required for a self-sustaining chain reaction to take place whereby a split atom gives off two or three neutrons, which in turn bombard other atoms nearby which split and send out yet more neutrons, and so on. This process takes only a fraction of a second to affect all the fissionable material and it generates an enormous amount of heat and light.

In an atom bomb two lumps of uranium are kept apart and brought together only to produce the explosion. Besides heat and light, an atomic explosion produces an air pressure wave. It also emits alpha, beta and gamma rays, X-rays, stray neutrons which failed to impact with uranium atoms, and fission byproducts such as strontium-90 and cresium-137.

This kind of bomb, made up of at least 70 per cent U-235, was used at Hiroshima. The bomb, 'Little Boy', produced a blast yield equivalent to about 20,000 tons (20 kilotons) of TNT. The bombs which exploded at Alamogordo and Nagasaki used plutonium-239.

History

The inter-war pioneering theoretical work in nuclear physics was openly published and read by the physics community all over the world. Once World War II began, the fear among physicists was that Hitler's Germany could and would develop an atomic bomb. On the instigation of Leo Szilard, Albert Einstein wrote to the US President, Franklin Roosevelt, on 2 August 1939, 'I think that it is my duty to bring to your attention ... that extremely powerful bombs of a new type ... may be constructed.' He wrote a second letter about the same time as the US administration was handed a Memorandum drafted by Otto Frisch and Rudolf Peierls which had been shown to a British government committee. In it they noted, 'We have ... come to the conclusion that a moderate amount of uranium 235 would indeed constitute an extremely efficient explosive.'

On 6 December 1941 the US administration decided to construct an atomic bomb and the MANHATTAN PROJECT was mounted. Four years of feverish work by leading US and foreign physicists and engineers bore fruit at the first A-bomb test, on 16 July 1945, at Alamogordo. 'Thirty seconds after the explosion came ... the air blast ... followed ... by the strong, sustained, awesome roar which warned of doomsday and made us feel that we puny things were blasphemous to dare tamper with the forces heretofore reserved for the Almighty.'

When it was clear that Germany did not possess such a weapon, Szilard had again written to the President, this time warning of the dangers it posed to the world. Many physicists signed a petition opposing the use of the bomb on Japan (which had no uranium) without demonstrating it beforehand and giving them a chance to surrender. The suggestion was rejected, first because the test might not have worked; but more importantly because 9 August was the deadline for an agreement made by the USSR to its allies for it to declare war on Japan. The USA and Britain wanted above all to obtain

Japanese surrender before the USSR had any chance of occupying Japan. As P M S Blackett, the Nobel Prizewinner for Physics, noted, 'The dropping of the atomic bomb was not so much the last military act of the Second World War as the first act of the cold diplomatic war with Russia.' Eisenhower declared more tersely, 'It wasn't necessary to hit them with that awful thing.'

Just five years earlier, in 1940, the moral climate in America had been such that Frisch and Peierls could write in their Memorandum, 'Owing to the spread of radioactive substances with the wind, the bomb could probably not be used without killing large numbers of civilians, and this may make it unsuitable as a weapon for use by this country.' After Little Boy fell on Hiroshima, Robert J Oppenheimer said, 'the physicists have known sin and this is a knowledge they cannot lose.'

The very first resolution of the General Assembly of the newly founded United Nations set up the Atomic Energy Commission, the express purpose of which was 'the elimination from national armaments of atomic weapons'.

atomic demolition munitions (ADM) The name given to a nuclear mine that can be exploded either underground or underwater. The US Army and the Marine Corps have two types deployed: Medium ADM in the 1–15 kt range (there are approximately 300 of these in service), and the low-yield Special ADM (SADM) which can be carried in a soldier's pack (again, about 300 of these are in use).

Atomic Energy Act, 1946 The Act, passed 1 August 1946, was promoted by US Senator Brian McMahon as an alternative to a bill formulated by the US Army. The Army's bill had proposed a commission – to safeguard and direct the US atomic energy programme – to be composed of five civilians and four serving officers. The army bill had created an outcry over fears of military interference with research, and restrictions in the name of security.

Although the new Act secured civilian control via a commission composed of cabinet officers and federal officials, it was no less draconian from a security point of view. Its task was 'to conserve and restrict the use of atomic energy for the national defense, to prohibit its private exploitation and to preserve the secret and confidential character of information concerning the use and application of atomic energy'. Its 'restricted data' covered all information about the manufacture and use of atomic weapons, with harsh penalties, up to and including the death sentence, for transgressors.

In addition, it stated, 'Until effective and enforceable international safeguards against the use of atomic energy for destructive purposes have been established, there shall be no exchange with other nations with respect to the use of atomic energy for industrial purposes.' This clause embraced not just the USSR, but also America's wartime allies, Britain and Canada.

Atomic Energy Commissions (AECs)

The first atomic energy commissions were set up in states which either had or were developing military atomic capability: USA, UK and the USSR. They were quickly joined by France, Canada and India.

From the start their aim was the prospect of limitless cheap electricity – the use of the atom for peaceful purposes. This prospect (aided and abetted by Eisenhower's ATOMS FOR PEACE programme), together with the desire of many scientists to keep abreast of the most up-to-date developments in nuclear physics, and the more secret desire of certain states to develop military nuclear capacity, produced in the 1950s a burgeoning of AECs across the world: Germany, Japan, Belgium, Italy, Spain, Brazil, Argentina, the Philippines. Here, it was felt, was the source of energy that would permit developing nations, poor in natural energy sources, to make the leap to modernity.

There was also the prospect of money to be made through the sale of atomic power stations. The height of this optimism came in a 1974 report of the International Atomic Energy Agency (IAEA); this projected a potential demand in the developing countries alone of 140 plants of between 500 and 600 megawatts. Too often no effective cost-conscious comparisons were made with traditional energy sources, while the national electrical grids of most of these countries were too small to cope with such large single power units and their request for smaller plants was not met by the big exporting companies.

In the USA, the AEC had poured money into no less than 30 reactor systems of which only two, Westinghouse's PRESSURIZED WATER REACTOR and General Electric's BOILING WATER REACTOR, were commercially viable. To sell even these it was necessary sometimes to resort to massive bribery (as in the Philippines, South Korea, Argentina). In the case of the Philippines, the Westinghouse reactor, which had never been subjected to independent regulatory review, was to be sited close to several volcanoes and was an economic nonsense; finally it was cancelled.

Lastly, although one aspect of the work of the IAEA was to monitor the production of plutonium in the world's nuclear power stations, this did not stop India extracting enough to transfer it, quite illegally, into a bomb-making programme.

Atomic Weapons Research Establishment (AWRE)

Sited at Aldermaston, Berkshire, it is one of over 30 research and development establishments for all sections of the UK Ministry of Defence. Its main function is to design and develop nuclear warheads and to service existing warheads. It also collaborates with the USA under the 1958 Agreement on the 'Uses of Atomic Energy for Mutual

Defence Purposes'. It has two research reactors and undertakes work on beryllium technology, plutonium, chemical high explosives, the detection of atmospheric and underground nuclear tests, the effects of nuclear weapons on military targets and equipment, and radiological defence.

Atoms for Peace (AfP) President Eisenhower launched Atoms for Peace at a speech to the United Nations General Assembly on 8 December 1953. In it he called for an 'atomic pool' to 'strip the weapon of its military casing and adapt it to the arts of peace.'

AfP developed in two ways. First, as a sidestepping response to the Candor Report's suggestion that the American people be warned of the present dangers of the arms race, and be appraised of the US's own stockpile. Second, as a way of demonstrating American goodwill to other nations while scoring a propaganda victory in the Cold War. The idea was for the atomic powers to hand over some of their stockpiled fissile material to an 'atomic pool' for distribution for peaceful purposes. 'The amount', suggested Eisenhower, 'could be fixed at a figure which we could handle from our stockpile but which would be difficult for the Soviets to match.'

The Soviets did not even try; their reply was harsh and to the point: the USA had ignored the key question, the need to dismantle all stockpiled atomic bombs. The 'atomic pool' idea was dead.

However, the rest of the world, partly as a result of a vast publicity campaign orchestrated by Eisenhower's speech writer, C D Jackson, partly because of a genuine yearning for peace, was swept away with enthusiasm for 'the peaceful atom'. Many countries signed bilateral agreements, mainly with the USA, to obtain know-how and fissile material, usually for power plants. The atom was credited with almost magical powers, almost all of them spurious: 'Nuclear Device will fight Cancer' and 'Atomic Locomotive Designed' were typical headlines of the period.

However, the possible linkage between 'the peaceful atom' and 'the warlike atom' – proliferation, so carefully spelt out in the Acheson-Lilienthal Plan seven years earlier – was completely absent from the AfP initiative. There were no safeguards, only the good word of the recipient states. In the heady days of the first AfP Conference in Geneva in 1955, such problems seemed far away as scientists from 73 countries, including the USSR, swapped information around a working model atomic reactor from the USA. The optimism lasted until around 1957 and included the fanciful Project Ploughshare scheme wherein the world would benefit from controlled atomic explosions to flatten mountains, alter river flows, and so forth.

The world paid a high price, both in money and the spreading danger of proliferation, for the euphoria generated by the AfP initiative. The cynicism of the project's initiators is aptly demonstrated by the fact that at around the same time they took another decision: to defend the USA almost exclusively with nuclear bombs.

B1-B bomber

The B-52 bomber – that venerable old warhorse of the US strategic arm – will be replaced by the B1-B. The aircraft rose from the ashes of the scrapped B1 which had been cancelled by President Carter in June 1977 but revived by President Reagan in October 1981 with a decision to procure 100 B1-Bs. The first production delivery is scheduled for June 1985 and the first squadron should be operational by the following year (though the whole programme may be reviewed due to the crash in mid-1984 of one of the prototypes). The full complement should be on station by 1988. By the 1990s the B1-B will be adapted as a cruise missile launcher.

The B1-B carries a wide range of nuclear and conventional weapons. The nuclear payload will be approximately twice that of the B-52. A typical nuclear load will have 8 internally housed air-launched cruise missiles, 14 externally mounted short-range attack missiles and 16 gravity bombs.

Specifications

Range: 9,600 km (combat radius)

Speed: up to Mach 2

Number planned: 100

B-52 bomber

The B-52 Stratofortress is the USA's main long-distance strategic bomber. Although the aircraft has been in operation since June 1955, more recent models – B-52G and B-52H – have undergone radical upgrading of weapons delivery (the introduction of air-launched cruise missiles and short-range attack missiles in addition to the nuclear bomb load) and defensive systems. President Reagan, in his Strategic Program of October 1981, announced the retirement of the oldest model – B-52D – by 1983. The G and H are being adapted as air-launched cruise missile launchers by 1986.

Specifications

Range: B-52D 9,900 km

B-52G 12,000 km

B-52H 16,000 km

Speed: Mach .95

Nuclear payload: maximum load 24 weapons. Typical B-52G/H would be 4 gravity bombs and 6–8 internal SRAMs.

Number deployed: B-52D – 31

B-52G – 151

B-52H – 90

Balashika Military Defence College, USSR

Military civil defence college in the USSR. Graduates from it have been entering the 50,000-strong civil defence corps since 1969. Civil defence preparations are extensive in the Soviet Union, with perhaps 100,000 full-time civil defence staff spread out among local authorities and large workplaces.

ballistic missile A ballistic missile consists of a rocket booster, a guidance system and a payload (which may contain conventional explosive or nuclear warheads). The rocket booster operates for only 10–15 per cent of the flight time and either simply burns out or is shut off after the desired velocity and direction have been achieved, and usually falls away from the payload. The payload continues in an arched flightpath and is acted on mainly by gravity.

Although, technically, any missile which freewheels towards its target is 'ballistic', in practice the term is reserved today for rockets which leave the earth's atmosphere during a part of their flight. MIRVed and MARVed warheads are, strictly speaking, not ballistic missiles as the 'bus' carrying MIRVs or MARVed warheads can itself be manoeuvred in space to alter course after the main rocket engines have burnt out.

ballistic missile defence (BMD) As far as the USA is concerned, anti-ballistic missile systems (now known as ballistic missile defence or BMD) fall into two broad categories: *area* defence and *point* defence. The first attempts to defend a whole territory, but as this is practically impossible at present the only systems envisaged have been termed 'light area defence' against a possible attack from China, an accidental attack from the USSR, or a small attack from the same source after a pre-emptive US first strike. Point defence attempts to defend a localized position, such as a capital city or a nuclear missile site. Of the two, the former is paradoxically more aggressive in intent than the latter, which has a clearly deterrent potential.

In the 1960s both the Sentinel proposals of Robert McNamara and Nixon's Safeguard (both ballistic missile point defence systems), were attacked on grounds of cost, capability and the likelihood that the USSR would respond by MIRVing its warheads, as the USA was doing in reply to the Soviet installation of a GALOSH ABM system round Moscow. Safeguard was terminated after the signing of SALT I, which included the Anti-Ballistic Missile (ABM) Treaty. The ABM system at Grand Forks, North Dakota, was dismantled after an expenditure on it of $5.7 billion.

The terms of the ABM Treaty were very precise and, although it was renewed for a further five-year term as recently as 1981, US developments in BMD break the treaty's terms in numerous ways (denoted below by an asterisk). It is not impossible that the USA will activate the provisions for withdrawing from the Treaty, in which case all arms control negotiations will be paralysed.

The whole point of the ABM Treaty was, by restricting the USA and USSR to just two fairly localized systems each, to ensure that the peace was kept through the balance of terror, mutual assured destruction (MAD). But if it ever proves possible to intercept all Soviet bombers and missiles while the USSR cannot simultaneously defend itself against a US nuclear attack then the USA will have gained the freedom to attack with impunity. The BMD under development or in operation, when supplemented by a silo-killing strategy and anti-submarine forces, can be perceived by the USSR as moving the USA towards an invincible disarming first-strike capability.

Systems at present deployed are for warning only. They include BMEWS in Alaska, Greenland and Britain for counting MIRVs and computing their likely targets, Pave Paws for warning against submarine-launched missiles, and early-warning satellites.

The following systems are being developed:

1 High Altitude Large Optics (HALO includes Teal Ruby, a passive sensor which will employ a mosaic of 250,000 individual sensors with integral processing capability). HALO will be a huge space platform carried up by, and assembled from, the space shuttle; a gigantic, multi-mission surveillance post.

2 The Advanced Sensor Demonstration, a smaller version of HALO put on to a satellite in geosynchronous orbit.

3 Layered defence for shooting down missiles. The first layer is above 300,000 feet and the programme is designated Homing Overlay Experiment. It is proposed that 96 per cent of incoming missiles will be detected by space-based mosaic infra-red sensors and then destroyed by non-nuclear interceptor missiles (HIT – Homing Interceptor Technology). This is a form of light area defence. The second layer is below 50,000 feet. Incoming missiles would be detected by ground radar and destroyed by a gun-launched hypervelocity interceptor employing a small nuclear bomb. The main problem is to get the interceptor launched a mere 10 seconds after initial detection. This system is called Low Altitude Defense System (LoADS).

4 There are plans to destroy enemy missiles soon after they have been launched either from the air or from forward bases close to the USSR including possible sea-bed systems.

5 There is a variety of directed-energy weapons being developed (see STAR WARS). The most well-known is the high-energy laser (the 'killer' laser). But also under development is an X-ray laser, made up of subatomic particles (which could detonate a warhead in flight) and a highly accurate neutron particle beam. All of these could function from space, the special properties of which would enhance the accuracy of the beam.

'bargaining chips'
see MULTILATERALISM

'Baroque Arsenal' A description of the highly complex aircraft, naval vessels and missiles which make up modern weapons systems, where each generation has become more overloaded with 'improvements' than its predecessor – a process known as 'technological creep'.

Mary Kaldor, the author of *The Baroque Arsenal,* argues that the principal reason weapons are as they are is a combination of military conservatism and the entrenched interests of weapons manufacturers to sell as much as they can of the traditional products they are already tooled-up to produce. This explains the 'ornate' quality of later generations of a product: the same old model but encrusted with sophisticated accoutrements. Most of these weapons have never been tested in battle.

Cheaper, more technologically advanced weapons, which are also easier to handle, would not be dependant on the very expensive platforms (planes, ships, tanks, etc) which are the mainstay of the principal producers; they would also undermine the traditional hierarchies of the military commands.

battlefield nuclear weapons Sometimes also known as tactical weapons, this category of lower-yield devices forms the bottom stratum of the nuclear pyramid. (High-yield intercontinental missiles and bombers form the top, or strategic, level; missiles such as ground-launched cruise and Pershing II missiles form the theatre or intermediate level.)

Apart from nuclear-capable strike aircraft, the battlefield armament is comprised of nuclear artillery, short-range air-launched missiles, short-range ballistic missiles and mines. Nuclear shells are in the 1–2 kt range (although the USA is developing a 4–5 kt version). Short-range air-launched missiles (SRAM) are in the 200 kt range (ie over ten times more powerful than the bomb dropped on Hiroshima).

Short-range ballistic missiles (SRBMs) range from 1–10 kt, although the USSR's FROG is reported to have a 200 kt yield. Nuclear mines can be as powerful as 15 kt or in the sub-kt range and small enough to be carried in a soldier's back-pack.

The present balance of tactical nuclear weapons (excluding aircraft) is:

	USA	+	NATO	USSR	+	Warsaw Pact
SRBM	144		224	2,022		335
SLCM	44		—	1,046		—
ALCM	200		—	1,685		—
SRAM	1,140		—	—		—
artillery	452		1,875	na		na
mines	600		na	—		—
totals	2,580		2,099	4,753		335
		4,679			5,088	

sources: *Military Balance 1983/84;* Cochran, Arkin, Hoenig, *US Nuclear Forces and Capabilities,* 1984

blackjack RAM-P bomber Recent information suggests that this highly secret USSR bomber will be larger than the US B1-B, although some observers feel that its weapons payload will be in the region of 16 tons, compared to the B1-B's 28 tons. The US Department of Defense is predicting an initial operational capability by 1987 with about 50 aircraft in service.

Specifications
Range: 12,800 km
Speed: Mach 2.3
Number planned: 100

boiling water reactor (BWR) A type of light water reactor. Steam is generated in the reactor core under pressure (68 atmospheres) at the low temperature of 300°C. Water circulated through the core generates steam which is dried and piped to the generators. Efficiency is 32.3 per cent. Fortunately, most of the radioactivity produced is due to N-16, which has a HALF-LIFE of only seven seconds. Fuel is uranium dioxide pellets, enriched by 2.2 per cent and clad in zirconium alloy. The BWR is in many ways the most primitive of all nuclear reactors.
see FAST-BREEDER REACTOR

Bradford School of Peace Studies Founded in 1974 at Bradford University with help from the Society of Friends (Quakers), it defines the scope of peace studies thus: 'By peace – or peaceful relationships – we mean a positive combination of justice with a lack of violence which enables two or more groups or nations to achieve together what they could not have achieved separately.'

The energies of the school are focused on 'three areas: peace and non-violence, inter-group relations, and geographical regions where peace is at risk'. While politics and sociology constitute the main areas of study, history, economics and psychology are integrated as disciplines into the different projects. The school produces three series of publications: *Peace Studies Papers; Peace Research Reports;* and *Peace Studies Background Briefing Documents.* It also produces a twice-yearly newsletter and its staff contribute to scholarly journals, the news media generally, and several of them have published books in the field.

School of Peace Studies, University of Bradford, Bradford, West Yorkshire BD7 1DP.

Britain as a nuclear power Compared to the USA or the USSR, Britain is a second-class nuclear power. However, the 'nuclear club' is still very exclusive with probably only seven member states. Although Britain developed its nuclear capability on its own (both for the A-bomb and the H-bomb) its nuclear forces are fully committed to

NATO's integrated military strategy, and are dependent on US satellite targeting information. Furthermore, the lynchpin of its nuclear weapons forces – Polaris and possibly soon Trident – are either purchased from the USA or manufactured in Britain under licence.

Figures can only be approximate but at present British nuclear capability is roughly as follows:

1 Strategic

● Four Polaris submarines each armed with 16 Polaris A-3 missiles carrying three non-independently targetable warheads, making 192 warheads in all; when the Chevaline updating programme is complete (scheduled for 1987 or 1988) there will be up to six MRVs per missile.

● Present government policy is to replace Polaris with four Trident submarines in the 1990s (the first is expected to enter service in 1992), each of which carries 16 Trident D-5 missiles, each with up to 14 MIRVed warheads. As Polaris warheads are not MIRVed the number of targets is limited to the number of missiles – 64. Trident would increase the number of targets to a theoretical 896. Polaris is stationed at Faslane, Scotland, as will be Trident.

If Trident were cancelled, the possible options would be to purchase US cruise missiles, collaborate on developing a Pershing III, or develop the British Aerospace P3T and P5T Sea Eagle into a British nuclear-armed cruise missile.

2 Tactical

a) Nuclear-capable planes:

● Interdictor Strike Tornado – the most likely replacement to Trident if the latter has to be cancelled (the other options are Pershing III or a British cruise missile); 220 Tornados are planned, but only a portion of these will be nuclear capable.

● 60 Buccaneers; 72 Jaguars; 30 Nimrods of which a Mark II is on the way (no other British nuclear-capable aircraft has its 5,000-mile range); 30 Sea Harriers with 60 more planned.

● 45 Sea King helicopters; four Wessex helicopters; 34 Lynx; 19 Wasps.

b) missiles:

● at least 60 Lance missiles stationed in West Germany.

c) artillery:

● at least 100 M-109 field guns capable of firing a 2 kt shell approximately 24 km.

● 16 M-110 field guns capable of firing a 10 kt shell some 29 km (both of these are stationed in West Germany).

Britain also hosts a number of important NATO and US command, control, communications and surveillance sites. There are an estimated 130 US bases, camps, depots, airfields and other facilities stationed in Britain.

Britain is party to a number of international treaties and agreements (eg ANTARCTIC, SEABED, HOT LINE, OUTER SPACE, TLATELOLCO, NON-PROLIFERATION TREATY). It is not, however, a party to SALT I or II or the more recent START and INF talks in Geneva.

UK Defence Spending

Date	£ million at current prices	£ million at 1982/83 cost terms	% GDP at market prices
1979/80	9,227	12,056	4.5
1980/81	11,180	12,374	4.8
1981/82	12,606	12,606	5.0
1982/83	14,411	13,406	5.3
1983/84	15,987	14,163	5.5
1984/85	17,290	14,588	5.6
1985/86	18,330	14,871	5.6

In the 1982/83 defence budget the cost of nuclear strategic forces was £327 million, or 2.3 per cent of the total. However the cost of Tornado had, for three years running, been 8 per cent of the total – 18 per cent of the equipment budget.

broken arrows
see NUCLEAR ACCIDENTS

burns from nuclear explosions
Although heat and light make up only 35 per cent of the total energy from a nuclear explosion, burns would be by far the most common of all treatable injuries of those who survived initially. Burns would result both from the heat and light of the detonation itself – very intense but of short duration though affecting a wide area – and from secondary fires which could coalesce into a firestorm. With even minor radiation the damage to a patient's immune system and to blood element regeneration results in a patient becoming prone to invasive sepsis, less satisfactory healing and, generally, an increased risk of death from burns that would ordinarily not be fatal.

The number of burn survivors and the seriousness of their burns could vary by a factor of 1,000 depending on the size of the bomb, whether it was a GROUND BURST or AIR BURST, the degree of opac ty in the air, the time of day, and the extent to which the population was pre-warned (ie indoors and wearing a lot of clothing).

Assuming a 1 mt explosion and just 2 miles visibility (it can often be 10 miles or more), second-degree (partial skin thickness) burns would be very common in a belt between 2½–6 miles from GROUND ZERO. Nearer in, third-degree burns would be more common but most people would die anyway from blast alone.

Someone with third-degree burns over 24 per cent of their body or second-degree burns over 30 per cent of their body will probably die unless treated adequately, but a severe burn requires more hospital treatment and facilities than almost any other injury: as many as 30 to 50 operative procedures over a period, and months of hospitalization and intensive care.

In the USA the cost of running three 30-bed burn hospitals for children is the same as for 19 orthopaedic hospitals. In the whole country there are only 1,000 so-called burn beds and the cost of a severe burn-case is between $200,000 and $400,000.

'The most conservative calculation of the thermal injuries resulting from an isolated one-megaton or "minimal nuclear explosion", with preservation of all US medical facilities and ... transportation, will completely overwhelm what we consider to be one of the most lavish and well-developed medical facilities in the world.' John D. Constable in *The Final Epidemic*, Chicago, 1981.

The report of the British Medical Authority echoes this judgement:
> The explosion of a single nuclear bomb of the size used at Hiroshima over a major city in the UK is likely to produce so many cases of trauma and burns requiring hospital treatment that the remaining medical services in the UK would be completely overwhelmed .... The NHS could not deal with the casualties that might be expected following the detonation of a single megaton weapon over the UK. It follows that multiple nuclear explosions over several, possibly many, cities would force a breakdown in medical services across the country as a whole. (*The Medical Effects of Nuclear War*, p. 124.)

see also EFFECTS OF NUCLEAR EXPLOSION

bus
see POST-BOOST VEHICLE

C³I
see COMMAND, CONTROL, COMMUNICATIONS AND INTELLIGENCE

Campaign for Defence and Multilateral Disarmament (CDMD)
The British Conservative Party launched this organization 'to clarify the issues and to counter misinformation and even falsehoods being put about both by the Soviet Union and by some of those who advocate Britain's unilateral (one-sided) disarmament – which could leave us defenceless in the face of the increasing Soviet threat.'

It is headed by Winston Churchill MP and is affiliated to the COMMITTEE FOR PEACE WITH FREEDOM. It puts out small sheets on different aspects of nuclear defence such as on Trident, 'Why Multilateral Disarmament?', 'Does Britain Need an Independent Nuclear Deterrent?' and on Cruise. It argues that the USSR has been moving ahead of the USA 'particularly in the number of missiles and in the size of warheads and their destructive power.' With US forces remaining static and the USSR forging ahead, one could not talk of an arms 'race'. The consequence of this 'has been to undermine the rough balance of power that used to exist between the USA and the USSR and between NATO and the Warsaw Pact'.

In the view of many, this information is either selective or tendentious. The USSR does indeed have a superiority in megatonnage and missiles deployed (especially land-based missiles). But it does not possess more than about two-thirds the number of warheads stockpiled by the USA.

Campaign for Nuclear Disarmament (CND) The first
British H-bomb was tested on Christmas Island in the spring of 1957. On 16 January 1958 a meeting to found CND was called at the house of Canon John Collins. Among those present were Bertrand Russell, J B Priestley, Kingsley Martin, Rose Macaulay, Sir Julian Huxley, Bishop Bell, Michael Foot, Sir Richard Acland, Ritchie Calder and James Cameron. Peggy Duff had organized the meeting and, together with Arthur Goss and Dr Sheila Jones, represented the National Committee for the Abolition of Nuclear Weapons Tests founded in early 1957.

At the first public meeting – 17 February 1958 – 5,000 packed Central Hall, Westminster. The following declaration emerged:

> The purpose of the Campaign is to press for a British initiative to reduce the nuclear peril and to stop the armaments race. We shall seek to persuade the British people that Britain must:
>
> a) renounce unconditionally the use or production of nuclear weapons, and refuse to allow their use by others in her defence;
>
> b) use her utmost endeavour to bring about negotiations at all levels for agreement to end the armaments race and to lead to a general disarmament convention;
>
> c) invite the co-operation of other nations, particularly non-nuclear powers, in the renunciation of nuclear weapons.

By 1960, local groups had risen to 450 and the Campaign's newsletter, *Sanity,* reached a circulation of 40,000. The high point in this, CND's first phase, was the 1962 Aldermaston March with some 150,000 participants.

The decline of CND dates from about 1963. The Cuban Missile Crisis had certainly frightened people who, until then, had supported nuclear weapons. But the crisis had been resolved in what was seen popularly to be a classic case of gutsy American deterrence, and the period of detente which followed anaesthetized public opinion. The fears over strontium-90 which had so exercised the public imagination in the late 1950s were largely allayed by the PARTIAL TEST BAN TREATY of 1963. In addition, CND seemed irrelevant to a young protest movement more concerned with the broader issues raised by the Vietnam War and 'revolution' – peaceniks not beatniks.

In 1972 CND had registered a mere 105 new recruits throughout the UK. In 1976, still with only 60 local groups, recruits had risen to 569. From being a large organization in decline CND saw itself as a small organization that was growing. The BBC's screening of 'All

Against the Bomb' and local showings of Peter Watkins' 'The War Game', together with dissatisfaction among Labour Party supporters at the Labour Government's failure to implement unilateralist election pledges and unease at the following Conservative Government's Cold War postures created a climate of nuclear unease, exacerbated by a growing realization that nuclear escalation was reaching massive proportions. However, it was President Carter's decision in 1977 to deploy the ENHANCED RADIATION WEAPON – the 'neutron bomb' – in Europe that galvanized opposition (CND's petition had 250,000 signatures, while in Holland over a million were collected). CND could now boast 4,000 members.

Membership grew steadily as a series of events began to convince many of the as yet uncommitted that Europe had been chosen by the USA and USSR as the nuclear killing ground. In May 1979 the Conservatives took office firmly committed to an expansion of Britain's nuclear capability. Later in that year the US Senate refused to ratify SALT II. On 12 December 1979 NATO announced plans to instal ground-launched cruise missiles. Early in 1980 it was learned that the previous Labour Government, far from disbanding British nuclear weapons had, without any debate in Parliament, secretly agreed to the Chevaline modifications to the Polaris A-3 missile, doubling the number of warheads. Francis Pym, the then Conservative Minister for Defence, announced in 1980 the intention to buy the Trident II D5 system from the USA involving a massive escalation in Britain's nuclear capability. But perhaps the most effective spur to CND membership was the Government's civil defence pamphlet *Protect and Survive* with its naive 'advice' and cosy tone. The 80,000 strong demonstration in October 1980 heralded a new period of vigorous anti-nuclear protest. In 1982 the Home Secretary, William Whitelaw, was forced to cancel the civil defence exercise, 'Hard Rock', after 24 of the 52 participant county councils had refused to co-operate (two years earlier, Manchester City Council had declared itself a nuclear free zone – and 200 councils have followed suit). The foundation of the Greenham Common Peace Camp, the adoption of unilateralist resolutions by the Labour Party, the formation of European Nuclear Disarmament (END), the mass rally of October 1983 when CND estimated that 400,000 marchers had gathered in Hyde Park, are all evidence of the power of 'and popular support for' the movement. Above all, CND would point to the table below as a manifestation of its influence:

CND membership

	1979	1980	1981	1982	1983
National	4,287	9,000	20,000	50,000	85,000
CND groups	150	300	700	1,000	1,250
Affiliated organizations	274	?	?	1,000	1,300

Canada as a nuclear power Canada 'is the first country in the world with the capacity to produce nuclear weapons that chose not to do so; we are also the first nuclear-armed country to have chosen to divest itself of nuclear weapons' (Prime Minister Pierre Trudeau before the UN General Assembly Special Session on Disarmament, May 1978.)

Canada, with its massive uranium deposits, agreed, in 1942, to sell nearly all its mined uranium to the USA for use in the MANHATTAN PROJECT. During World War II the British proposed that Canada work on a joint atomic power project; this was eagerly seized on, first by Chalmers Mackenzie, Canada's chief scientific advisor, then by Clarence Howe who ran the Ministry for Munitions and Supply and was later to set up Atomic Energy of Canada Ltd (AECL) to make power plants.

In April 1944 work began on the first heavy-water-moderated, plutonium-producing, natural-uranium reactor. ZEEP, as it was known, went into action in September 1945 and was the first controlled chain reaction outside the USA. In 1943 the Quebec Agreement, between the USA, Britain and Canada, pledged co-operation on post-war commercial use of atomic power as well as secrecy with respect to France and the USSR. This was reiterated in 1945, but General Groves restricted the co-operation to scientific data alone. With the passing of McMahon's Atomic Energy Act the USA cut off even this co-operation from its wartime allies. But in 1954 the USA agreed to buy up all the plutonium produced as a byproduct of Canada's heavy-water reactors for use in the USA's military programme, thus providing a sound financial basis for developing a commercial power plant programme.

The first nuclear power reactor order came in 1959 – the Douglas Point reactor – and by the mid-1970s six Canadian Deuterium Uranium reactors (CANDUs) had been exported. The British Central Electricity Generating Board had been interested but had in the end chosen gas-cooled reactors. Large profits were not forthcoming; a sale to Argentina was made at a loss.

In May 1974 India exploded an atomic bomb at Pokaran. Canada had supplied a heavy-water reactor to India without any safeguards, in the benign days of 'atoms for peace'. It was from that reactor that the plutonium for the Indian bomb had come. From then on Canada took the lead in pressing for stronger safeguards, by refusing to supply fuel or equipment to unsafeguarded plants, but never to the extent of completely refusing to export reprocessing and enrichment plants.

In 1962 Canada became part of the Non-Nuclear Club, a bloc of mainly NATO and Warsaw Pact countries which undertook to forgo developing a nuclear military capacity even though they had the technology to do so. However, this has not stopped Canada remaining within NATO, nor has it prevented the Federal Government from permitting the USA to test-flight cruise missiles over areas of Canada that geographically resemble the Russian steppe.

'Carte Blanche' In 1955 a NATO nuclear war-game, 'Carte Blanche', was held in West Germany, the Netherlands and north-east France. It simulated the effects of 335 tactical nuclear explosions (each in the sub- or low-kiloton range), 268 of which were in West Germany. It was estimated that about 1.7 million Germans would be killed by blast and immediate radiation; 3.5 million would be 'incapacitated'.

Center for Strategic and International Studies Based at
Georgetown University, Washington DC, the Center has been influential in shaping President Reagan's foreign and nuclear policy. It has supplied the Reagan administration with its UN Ambassador, Jean Kirkpatrick, and its first National Security Advisor, Richard Allen.

The Center's senior advisors are James Schlesinger, Zbigniew Brzezinski and Robert G. Neumann. Its counsellors are Henry Kissinger and Robert Henle. It publishes some 80 titles a year and has three main publications: *The Washington Quarterly*, edited by Walter Laqueur, *The Washington Papers*, and various pamphlets in the *Significant Issues Series*.

One of the Center's senior fellows, Edward Luttwak, is one of the administration's most fervent critics from the right. He accuses Reagan and others of 'appeasing the protesters, the churchmen and the media. From those who once could explain quite lucidly the fundamental and unchanging reasons for the inevitable failure of arms control, we now hear only great declarations of their love of peace, their revulsion against war, and their sincere dislike of nuclear weapons'.

Central Electricity Generating Board (CEGB) The
Central Electricity Generating Board is the British nationalized agency for the production and distribution of electricity. As such it is one of the largest utilities in the world, with a capital investment equal to the sum of all other British nationalized industries with the exception of steel. Its delayed but eventual decision to abide by the Atomic Energy Authority's advice and build an advanced gas-cooled reactor at Dungeness 'B', proved an expensive disaster which also put paid to the British nuclear-power industry's export chances. The CEGB made the mistake first of underestimating electricity demand in the 1960s and then of overestimating it for the 1970s. However, the new, larger power stations, although relatively efficient when they worked, spent so many months of each year out of action that supply did not significantly exceed demand. The CEGB runs as many nuclear powered reactors as the USSR, second only to the USA. It is also responsible for the nuclear reprocessing plant at Sellafield which has been plagued by safety problems since 1957.

Chevaline The name given to the upgrading programme designed to improve the nuclear fire-power of the UK's aging Polaris submarines. The programme was started in the late 1960s and will be completed in 1987/8 at an estimated cost of £1,000 million.

Before Chevaline improvements, every Polaris A-3 missile carried three MRV'd warheads, each 200kt (192 warheads). Now each missile is armed with six MRV'd warheads in the 50 kt range (384 warheads). Not all the warheads will necessarily be armed; some may be decoys whose function is to confuse the Soviet anti-ballistic missile defence network (GALOSH) around Moscow.

China as a nuclear power In October 1964 China exploded its first atomic weapon at Lop Nor in Sinkiang Province.

The Chinese nuclear programme had been geared exclusively to military aims until the late 1970s, and the USSR spared China almost nothing, training its scientists, engineers and designers at the Dubnu Joint Institute for Nuclear Research, and sending to China its own experts, equipment and materials. But the Chinese, led by the powerful Chairman of the Scientific Planning Commission, Nierh Jung-chen, were determined to become scientifically independent. 'There are people who feel', said Nieh, 'that as long as we receive assistance from the Soviet Union and other fraternal countries there is no need for us to carry out more complicated research ourselves .... This way of thinking is wrong.'

In July 1958 the first Chinese nuclear chain reaction took place in a Soviet-made reactor. The next reactor was Chinese made, and the third was Chinese designed. The first Chinese nuclear bomb used U-235 rather than plutonium. This implies that they had built their own uranium enrichment plant.

The present stockpile is estimated at 942 devices, of which probably some 200 are missiles. During 1982 China launched a three-stage liquid-fuelled rocket and test-fired a ballistic missile from a submarine. Unlike most countries, however, military expenditure, while increasing substantially between 1977 and 1979, has since been rather stable as a percentage of GNP.

China has not signed many of the international treaties and agreements (see ARMS CONTROL AND ARMS LIMITATION) and abstained on the UN freeze motion. However, of late she has been giving much more support to the European peace movements and in 1984 invited a CND delegation on an official visit.

'China syndrome' Term coined by US nuclear reactor engineers to describe a situation where the fuel element in a reactor melts down into a molten mass due to a malfunctioning of the cooling mechanism. The molten core could sink right through the reactor containment, carry on through the earth's crust and come out, so they estimated, somewhere in China.

circular error probable (CEP) A measure of a missile's accuracy represented by the radius of a circle around a target point within which there is a 50 per cent probability of the missile landing. see MISSILE ACCURACY, LETHALITY, TWO-ON-ONE CROSS-TARGETING, COUNTER MILITARY POTENTIAL, CUBE-ROOT LAW

civil defence Whether nuclear armed governments make extensive civil defence provision (USSR) or practically none (USA), they have to face the paradoxes embedded in the concept. On the one hand, having made so much of the deterrent power of nuclear weapons it is almost an admission of defeat to take extensive civil defence measures. On the other hand, in order to convince a potential enemy of one's determination to use nuclear weapons if necessary, preparation must be made to withstand a nuclear exchange. Civil defence, then, becomes part of a war-fighting preparation, and to mobilize it might well be construed by an enemy as an aggressive act. Another paradox is that governments cannot afford to protect their populations against the degree of destruction necessarily involved in even a relatively minor nuclear exchange and yet they must suggest that survival is possible.

Britain

The doctrine can be paraphrased as 'A little, no matter how inadequate, is better than none.' In 1980, Lord Belstead, then head of civil defence affairs at the Home Office estimated that £60,000 million would be the cost of providing adequate shelters. The total budget for all civil defence, 1983/84, is 'about £67 million' according to Ministry of Defence figures. The declared aims of 'home defence' are:

1 To secure the UK against any internal threat.
2 To mitigate the effects of conventional, nuclear, biological or chemical warfare upon the civil population.
3 To provide alternative government machinery at all levels.
4 To enhance the basis for national recovery in the post-attack period.

Most of the effort has gone into **3.** An administrative pyramid has been established of 12 regional HQs, 18 sub-regional HQs, and a seat of national government at Corsham near Bath. Each sub-region would be controlled by a senior civil servant with about 200 assistants (civil servants). Further down the pyramid would come county and district HQs administered by the chief executive of the local authority. At the very base would be parish councils and ad hoc ward or neighbourhood groups. Government circulars make it clear that point **2** is the lowest priority, point **1** the highest. The population must rely on self-help and DIY. The government would issue early warnings and provide advice with booklets such as *Domestic Nuclear Shelters, Civil Defence, Why We Need It* and *Protect and Survive* (now being revised). In the first 14 days after an attack there would be little attempt to help survivors. For example, government circular ES 1/1977 points out to hospital staff: 'It would be essential that staff, vital to the long-term recovery of the country, should not be wasted by allowing them to enter areas of high radioactivity and no staff should leave shelter.' Those casualties who reached hospital would be treated only if it were thought that they had a chance of surviving longer than seven days.

USSR
A civil defence corps of about 50,000 is organized under the Ministry of Defence. A military civil-defence college has been established at Balashika and graduates have been entering the civil defence corps since 1969. Each local authority or large-scale factory employs full-time civil defence staff, of whom there are believed to be 100,000.

USA
'Dig a hole, cover it with a couple of doors, and then throw three feet of dirt on top .... It's the dirt that does it ... if there are enough shovels to go around, everybody's going to make it.' T K Jones, Deputy Under Secretary for Defense for Strategic Nuclear Forces.

Switzerland
Protection is primarily geared to counter fallout drifting in from other countries although some Swiss shelters will afford a high degree of protection against blast and initial radiation. The Swiss Government claims to have shelter space for 90 per cent of its population (mountain motorway tunnels as well as the legal requirements to provide shelters in private accommodation under construction – a law recently adopted in France). As in Sweden, most citizens are obliged to train either in the military or in the civil defence corps.

see SQUARE LEG, HARD ROCK, EFFECTS OF NUCLEAR EXPLOSIONS, BURNS

Club of five
see URANIUM SUPPLY CONTROLS

Coalition for Peace through Security
Founded in Britain in 1981 by Edward Leigh MP, Tony Kerpel and Francis Holihan, its aims are very similar to its near-namesake in the USA, but its weight is very different. One of its principal tasks, both during and after its launch conference, was to convince the Conservative Party of the need to adopt the sort of campaigning methods used so successfully by the American COALITION FOR PEACE THROUGH STRENGTH in both congressional and presidential elections. Dr Julian Lewis of the Freedom Association became its research director in 1982 and, soon after, an ad hoc Committee for Peace with Freedom was formed (under the wing of Winston Churchill MP) linking all the anti-disarmament campaigning groups.
see also COMMITTEE FOR A FREE WORLD

Coalition for Peace through Strength (CPS) Formed in the USA in the late 1970s by the powerful private lobbying organization, the American Security Council (ASC). The CPS unites over 100 organizations, ranging from the World Federation of Cossack National Liberation Movements to the quietly influential conservative Caucus Inc. It includes 2,000 retired admirals and generals and over 200 congressmen.

It successfully fought against the US Congress adoption of SALT II, which it described as a policy of 'unilateral nuclear disarmament and retreat'. Later, in President Reagan's presidential election campaign, it used the ASC's 'voting index' of congressmen deemed soft on defence to computer-mail their constituents. Finally, it introduced a resolution into Congress calling for a national strategy based on 'overall military and technological superiority over the Soviet Union'. It publishes the journal *Protect or Perish*.

see also COALITION FOR PEACE THROUGH SECURITY.

cold launch The missile is propelled from the tube or silo by a gas generator – a small rocket motor not attached to the missile proper. The rocket's main motors are ignited after clearing the silo's muzzle. By pushing the missile into motion in this way a large saving can be made in the missile's on-board fuel which, in turn, increases its range. Cold-launch silos also have the advantage that a second rocket can be fired from them fairly quickly.

collateral damage Accidental or intentional damage may be suffered by people and property as a side effect (collaterally) of a nuclear attack on a military target. Some supporters of the ENHANCED RADIATION WEAPON point to its relatively low collateral impact due to its reduced blast.

Comiso The NATO nuclear modernization decision of December 1979 proposed that Italy should take 112 ground-launched cruise missiles (GLCMs). The site chosen was at the Magliocco air base near Comiso, Sicily. Although the site was not fully prepared, some cruise missiles were duly flown in at the end of 1983. This was partly to meet West Germany's stipulation of 'simultaneity', ie that at least one Western European NATO state which did not possess nuclear missiles itself (in other words not Britain) should receive GLCMs or Pershing II at the same time as West Germany.

While the range of the GLCMs sited there would allow them to strike the Balkans and possibly Georgia, they most evidently threaten countries in the Middle East and North Africa.

Comiso has been the scene of mass actions by local committees, and 1,000,000 Sicilians out of a total population of 4,000,000 have signed protests against the siting of cruise missiles on their island.

Command, Control, Communications and Intelligence (C³I)

US C³I

In 1962 US Secretary for Defense, Robert McNamara, announced the creation of the National Military Command System (NMCS) which he defined as 'the facilities, equipment, doctrine, procedures and communications provided specifically for use by the National Command Authorities ... in providing national strategic direction of the Armed Forces of the United States.' It is serviced by the Worldwide Military Command and Control System (WWMCCS – 'Wimmex').

Structure

The system comprises a network of command-and-control centres, communications links, data-processing facilities and accepted procedures intended to permit the deployment of US strategic nuclear forces under the command of the NCA. It involves between 25,000 and 30,000 personnel.

Listed below are the core sections of the US C³I:

National Command Authority (NCA)

President and Secretary of Defense

National Military Command System

National Military Command Center in the Pentagon (War Room)

Alternate National Military Command Center (Underground)

National Emergency Airborne Command Post (NEACP or 'Kneecap')

Subordinate Commands

Strategic Air Command (SAC)

North American Aerospace Defense Command (NORAD)

Theatre HQs

All of these constitute the Worldwide Military Command and Control System. Linking it all together is the Defense Communications System and the Minimum Essential Emergency Communication Network (MEECN). Overall control is exercised by the National Command Authority which consists 'only of the President and the Secretary of Defense or their duly deputized alternates or successors'. The chain of command passes from the National Command Authority through the Chairman of the Joint Chiefs of Staff to the executing commander.

Communications systems

The Worldwide Military Command and Control System is set up to 'provide the constituted national authorities with the information needed for accurate and timely decisions and the reliable communications needed to transmit their decisions to the military forces under all conditions of peace and war'.

It consists of 43 different communications systems including underwater cables, land lines, radio systems, satellite relay systems, etc. Most are part of the Defense Communications System which has some 600 facilities with over 50,000 individual circuits totalling 30,000,000 miles, five satellites and 100 satellite ground terminals.

If all else fails there is an Emergency Rocket Communication System of 12 Minuteman II missiles which carry UHF radio packages instead of warheads. These can be launched into a very high trajectory to provide 30 minutes message-transmission time for Strategic Air Command and the submarine force.

Surveillance, warning and assessment

This is headed by the Defense Support Program – three satellites which provide 30 minutes warning of an attack by intercontinental ballistic missiles (ICBM) and 10–20 minutes warning of a submarine-launched ballistic missile (SLBM) attack. For an account of the other facilities in this part of the US C³I system, see NORAD.

Soviet C³I

The overall architecture of the Soviet C³I system is similar to that of the USA. The ultimate control resides with the Politbureau of the Communist Party. The Soviet High Command consists of:

The Council for Defence

The General Secretary, the Minister of Defence and other top political and military leaders.

The Main Military Council

In the event of war this would become the HQ for the Supreme High Command and would implement the military-political tasks determined by the Council for Defence. In peacetime, it is responsible for Soviet strategy.

The General Staff

This is responsible for 'the coordinated actions of the main staffs of the services of the Armed Forces, the staff of the Rear Services, the staff of the Civil Defence, the main and central administrations of the Ministry of Defence, the staffs of the military districts, groups abroad, air defence districts and fleet'.

There are five separate forces in the Soviet Armed Forces: Strategic Rockets Force, Ground Force, Troops of National Air Defence, Air Force and Navy (in that order of precedence). The three High Command bodies and the HQs of all five forces are located in Moscow. The USSR places great importance on the survivability of the leadership in time of war and shelters have been constructed for about 110,000 members of the leadership – Party and governmental, national and regional, military and civilian

Communications systems

Soviet communication links are by land lines, satellites, microwaves and other radio systems. The system used to depend on HF radio, but this is being discontinued because of its vulnerability to electromagnetic pulse (EmP). Very low frequency waves are used and there is a significant reliance on satellites, of which there are three systems:

1 36–48 small satellites in circular orbits and with life-spans of two to three years;

2 the *Molniya* series which follow highly eliptical orbits with apogees in the northern hemisphere, providing 8–10 hours a day of communication link;

3 satellites in geo-stationary orbit.

There are 26 very low frequency stations, five with outputs of 500 kw, giving a worldwide coverage.

Surveillance, warning and assessment

Early warning is provided by satellites, over-the-horizon radar and search-and-track radars with a range of 3,200 nautical miles.

command disable system (CDS) A safety device stored in some nuclear warheads which, when activated by an appropriate command code, will destroy critical components in the warhead and thus disarm it.

see also PERMISSIVE ACTION LINKS and DUAL KEY.

Committee for a Free World This anti-arms-negotiation organization founded in February 1981 has offices in London and New York. The London office is shared with the COALITION FOR PEACE THROUGH SECURITY. Its executive director is Midge Decter who has forceful views: 'We have the option to do everything in our power to undermine the economic political and military strength of our enemy – and as it happens this is a time of golden opportunity so to do; or we have the option of accommodating ourselves to the ever increasing spread of the enemy's power ...'

Decter is against any form of arms negotiations, which she has termed 'the talisman of the self-deceived'. see also COALITION FOR PEACE THROUGH STRENGTH

Committee on the Present Danger (CPD) Formed in March 1976 with the aim of warning the American public that the Soviet Union was preparing to fight and win a nuclear war, its strategic conclusion was that the USA must do likewise. Its key personnel included Paul Nitze, whose appointment as chief SALT negotiator was likened, by the historian Barbara Tuchman, to 'putting Pope John Paul II in charge of abortion rights', Eugene V. Rostow, former Defense Secretary James Schlesinger and Richard Pipes. It was later joined by Ronald Reagan. After Reagan's election to the White House, he installed no fewer than 32 CPD members in his administration.

Comprehensive Nuclear Test Ban Treaty The 1963 Partial Test Ban Treaty (PTBT) had begun life in spring 1962 as a proposal from several non-aligned countries for a comprehensive test ban. The verification mechanics proposed using existing observation stations, thus cutting through the problems raised by the superpowers over the need for new monitoring facilities. The new-found urgency of the talks was due partly to the worldwide outcry over the resumption of testing and later to the shock of the Cuban missile crisis in October 1962.

The USSR conceded up to three on-site inspections and to the siting of three automatic recording stations. However, this was not enough for the USA which continued to insist on eight annual inspections. It has since been shown that seismographs can readily distinguish between a naturally caused tremor and one caused by a nuclear test and, consequently, that three inspections would have been sufficient. The talks foundered.

Instead of a comprehensive ban the USA and the USSR swiftly negotiated the PTBT which, although it paid lipservice to the need to proceed towards a comprehensive ban, and raised worldwide hopes in that direction, became in effect the first agreement between the superpowers to set out the ground rules for their own nuclear arms race while excluding the rest of the world from such negotiations.

A comprehensive test ban in 1963 would genuinely have slowed down the arms race; such a ban today would not have the same effect because the major powers do not need to test weapons, even underground, while they are being developed to the same extent as before.

Conference of the Committee on Disarmament
see EIGHTEEN NATIONAL DISARMAMENT COMMITTEE

congressional agencies The different branches of the US government, as well as of its armed services, produce an enormous quantity of literature including weekly abstracts, monthly magazines, quarterlies and annuals, many derived from the numerous hearings of Committees of Congress. Four major agencies prepare reports for Congress:

The Congressional Budget Office (CBO)
Established in 1974, it provides information on budget and fiscal programmes, budget analysis and spending alternatives. Its analyses usually include background on a given issue, its present status, and alternatives for the future. The National Security and International Affairs Division provides Congress with alternatives with regard to force structure and procurement decisions. Copies can be obtained from:
Office of Intergovernmental Relations, Congressional Budget Office, House Office Building Annex no. 2, Second and D Streets, S.W., Washington DC 20515.

The General Accounting Office (GAO) and the Office of the Comptroller General.

The International Division reviews governmental participation in assistance programmes and foreign policy, security and defence. The Science and Technology Division reviews defence and nuclear research and development. The GAO monitors the status of major weapons systems being acquired, assessing cost, development, production and deployment schedules. It published the *Monthly GAO Document: Catalog of Reports, Decisions, and Opinions, Testimonies and Speeches* and an annual report, *Summaries of Conclusions and Recommendations on Department of Defense Operation.* Copies can be obtained from:

US General Accounting Office DHISF, Box 6015 Gaithersburg, MD 20760.

The Office of Technology Assessment (OTA)

Established by Congress in 1972, it analyses the impact of technology, identifies alternatives and publishes the *Annual Report to the Congress by the OTA.* Perhaps its most important publication has been *The Effects of Nuclear War,* which is of especial interest to people in Britain because its methods and conclusions differ markedly from the assumptions made and conclusions reached by the Home Office. SCIENTISTS AGAINST NUCLEAR ARMS (SANA) based many of its assumptions about the effects of nuclear explosions on the research and findings in this publication, when they were estimating the effect of a 200 mt attack on Britain at the time of the abortive HARD ROCK home defence exercise and CND's 'Hard Luck' rejoinder. SANA's conclusions were adopted, more or less unaltered by the British Medical Association in preference to those of the Home Office, and it looks increasingly likely that the Home Office will alter its estimates to fall in line with the OTA. Its address is: Office of Technology Assessment, US Congress, Washington DC 20510.

The Congressional Research Service (CRS)

This is an arm of the Library of Congress. Its studies have a reputation for being unbiased and sophisticated. Many of them are published as committee prints or placed in the congressional record. It publishes a semi-annual 'CRS Documents in the Public Domain'. Less substantial reports are published as CRS Issue Briefs.

Much of the documentation from these four agencies is well-indexed in the *CIS Index/Abstracts* which is the best single tool for any researcher on military, nuclear or foreign policy matters. It can be obtained from the Government Printing Office (GPO) as can many, but by no means all, of the publications produced by the congressional agencies.

correlation guidance systems
see MISSILE ACCURACY

costs

1 The costs for nuclear weapons' production and procurement, running costs, and research and development for any country can only be approximate, first because the figures are generally not available, secondly because so much of the C³I and other overhead costs are shared with conventional forces. Individual projects, however, often turn out more costly than their estimates.

2 Military costs within NATO are calculated by adjusting for inflation using the consumer price index. Thus the military budget is compared with the civil resources which have been forgone.

3 Figures for military expenditure in the Warsaw Treaty Organization (WTO) are, especially for the USSR, sometimes available only after a delay of some years and never in sufficient detail. The Central Intelligence Agency (CIA) estimates Soviet expenditure by calculating what it would cost the USA to duplicate the Soviet effort. This can produce absurdities, such that, for example, if the US cost of living index goes up then so does Soviet military expenditure by the same percentage. The STOCKHOLM INTERNATIONAL PEACE RESEARCH INSTITUTE (SIPRI), calculating on a different ratio between the rouble and the dollar, put Soviet expenditure at $61 billion for 1976 compared with a CIA estimate of $130 billion and a US expenditure of $102.2 billion.

4 Nuclear weapons are, in fact, not expensive compared with conventional weapons. The British Government estimates that the cost of its nuclear forces has been between 2 and 10 per cent of the defence budget over the past 25 years. In 1983 it announced that 'Our nuclear forces cost us well under one half of one per cent of total government expenditure.' In the USA the Pentagon spends as much on military pensions as it does on strategic systems.

5 There appears to be an inverse ratio between arms spending and capital investment as a whole and manufacturing productivity in particular, with Japan at one end of the spectrum and the USA followed by Britain at the other. Moreover, equivalent sums create more jobs in civil projects than military ones. Finally, military R & D drains away huge resources of money and expertise from civilian innovation.

6 Here are some examples of the costs of weapons (1983 prices):

● one Trident D-5 submarine with its missiles; $2.5–3 billion
● one F-14 fighter: $22 million
● one average guided-missile destroyer: $195 million.

NB A bomber costs 200 times as much as a World War II bomber, a fighter 100 times as much, and an aircraft-carrier 20 times as much.

7 Some social cost comparisons:

● 1982 world military spending was around $650,000 million – equivalent to the income of 1,500 million people in the 50 poorest countries of the world

● the cost of one fighter plane could innoculate three million children against six common childhood diseases
● one year's defence contracts to American universities were worth 50 per cent more than the entire education budget of Pakistan (population 84 million).

8 Some statistics for certain countries at 1982 levels:

(a) = population in millions; (b) = defence spending in $ million; (c) = $ million defence spending per capita; (d) = defence spending as percentage of GNP; (e) = change in defence spending between 1975 and 1981 as percentage of GNP

Country	(a)	(b)	(c)	(d)	(e)
Britain	56	26,200	468	5.4	+ 10
USA	230	216,000	938	6.1	+ 5
France	53.8	22,677	421	4.1	+ 5
Australia	15	4,229	317	3.0	− 7
Japan	118	10,045	89	0.9	no change
East Germany	16.7	7,390	441	7.7	+ 40
Poland	36	5,410	151	4.3	+ 13

source: *Military Balance, 1982/83*

9 Defence spending in the power blocs in 1982 (at 1980 prices and exchange rates):

	$ million
USA:	169,691
Other NATO:	116,056
Total NATO:	285,747
China:	39,400 (estimated)
USSR:	135,500 (estimated)
Other WTO:	12,780 (estimated)
Total WTO:	148,280 (estimated)
Total world:	$618,744 million

source: SIPRI, 1983.

Several points emerge:
a) Total NATO expenditure is just over 46 per cent of the world total compared with 24 per cent for the WTO.
b) Other NATO expenditure was 68.4 per cent of that of the USA whereas in 1979 it was 78.7 per cent.
c) Only Britain and Italy have expanded military expenditure at the 3 per cent a year agreed on by NATO ministers in 1977, whereas the USA has expanded at a rate in excess of 4 per cent a year between 1978 and 1982.

counterforce An expression used to describe nuclear attacks directed against military targets. These include not only ports, airfields, barracks and arms dumps but more especially command-and-control centres, submarines, and hardened silos containing missiles. Counterforce is contrasted with COUNTERVALUE which is a nuclear attack directed against population centres and industry.

Both the USA and USSR have always targeted military installations. What has changed is the precision of the guidance systems employed in nuclear missiles – with the USA having a commanding lead at present. Only very accurate missiles have much chance of destroying a hardened silo or underground command centre. Although counterforce weapons are not necessarily FIRST STRIKE weapons, counterforce as a strategy does have offensive first strike connotations; for many of the targets would have to be destroyed *before* the missiles within them could be fired, otherwise their destruction would be pointless. It has to be stressed that counterforce targeting is at the very core of strategic doctrine on both sides. The real military 'action policy', even for smaller nuclear states such as Britain and France, is geared to this end whatever their 'declaratory policies' may say.

see STRATEGIC DOCTRINE (WESTERN), STRATEGIC DOCTRINE (SOVIET), SINGLE INTEGRATED OPERATIONAL PLAN, DETERRENCE, COMMAND, CONTROL, COMMUNICATIONS AND INTELLIGENCE

counter military potential (CMP)

An expression used to gauge the effectiveness or LETHALITY of a nuclear warhead in destroying a HARD TARGET (such as an ICBM silo or a C³I centre). The sheer size of a warhead's yield is here not so important as the accuracy in relation to yield and the degree of target hardness. CMP is expressed as:

$$CMP = \frac{(Yield)^{\frac{2}{3}}}{CEP^2}$$

As missile technology improves and CEPs (CIRCULAR ERROR PROBABLE) become increasingly reduced, the CMP of a missile system approaches almost 100 per cent chance of success. The problem, however, is that it is still difficult to predict accuracy *in operation*. Military strategists have to rely heavily on computer models and limited live tests. The International Institute of Strategic Studies suggests that the degree of variance between theory and reality may be plus or minus 50 per cent – a chilling thought for any strategist contemplating a disarming FIRST STRIKE where total success is essential if the attack is to avoid massive retaliation.

see MISSILE ACCURACY, EQUIVALENT MEGATONNAGE, FIRST STRIKE, SINGLE-SHOT PROBABILITY OF KILL

countervailing strategy
see STRATEGIC DOCTRINE (AMERICAN)

countervalue
In contrast to COUNTERFORCE (nuclear attack

against specifically military targets) countervalue strikes are aimed at civilian targets: cities and industrial complexes.

coupling Coupling, in strategic parlance, is seen as part of DETERRENCE THEORY and supposes that American nuclear forces will act as an insurance policy against Soviet nuclear aggression in Europe. The theory has it that if the USA is coupled to NATO with a commitment to use its nuclear capability – in the full knowledge that any strike against Russia will involve retaliation against the US homeland – this will ensure that there will never be an irresponsible use of US nuclear weapons in Europe. In addition, with America's nuclear might behind it, Europe is safe from Soviet nuclear superiority. For these reasons, the West German government, under Helmut Schmidt, was foremost in urging the USA to deploy Cruise and Pershing II missiles in Europe.

The critics of coupling argue that a consolidation of US nuclear forces turns Europe into a US FORWARD BASED SYSTEM which, far from guaranteeing European security, threatens it. Superpower self-interest, they claim, would also ensure that any European nuclear war would not escalate to a US/USSR intercontinental exchange. In the words of US Rear-Admiral Gene LaRocque:

> There isn't any question, if there's a trade off we'd rather trade the Russians London or Bonn than we would Washington or Boston. No there isn't any question. That's just the nature of international politics. That's one of the reasons too, that we're pushing the British people to accept more of our nuclear weapons, which will be totally under US control, and, of course, if the Soviets want to knock them out they'll be firing at targets in the United Kingdom rather than in the United States ... We fought World War I in Europe, we fought World War II in Europe and if you dummies let us, we'll fight World War III in Europe.

cruise missile A pilotless missile, guided either by on-board guidance systems or by remote control from a command base. It is normally powered by small, high-efficiency engines which, unlike the ballistic missile, are used to power the cruise missile through all or almost all of its flight. It also uses aerodynamic surfaces for lift in the same way as a conventional aircraft (in other words, it flies). Also in contrast to the ballistic missile, the cruise missile flies at very low altitudes (thus making radar detection difficult) without ever leaving the earth's atmosphere. Cruise missiles can be launched from aircraft AIR-LAUNCHED CRUISE MISSILES (ALCMs), from ships and submarines SEA-LAUNCHED CRUISE MISSILES (SLCMS), or from the ground GROUND-LAUNCHED CRUISE MISSILES (GLCMs). (It is the American version of the GLCM that has become popularly known as 'the Cruise'.)

Historically, the cruise missile goes back to the 'aerial torpedo' developed by Dr Elmer Sperry in 1915 and the V-1 flying bombs of World War II. Both the US and the USSR pursued development programmes for the cruise after the war was over. The early American successes in this field included the *Regulus* (submarine-launched), the *Matador* and the *Mace* (ground-launched), and the *Snark* and *Hound Dog* (air-launched). All of them were large in size, and were severely limited by lack of range and high levels of inaccuracy, so much so that the US Government dropped the cruise programme in the late 1950s to concentrate resources on the then more promising ballistic missile.

However, during the 1960s a number of technological break-throughs provided ways of overcoming the cruise missile's defects and the development programme was revived in the early 1970s. Improvements in the miniaturization of the warheads and advances in the engines of the missile greatly improved its range. But the most significant improvements were to the guidance systems. The combination of INERTIAL GUIDANCE and TERRAIN CONTOUR MATCHING (TERCOM) turned the cruise missile into one of the most accurate weapons yet devised; after a journey of some 2,500 km, the US cruise missile can land within 50 m. of its target.

In 1977, the US Defense Department set up the Joint Cruise Missiles Project to monitor and encourage the development of all the cruise missiles, particularly the air-launched version for the US Air Force. The cruise missile is particularly favoured because of its comparative cheapness – about $2–6 million per missile instead of over $100 million for an MX ICBM. Nevertheless, the total cost of the current US cruise programme is estimated at approximately $25 billion.

Unlike the US, the Soviet Union continued to develop its versions of the cruise missile after the end of World War II, deploying a number of sea- and air-launched cruise, such as the air-launched AS-3 Kangaroo and the AS-4 Kitchen missiles, and the sea-launched SS-N-3 Shaddock missile. These all suffer from the same defects as the early American versions – limited range and inaccuracy. Like the Americans, the Soviets have made many developments in the field of cruise missiles to rectify some of the early missile's problems. The latest versions (for example, the AS-6 Kingfish and the SS-N-19) are still relatively limited in range, though they are more effective as a consequence of their improved guidance systems and high speeds.

see also GROUND-LAUNCHED CRUISE MISSILES, AIR-LAUNCHED CRUISE MISSILES, SEA-LAUNCHED CRUISE MISSILES, ADVANCED STRATEGIC AIR-LAUNCHED MISSILE, ADVANCED CRUISE MISSILE PROGRAM

cube-root law At the heart of a missile's LETHALITY (its ability to destroy HARD TARGETS) and thus of many aspects of STRATEGIC DOCTRINE, such as FIRST-STRIKE CAPABILITY, is the relationship between accuracy and yield. To paraphrase a complicated mathematical equation: if the accuracy of a missile CIRCULAR ERROR PROBABLE (CEP) is halved, the missile's lethality increases eight times (a cube-root relationship). For example, the Soviet SS-18 ballistic missile has a CEP of 425 m. The Pershing II, on the other hand, has a CEP of 30 m, which means that the Pershing has 2,843 times greater chance of destroying its target than an SS-18. In essence, the blast effect of an SS-18 is diffused over a wider area, while that of a Pershing is concentrated.

see COUNTER MILITARY POTENTIAL, EQUIVALENT MEGA-TONNAGE, CIRCULAR ERROR PROBABLE, MISSILE ACCURACY, TWO-ON-ONE CROSS TARGETING

damage limitation An innocent-sounding term coined by the Pentagon. Actually it means COUNTERFORCE strategy. The 'damage' to be 'limited' is to American cities and military sites. To achieve this requires the destruction of enemy forces before they can be used. When referring to Soviet counterforce capability the Pentagon term employed is 'war-fighting'. In fact the two terms are identical.
see also STRATEGIC DOCTRINE (SOVIET)

deep basing (DB) One plan for protecting the US MX ICBMs from pre-emptive nuclear attack was to build a system of deep tunnels which could take either single missiles or a number at one time. For example, the Mesa Concept envisages the creation of a network of interconnecting tunnels some 2,000–3,000 feet below a hill. However, such protection reduces the reaction time and is enormously expensive to build.

see also MULTIPLE PROTECTIVE STRUCTURE ('Race Track') and DENSE PACK basing.

deep strike NATO plans for the defence of Europe are undergoing great changes at present. Since the 1950s its policy has been to hold a line along the East–West border (see FORWARD BASED SYSTEMS) and wear down the invader with massive use of fire power. This policy of forward defence is now enhanced by the doctrine called deep strike, the colloquial term for follow-on force attack.

It is assumed under deep strike that any attacking Soviet or Warsaw Treaty Organization (WTO) forces would advance in waves. The object of this strategy is to block off and destroy the second and succeeding waves of troops, tanks, etc while they are still in WTO territory, possibly some hundreds of miles in the interior. Also attacked would be land communications, logistical supplies and C³I systems. What is new is the means for accomplishing this: highly advanced conventional weapons with the entire battlefield 'managed' by sophisticated computer systems, which together are referred to as Emerging Technology (ET).

The new weapons include PRECISION-GUIDED WEAPONS and

equally accurate missiles with extremely powerful conventional warheads with a yield equivalent to 2–5 kt. The US is planning the production of 6,000 Corps Support Weapon System (Assault Breaker) missiles as well as a multiple launch rocket system.

Several questions surround deep strike. It is expensive. General Rogers (Supreme Commander, NATO forces) has requested an extra 4 per cent a year in the military budgets of NATO governments (with which they are unlikely to comply). The technology is overwhelmingly dependent on fragile communication and computer equipment which could easily go wrong, be destroyed, degraded or simply be jammed. The WTO forces look as if they are changing their tactics, through the creation of operational manoeuvre groups near the front lines, which do away with the previous tactic of wave upon wave of offensive echelons and this puts into question the whole raison d'etre of deep strike.

The attraction of deep strike lies in its claim to raise the nuclear threshold. While some of its proponents are urging cutbacks in or even the elimination of tactical nuclear weapons (TNW) few cuts are likely; those that have been made were of already obsolete weapons. Possible FIRST USE is and will remain NATO policy. If nuclear weapons are fired by NATO they are unlikely in the first instance to be TNW because, with their short range, they would explode in West Germany and would be 'self-deterring'; Cruise or Pershing II would more likely be used in a deep strike role.

Deep strike is, in fact, a part of a wider doctrine called Airland Battle, which puts considerable emphasis on offensive manoeuvring as opposed to static linear defence. Its essence, however, is the integration of plans for 'conventional, nuclear, chemical and electronic' capabilities. The firebreak between conventional and nuclear weapons is now almost non-existent; not just because the conventional weapons can be the equal of small nuclear weapons in destructive yield, nor because nuclear weapons are already so embedded in force structures and military planning that their use is a foregone conclusion should a war break out, but also, now, because both types of weapons as well as others have been integrated into a technologically advanced totality, and systematized into a method of warfighting that henceforth will be taught to every soldier in the European sector of NATO.

Nuclear weapons are characterized both by their aggressive nature and by their destructive potential. Deep strike weapons, even if they were non-nuclear, would have the same characteristics. By making a fetish of nuclear weapons it is possible to imagine that conventional warfare would be tolerable by comparison. The new generations of conventional weapons show this to be an illusion; in the war zone their destructiveness could be equal to that of any 'limited' nuclear war.

defcon
see QUICK REACTION ALERT

defence communications system
see COMMAND, CONTROL, COMMUNICATIONS AND INTELLIGENCE

defence contractors To list the involvement of even the top ten US defence contractors is beyond the scope of this work. It is proven beyond doubt that high expenditure on defence produces smaller average growth rates of the economy as a whole (Gross Domestic Product) and lower rates of investment in civilian projects. A sum of money invested in a military project will also lead to the generation of fewer jobs than it would if it was invested in any other branch of industry or social services. Defence contracts distort the research carried out in most American (and British) universities and tie up the time and energy of tens of thousands of the best trained minds available. Lastly, for the USA, by its concentration in just a few states (in 1981, 67.2 per cent of the value of prime defence contracts was distributed within 13 states) divisions between rich and poor states are accentuated and job opportunities for less skilled workers in areas dominated by the defence sector are diminished.

In 1982 the US Department of Defense issued contracts to the top ten defence contractors as follows:

	$, million
General Dynamics	5,891
McDonnell Douglas	5,530
United Technologies	4,208
General Electric	3,654
Lockheed	3,498
Boeing	3,238
Hughes Aircraft	3,140
Rockwell	2,690
Raytheon	2,262
Martin Marietta	2,008

In addition, many contractors receive large reimbursements from the government for R&D they have carried out themselves. Many of these corporations depend on Department of Defense contracts for more than half their income. For example, General Dynamics, given below as an example of the industry, between 1975 and 1979 had 67 per cent of its contracts tied up in defence.

General Dynamics
One of the largest defence contractors, it is based in Dallas-Fort Worth in Texas, with its Electric Boat Division in Connecticut. Its most successful recent weapons product is the Tomahawk cruise missile. It has recently been involved in the following projects:
1 Its Electric Boat Division constructs the US Trident submarines.
2 The US Air Force wanted it to produce 100 updated F-111s – the re-named FB-111H – which, as a medium bomber, would not have

counted against the US quota of heavy bombers in any future SALT agreement. But the House rejected funds and the programme was deferred, though could be reactivated.

3 It lost out in ten competitive 'fly-offs' between the Boeing-built ALCM-B and its own TALCM (both air-launched cruise missiles) during 1979–80. The prize was to build 3,418 ALCMs.

4 However, a Tomahawk similar to the TLAM/N land-attack cruise it already supplies to the Navy was chosen as the prototype for ground-launched cruise missiles.

5 It is building a very accurate medium-range air-to-surface missile (MRASM), with a different version for the Navy and the Air Force, and an anti-ship MRASM is planned to go into service in 1986, equipped with a new imaging infra-red guidance system. It is also building an anti-submarine warfare/stand-off weapon with a range of 480 km.

6 It is engaged in a feasibility study for an intercontinental cruise missile.

In 1969 a survey showed that 113 of 2,122 former top military officers working for the leading 100 defence contractors worked for General Dynamics.

defence planning committee
see NORTH ATLANTIC TREATY ORGANIZATION

defense mapping agency
see TERRAIN CONTOUR MATCHING (TERCOM)

delivery vehicles The self-propelled, piloted or stationary transporter which delivers a warhead or free-falling bomb from its original site towards its target. The most common delivery systems are ballistic missiles, cruise missiles, bombers and fighter planes. Also included would be certain helicopters, nuclear-tipped torpedoes, and field guns capable of firing tactical nuclear shells.

dense pack A proposed method for deploying Peacekeeper (MX) missiles, at the Warner Air Force Base, Cheyenne, Wyoming, and announced in April 1982. The dense pack option would involve 100 MX in super-hardened capsules, 600 m. apart. By packing the MX silos close together the idea is that any Soviet attack would destroy only one silo. For, in so doing, it would create such an ELECTROMAGNETIC PULSE (EMP) effect, as well as such dust and debris in the atmosphere, that Soviet missiles arriving later would either malfunction or be destroyed (FRATRICIDE). The MX missiles would then, so the theory goes, rise slowly through this atmosphere and not be affected.

The problem with dense pack is that no one can be sure that the MX missiles would be unaffected by EMP at the moment of blast-off. Although the US Air Force maintains that up to 70 per cent of dense-pack MX would survive, in fact a complete rocket with all its electronic circuits could be more difficult to shield from EMP effects than a hardened incoming warhead.

Dense pack may run counter to SALT I and II which state that 'each party undertakes not to start construction of additional fixed ICBM launchers'; but the US has replied that the launchers are not fixed: 'the hole in the ground is fixed but the launcher moves with the missile'. Soviet officials also object to it on the grounds that, according to them, SALT II involved 'an obligation not to create additional silos for intercontinental missiles'.

de-nuclearization Anti-nuclear organizations, such as CND, define de-nuclearization as:

a) the decision to remove the nuclear forces of an ally from one's own territory (see CANADA AS A NUCLEAR POWER);

b) the decision to dismantle all reprocessing plants, fuel enrichment plants, nuclear power stations, and mining operations from one's own territory – all of these being parts of the uranium-plutonium fuel cycle;

c) the decision to destroy or dismantle nuclear and thermonuclear warheads in one's own state's possession;

d) the decision to argue that any military alliance of which one's state is a part should likewise take unilateral, bilateral or multilateral steps to reduce and eventually eliminate its nuclear arsenal;

e) the decision to terminate all research and development on nuclear technology for military purposes.

deterrence theory Deterrence is the most important single concept in any discussion of nuclear weapons, and the most widespread justification for their existence. In essence, the concept is very simple: 'The creation by a state seeking to prevent military aggression of a situation in which the potential costs of the aggression risk outweighing the potential gains.' (H. J. Neuman, *Nuclear Forces in Europe,* International Institute of Strategic Studies, London, 1982.) However, when applied to a rapidly changing world, the principles of deterrence become exceedingly complex and somewhat confused.

Five main phases in deterrence doctrine can be identified to date:

1 The idea of deterrence in terms of 'massive retaliation' was the motivating force from 1949 (when the USSR developed its own atomic bomb) to the mid-1960s when both sides reached a point where they could inflict overwhelming damage on each other. Each side also felt the need to close a gap they both identified as being potentially fatal. Thus, new and more advanced weapons were developed.

2 In the mid-1960s the emphasis shifted from deterrence of all nuclear war. The thinking now centred on the question that if a nuclear war was to be fought, a distinction had to be made between 'acceptable' and 'unacceptable' damage. Robert McNamara, US Secretary of

Defense in the Kennedy Administration, defined unacceptable damage as the destruction of between 50 and 75 per cent of industrial capacity and between 25 and 33 per cent of the population.

The search for nuclear supremacy was primarily in terms of numbers of weapons. The inevitable consequence was OVERKILL – a huge increase on the 200 strategic weapons deemed to constitute MUTUAL ASSURED DESTRUCTION – in order to ensure national 'security'.

3 FLEXIBLE RESPONSE was adopted by NATO in 1967 and was designed to deter Warsaw Treaty Organization (WTO) forces at 'local' levels. It assumed two things (**a**) the ability to achieve dominance at each level of escalation; (**b**) that the enemy would recognize the 'rules' and, by inference, refrain from escalating up to superpower exchange. The USSR has always rejected these rules in favour of massive retaliation in response to any FIRST USE by NATO forces. Deterrence theory now moved from an attempt to prevent any nuclear exchange of any kind to an agreement only to limit any nuclear exchange in order to prevent an intercontinental nuclear war.

4 In order to 'deter' the enemy from making a nuclear strike it is now thought necessary to achieve FIRST STRIKE dominance. Security in numbers of weapons has been replaced by the need to improve accuracy and lethality, so attempts are made to make more and more advanced weapons.

5 On 23 March 1983 President Reagan announced a major reversal in deterrence theory. His STAR WARS defensive project aimed to neutralize attacking missiles before they reached the USA. The ANTI-BALLISTIC MISSILE TREATY (1972) had sought to strengthen deterrence by limiting the superpowers' ability to defend themselves against nuclear missiles and by so doing to preserve the balance of mutual destruction. If one side could effectively shield itself from attack (or at least greatly reduce the effects of a nuclear exchange) while at the same time could increase its ability to take out enemy weapons and command posts, then a clear war-winning chance would have been created. Naturally, the Reagan Administration dismisses any such aggressive intention. In the words of Defense Secretary Caspar Weinberger (March 1983): 'Deterrence would be strengthened because we would remove an aggressor's capability to attack us rather than merely threatening retaliation after an attack had taken place.' Or as President Reagan put it: 'We would protect our people, not avenge them.'

disarmament As an aim this should not be confused with ARMS LIMITATION AND ARMS CONTROL talks or agreements, the aims of which are primarily to restrict, order and set limits on the growth of nuclear arsenals and to prevent their PROLIFERATION.

Disarmament can, of course, refer to nuclear weapons, biological and chemical weapons, or conventional weapons. At present, as regards nuclear weapons, no state in possession of them has taken any significant unilateral, bilateral or multilateral disarmament action. Nor does the prospect of their doing so look likely unless (a) the peace movements are able to force through a programme of progressive disarmament measures, or, (b) the states concerned become so dismayed by the prospects of mounting costs, internal dissent, dangerous proliferation, military ineffectiveness, and the threat of global suicide should they ever be used even in fairly limited exchanges (see NUCLEAR WINTER) that they begin to take urgent steps to reduce their arsenals. UNILATERAL DISARMAMENT decisions, while in no way guaranteeing that other states would follow, could at least begin to reverse the current trend of the arms race and demonstrate that it is possible to 'learn to live *without* the bomb'. Unilateral initiatives are entirely possible within the framework of BILATERAL or MULTI-LATERAL arms negotiations. They unblock a frozen situation and by showing evident good will help to build up a climate of trust from which reciprocal gestures first on minor matters, later on more important issues can follow one upon another.

doomsday clock This is the name given to the clock on the logo of the Bulletin of Atomic Scientists. The latter work with, and some of its members belong to, the PUGWASH MOVEMENT, but the two movements are different and the doomsday clock was not, as is often thought, started by the Pugwash Movement. The clock symbolizes the growing danger of nuclear war from year to year by moving the minute hand closer and closer to midnight (midnight equalling the moment of nuclear war). Currently it stands at three minutes to midnight. Some would say that this sombre idea risks the fate of Jeremiah the Prophet: ridicule if the clock finally reaches midnight and the world survives; thanks from nobody if, on the other hand, it is proved right.

dual capable The term applied to a missile or bomb which has the capacity to be nuclear armed or conventionally armed. The dual-capability of strike aircraft, cruise missiles and artillery increases the difficulty of making direct comparisons between the Soviet and the US nuclear forces. For example, most of the Soviet air-launched cruise missiles are capable of carrying both nuclear and conventional warheads. This is proving one of the stumbling blocks in arms negotiations between the two superpowers.
see also FUNCTIONALLY RELATED OBSERVABLE DIFFERENCES

dual key On some nuclear weapons it is necessary for two complementary codes to be inserted into the weapon's command system before the warhead can be activated. For some US nuclear weapons deployed in Europe, the dual-key arrangement has come to mean that a warhead can be activated only by a code held by the US custodial team (in charge of the warhead) and the allied host (responsible for the delivery system). Some warheads are protected against accidental or illegitimate arming by PERMISSIVE ACTION LINKS (PALs) which disarm the warhead in the event of unauthorized coding.

Not all US nuclear weapons in Europe are deployed co-operatively. For example, the British Government rejected a dual-key option for those GROUND-LAUNCHED CRUISE MISSILES based at Molesworth and Greenham Common on the grounds of expense, preferring to rely on an historical 'understanding' that the weapons would not be used unilaterally by the US without first having consulted the British Government.

effects of nuclear explosion To avoid repetition, fuller accounts of particular aspects of the effects of nuclear explosions can be found under the following headings: FISSION, FUSION, ENHANCED RADIATION WEAPON, BURNS, RADIATION, FALLOUT, GROUND BURST, AIR BURST, ELECTROMAGNETIC PULSE (EMP), NUCLEAR WINTER, OVERPRESSURE, HIROSHIMA, NAGASAKI. The effects of an explosion will vary considerably according to the size of the bomb or warhead, whether the explosion is a ground burst, an air burst or a high-altitude burst, and whether the bomb is fission only, fission–fusion–fission, or an enhanced radiation weapon (ERW).

Briefly, the size affects the extent of damage of all kinds, although this extent does not grow proportionally with size (see EQUIVALENT MEGATONNAGE). A ground burst will produce the worst blast damage at close range and also the worst fallout because of the earth and other surface debris that is dragged up into and vapourized within the fireball. An air burst would spread its heat flash, and therefore its burn effects and secondary fires, over a wider area than a ground burst, while a high-altitude burst would spread the effects of EMP over the widest possible area.

Fission bombs produce more and longer-lasting radioactive fallout than fusion bombs. The dirtiest bombs of all are the fission–fusion–fission variety, because the outer shell is made of uranium-238, thus producing highly radioactive fallout. A fission bomb cannot achieve megaton capability, because it is difficult to keep large quantities of the fissile material, uranium-235, sufficiently separated to prevent a chain reaction from starting. Hydrogen (fusion) bombs are much more powerful, first because fusion releases three times as much energy as a similar quantity of fissionable material, secondly because deuterium and tritorium can be stored in large quantities without becoming critical.

The second set of variables which can alter the effects of a nuclear explosion relate to topography, the proximity, density and type of buildings, the amount of water in the atmosphere, the opacity of the air, whether the explosion is at night or in the day, the temperature of different air layers, and wind direction and speed. To take one example: a 100 kt explosion at 50,000 feet could cause flash blindness (temporary) at a distance of 20 miles from GROUND ZERO in daytime and 70 miles at night; indeed, at night it could cause retinal burns 27 miles away.

General effects

1 About 35 per cent of a nuclear fireball's energy takes the form of intense heat and light – the heat FLASH. This would ignite most combustible materials within the fire zone. (Range for charred skin: 8 miles.*)

2 Blast from a nuclear explosion has two effects. The first is a sudden compression of the wall of air pushed out from the explosion. This increases the air pressure above the normal 14.7 psi and is called static OVERPRESSURE. It can crush buildings at just 4 psi (above normal) and can kill people at over 30 psi (above normal, though with psi at that level people would certainly be killed from other causes). The second effect is dynamic pressure or drag pressure – very high winds of hundreds, even thousands of miles per hour. These have devastating results, though some people argue that they would snuff out the fires just ignited by the heat flash. Once the atmospheric pressure returns to normal as the blast wave moves on, many buildings, the internal atmospheric pressure of which had been increased by the wave, would simply explode. (Range of devastation for above-ground buildings: 2.5 miles.*)

3 Radiation takes two forms: initial ('prompt') radiation, consisting of deadly neutrons and gamma rays, is intense, short-lived and limited in range; and residual radiation, mainly fallout, which gets less and less deadly with time. (Range of lethal – 500 rads – initial radiation: 1.6 miles.*)

4 Electromagnetic pulse (EMP) would wreak havoc with electrical and electronic systems.

5 NUCLEAR WINTER: if even a modest nuclear exchange occurred, there is a strong consensus amongst scientists that the smoke from the resulting fires would blot out the sun, resulting in sub-arctic temperatures for possibly a year, followed by ultraviolet radiation from the sun's rays due to the partial destruction of the ozone layer.

6 The survivors – and how many are posited to survive for different configurations of attacks of varying megatonnage varies enormously according to the statistical assumptions employed – would then face the long-term effects of fallout on food and water, plant and animal life, and themselves, and devastation of the social and economic infrastructure.

* An asterisk signifies that these figures are based on an air-burst explosion of a 1 mt warhead at optimum height.

source: calculated from *The Effects of Nuclear Weapons,* 3rd edn and quoted in Peter Goodwin, *Nuclear War. The Facts,* 1981, p. 31

Eighteen Nation Disarmament Committee (ENDC)

In September 1961 the USA and USSR agreed to set up such a committee, which began its first session in Geneva in March 1962. By 1965 its sessions had become dominated by the issue of PRO-LIFERATION. It has been the main forum for multilateral arms control negotiations and, in 1969, was enlarged to 26 members and re-named the Conference of the Committee on Disarmament.

France has a seat but has never occupied it. The other members are: USA, Canada, Britain, Italy, Japan and the Netherlands; the USSR, Bulgaria, Czechoslovakia, Hungary, Mongolia and Romania; and Argentina, Brazil, Burma, Egypt, Ethiopia, India, Mexico, Morocco, Nigeria, Pakistan, Sweden and Yugoslavia.

The Conference of the Committee on Disarmament, later expanded to 35 nations, is required to formulate all its recommendations by consensus. The themes that appear on its agendas 'at least constitute agreements to formulate agreements' and include such questions as a comprehensive test ban treaty, new types of weapons of mass destruction such as radiological weapons, the cessation of the nuclear arms race, nuclear disarmament, and so on.

While no nuclear arms control treaty has so far emerged, many issues have been clarified. The Chinese delegation observed in August 1981 that 'the statements made by the various delegations ... have made clearer the points in common as well as the points of divergence ... which will undoubtedly help the future consultations and considerations'.

electromagnetic pulse (EMP)

This is the term applied to the sharp and extremely powerful surge of electromagnetic energy produced by a nuclear explosion. Its sheer power and the speed with which it is absorbed by any unprotected wire or cable will burn out capacitors and transistors and overload power supply systems. If a nuclear bomb of 10 mt were exploded 200 miles above the USA the effect would be to destroy every electrical and electronic system in the whole of North America.

Although attempts have been made to 'harden' military (especially C^3I) installations against EMP no one can say how successful these have been. The Russians may have been aware of EMP long before the USA as a MIG-25 Foxbat, whose pilot had defected, was found to be equipped with tiny vacuum valves instead of the normal transistors.

see also FRATRICIDE, EFFECTS OF NUCLEAR EXPLOSION

emergency rocket communications system

see COMMAND, CONTROL, COMMUNICATIONS AND INTELLIGENCE

enhanced radiation weapon (ERW) – neutron bomb

By miniaturizing the fission (atomic) trigger for a small H-bomb and by not surrounding the bomb with a shell of U-238, the amount of long-lived radiation particles given off in an explosion can be greatly reduced. Such a weapon gives off mainly heat, blast and neutron particles, the radiation effect of which is short-lived and prompt.

Invented in 1958 by Edward Teller, 'father' of the H-bomb, the development of the ERW was initially justified in terms of anti-ballistic missile defence development. After the ABM Treaty of 1972 this rationale collapsed and it emerged as an anti-tank weapon, the neutrons being capable of penetrating armour plating. It has since been suggested that if tank armour were hardened with zirconium alloy, or other alloys used for the construction of fuel rods in nuclear reactors, tanks would be immunized against neutron bombardment.

The Carter administration planned to deploy the 'neutron bomb', as it became known, in Europe on Lance missiles and in 8-inch artillery shells after a NATO agreement in 1977. However, public hostility was so great (the current phrase was 'the bomb that destroys people but not buildings') that Carter had to rescind its deployment. In August 1981 President Reagan gave the go-ahead for enhanced radiation weapons to be added to the US arsenal, though it was understood that these would not be deployed in Europe without NATO consent.

EnMod Convention (1977)

EnMod Convention (1977) The Environmental Modification Convention was signed or ratified by 31 states, including the USSR and the USA. It banned the use of hostile techniques to change climactic patterns, ocean currents, the ozone layer or the ecological balance. The fact that a nuclear exchange would almost certainly produce a NUCLEAR WINTER effect should be grounds for litigation against nuclear weapon states under the terms of this Convention. Since 1979, the Committee on Disarmament has been discussing the prohibition of radiological weapons other than a nuclear explosive device, specifically designed to employ radioactive material as a primary cause of destruction.

enriched uranium

enriched uranium Natural uranium contains only 0.7 per cent of the fissionable isotope uranium 235; virtually all the rest is uranium 238. However, for the construction of a fission bomb employing uranium about 70 per cent of the uranium must be U-235 (for nuclear fuel for power stations the figure is 3 per cent). This can be obtained by enrichment. This was first accomplished by a gaseous diffusion technique in which the lighter isotope, U-235, diffuses through a membrane more rapidly than U-238. This process can be repeated, using naturally occurring uranium until the required amount of U-235 has been obtained. The residue, almost entirely U-238, is called 'depleted uranium'.

The gaseous diffusion method has all manner of drawbacks: it is good for enriching to weapon-grade levels but wasteful for the 2 to 3 per cent required for nuclear fuel; the plant has to be built on a huge scale; worst of all it consumes electricity at a spectacular rate. By the

1950s such plants in the USA were drawing off 10 per cent of the country's electricity, almost all for bomb-grade uranium (this immense expenditure of energy is one of the hidden costs of nuclear weapons).

Another and much cheaper method of enriching uranium is the gas centrifuge system which separates U-235 from U-238 by putting uranium gas into a large, rapidly spinning, machine and pushing away the heavier isotope. It was one component of the MANHATTAN PROJECT but was not successfully developed until much later. It consumes only 5 per cent of the electricity used by the gaseous diffusion process. Laser enrichment is the most likely method in the future.

see NUCLEAR FUEL CYCLE

equivalent megatonnage (EMt) The destructive capacity of a missile cannot be expressed in terms of its yield alone. A 10 mt warhead is not simply ten times more powerful than a 1 mt warhead. Hence a more accurate calculation of a missile's ability to destroy a SOFT TARGET (as against a protected or HARD TARGET) is expressed as two-thirds power of its yield – $Y^{\frac{2}{3}}$.

The International Institute of Strategic Studies adds that 'EMt may overstate the effectiveness of very large weapons, because the area of potential destruction is likely to exceed the area of the target destroyed.'

see MISSILE ACCURACY, CIRCLE OF ERROR PROBABLE, COUNTER MILITARY POTENTIAL, LETHALITY, SINGLE SHOT PROBABILITY OF KILL

escalation dominance Seen, in DETERRENCE THEORY, as the ability of one combatant to maintain superiority at each level of a nuclear exchange, some feel, more sceptically, that escalation dominance, far from being part of deterrence, is a euphemistic term for nuclear war-fighting and war-'winning'.

European nuclear balance Ideally, calculation of any nuclear balance should be dynamic and qualitative, based on assessments of survivability, penetrability, reliability, targeting options, accuracy, etc. As this is well-nigh impossible we must fall back on a quantitative approach.

Even this has its problems: should the French and British forces be included, on the basis that they are there, that they are in Europe, and that they are targeted on the USSR? Or should they be excluded on the grounds that they are national defences of 'last resort' – strategic forces? If they are included, should their MRVed warheads count as one warhead only or as three or, in the case of Chevaline, possibly six warheads? Should the Soviet SS11s, SS19s and SS-N-5s, which have been targeted on Europe but perhaps have been re-assigned, be included? And should the 400 US Poseidon warheads allocated to Supreme Allied Command, Europe, but already accounted for in the SALT talks be included, on the basis that they are targeted on Europe? Then again, should one count warheads or launchers? Should one use equivalent megatonnage as a measure? Lastly, with such a wide discrepancy between the capability of different aircraft claimed (by the adversary) as opposed to admitted (by the state that flies them), should such aircraft be included in the general calculation?

Finally there is the problem that the USSR is, after all, a European power by virtue of its geographical position, while the USA is not; in other words, the USSR can be hit by long-range theatre nuclear weapons, while the USA, apart from Alaska, would be untouched by them.

If we exclude nuclear capable aircraft, US SLBMs, Soviet strategic weapons and Cruise and Pershing IIs then the nuclear balance is 2–2.5:1 in favour of the USSR. With aircraft it is still around 2.5:1. If US Poseidon warheads are added to the French and British missiles with MRVs counting as one warhead only, and if on the Soviet side the 30 SS-N-5s are included with the SS20s, then we obtain 578 warheads in the West and 564 in the East. With the advent of Cruise and Pershing II, the balance is changing, and will change still further with the completion of the Chevaline programme and the deployment of a new generation of French missiles. By the early 1990s, before the arrival of the British Trident submarines, the combined equivalent megatonnage of the British and French systems could be almost twice as powerful as the Soviet SS-20 force.

Even now the European balance has been seriously upset by the start of a flow of GLCMs and Pershing IIs to Germany, Britain and Italy at the end of 1983. The USSR walked out of the Geneva talks on Intermediate Nuclear Forces. This, after all, was the first time US land-based theatre missiles had been present on the European continent since the withdrawal of Mace missiles 15 years earlier.

The US ZERO OPTION position had been to agree not to deploy Cruise and Pershing IIs if the USSR would scrap all its SS-20s. This would have left the USSR in Europe with outdated and inaccurate SS-4s and 5s and 30 SS-N-5 Serbs facing the French and British submarine forces and 40 US Poseidon SLBMs, each armed with ten MIRVed warheads (excluding aircraft on both sides).

Nuclear-tipped artillery and short-range missiles have not been mentioned on either side. Soviet policy is to store these within Soviet territory; Nato policy is to keep them, sometimes in a high state of readiness, in Central Europe.

To demonstrate the complexity of trying to calculate the objective European balance, six estimates are reprinted below from different sources (all save the SIPRI estimate are taken with thanks from Andrew Kelly, *Not by Numbers Alone*, pp. 39–43).

Long-range theatre nuclear missiles

Country	Missile designation	Year deployed	Range (km)	CEP (m)	Warheads	Inventory	Programme status
USSR	SS-4 Sandal	1959	1,800	2,400	1 x mt	232	phasing out
	SS-5 Skean	1961	3,500	1,200	1 x mt	16	phasing out
	SS-20	1976/77	5,000	400	3 x 150 kt MIRV; 1 x ?	333	approx 50 more each year
	SS-N-5 Serb	1963	1,200	na	1 x mt	30	3 each on Golf II subs (6 such subs in Baltic since 1976)
USA	Pershing II	1983	1,800	40	1 x ? (low kt)	?	108 launchers by 1985
	GLCM	1983	2,500	50	1 x ?	?	464 missiles by 1988
UK	Polaris A-3	1967	4,600	800	3 x 200 kt MRV	64	on 4 SSBNs, being replaced by Chevaline
	Trident II D-5	1990s	10,000	250	8 x 355 kt MIRV	0	replacing Chevaline in 1990s with 64 launchers on 4 subs
France	SSBS S-3	1980	3,000	na	1 x mt	18	on five SSBNs
	MSBS M-20	1977	3,000	na	1 x mt	80	on 6th SSBN; total including retrofits: 96 by 1992
	MSBS M-4	(1985)	4,000	na	6 x 150 kt MRV	0	

source: *SIPRI Yearbook, 1983*, p.34

The theatre nuclear balance: US view

US		USSR	
IRBM	0	IRBM	
		SS-20	250
		SS-4/5	350
		SS-12/22	100
		SS-N-5	30
bombers		bombers	
F-111 in Europe	164	Backfire Tu-26	45
FB-111 in US	63	Blinder Tu-16	350
F-4	265	Badger Tu-22	
A-6 & A-6	68	SU-17 & SU-24	2700
		Mig-27	
total	560	total	3825

Comment: (a) no intermediate or short-range missiles included, although a comparable weapon – the SS-12 – is included on the Soviet side; (b) all Soviet medium-range nuclear-capable aircraft included when probably only around 25 per cent have a nuclear role. Conversely, not all nuclear-capable aircraft included on US side; (c) of course all British and French forces and all sea-borne forces on both sides are excluded.
source: *New York Times,* 30 November 1981

Theatre nuclear balance: Soviet view

US and NATO		USSR	
IRBM		IRBM	
French IRBM	18	SS-20	243
French SLBM	80	SS-4/5	253
UK Polaris	64	SS-N-5	18
bombers		bombers	
F-111	172	Backfire Tu-26	
FB-111	65	Blinder Tu-16	461
F-4	246	Badger Tu-22	
A-6 & A-7	240		
French Mirage IVA	46		
UK Vulcan	55		
total	986	total	975

Comment: (a) unlike the US total, the Soviet calculation includes French and British forces; (b) Soviet figures for SS-20s and SS-4s and 5s are higher than US estimates; (c) the nuclear-capable bomber total is down on the US total while the strike aircraft are not mentioned, even though it is known that they are nuclear capable, so it is unlikely that none of them is assigned a nuclear role; (d) Poseidon warheads allocated to SACEUR are not included; (e) some of the SS-20s are located in a 'swing position' so they can be targeted on Europe or China; (f) the USSR in 1981 was claiming rough parity in Europe while the USA saw an imbalance of nearly 7:1.
source: Leonid Brezhnev, interview in *Der Spiegel,* no. 45, November 1981

The theatre nuclear balance: British view

European theatre, land-based missiles

NATO		USSR	
long-range		long-range	
Vulcan, F-111	200	SS-4, SS-5, SS-20	490
		Badger, Blinder,	350
		Backfire	
medium range		medium range	
Pershing I	180	Scaleboard/SS-22, Scud	650
F-4, F-104, Jaguar	650	Fitter, Flogger,	2000
Buccaneer		Fishbed, Fencer	
short range		short range	
Lance, Honest John,	1150	Frog/SS-21, 203mm.	950
155mm & 8 inch		Howitzers, 240mm.	
Howitzers		Mortars	
total	2180	total	4400

European nuclear balance

Comment: (a) calculation is by missile not warhead; the same is true for US and Soviet calculations. The British government does state that were warheads to be the basis the ratio in favour of the USSR would be more like four to one; (b) no sea-based systems are included on either side; (c) the French systems are totally excluded (d) like the US nearly all Soviet nuclear-capable aircraft are included without any estimate of how many fulfil a nuclear role.

source: 'Statement on the Defence Estimates', HMSO, London 1982.

The theatre nuclear balance: the International Institute of Strategic Studies view

Long and medium range systems for the European theatre

	NATO	NATO (including Poseidon)	WTO
Inventory	1,643		4,124
Warheads available	799	1,199	2,297
Arriving warheads	275	563	1,085

Comment: (a) allowance is made for the availability and reliability of missiles as well as assessing their capabilities for penetrating and surviving enemy defences; (b) including Poseidon warheads the Soviet lead in 'arriving warheads' is about 1.6:1; (c) the figures do not include weapons with a range shorter than 160 km of which NATO has a preponderance so the comparison here is, on the IISS's own admission, 'inevitably artificial'.

source: *The Military Balance, 1982*–83, International Institute of Strategic Studies, London, 1982

How Soviet hawks might view the military balance: long, medium and short-range nuclear systems in the European theatre

NATO	warheads	WARSAW PACT	warheads
long-range		*long-range*	
45 Poseidon SLBM	400	105 SS-20 IRBM	315
64 Polaris SLBM	192	435 SS-4/5 I/MRBM	435
80 French M-20	80	60 SS-N-5 SLBM	60
57 Vulcan bomber	114	30 Backfire bomber	120
33 Mirage IVA bomber	33	177 Badger/Blinder bomber	354
109 F-4 Fighter bomber	109		
78 F-111 E/F bomber	156		
10 A-6E Carrier-based Aircraft	20		
20 A-7E	40		
6 Etendard	12		
medium range		*medium range*	
180 Pershing 1A	180	487 SS-12/SCUD B SRAM	487
90 Lance	90	9 SS-N-4 SLBM	9
32 Pluton	32	54 Fencer Fighter bomber	108
30 Buccaneer bomber	60	161 Fitter	161
40 Jaguar	40	260 Flogger	260
15 Mirage IIIE	15	200 Fishbed	200
95 F104	95		
total long and medium range:		total long and medium range:	
984	1668	1978	2509
short range		*short range*	
Various systems	6,000	None able to hit W. Europe	
total	7,668	total	2,509

Comment: Mary Kaldor is attempting to show how, when different weapon systems are included, markedly different results are achieved (a lead by NATO of three to one). The dispute over the European balance is about just that: which weapons to include and which weapons can be regarded as equivalents in the opposing arsenal when the two sets of weapons coalesce around totally different strategies.

source: M Kaldor, 'Misreading Ourselves and Others', in K Coates (ed.) *Eleventh Hour for Europe*, Spokesman Books, Nottingham 1981.

European Nuclear Disarmament (END) Founded by Edward Thompson, Mary Kaldor and others together with the Bertrand Russell Peace Foundation in 1980. European Nuclear Disarmament has provided a steady flow of information on the European peace movements through its bi-monthly journal. It has stressed the need for the creation of a demilitarized zone in Europe both West and East and has criticized strongly the denial of human rights and freedom of political expression in Eastern Europe, the USSR and Turkey, while making every effort to disseminate the views of the independent peace groups so persecuted, such as Charter 77 and the Moscow Group for Trust. It has also helped to mount the two Brussels International Peace Conferences.

END is based in Britain. It is affiliated to CND but independent of it. It has done much to raise questions in a wider public about the nature of the politico-military blocs that cut Europe into two and threaten to make it the theatre of a nuclear war in which its inhabitants have no say, no interest, and from which few of them would survive. A Europe free from nuclear weapons 'from Portugal to Poland' is its goal together with the banning of nuclear systems from Soviet Europe and sea-borne nuclear systems from Western Europe.

Some END writers stress the ambiguous nature of the two blocs – that although they now polarize the two halves of Europe against each other, their founding on both sides was quite largely caused by a need to pull together a sphere of influence and prevent other influences from becoming dominant: the western Communist Parties, nationalist movements in Eastern Europe, and a unified, social-democratic neutralist Germany.

eurostrategic weapons
see THEATRE NUCLEAR WEAPONS

extended deterrence This refers to the role US nuclear weapons would play in deterring attacks other than all-out attacks and those against the USA itself; more specifically, attacks on a European NATO ally. What is at stake is the preparedness of the USA to defend western Europe with nuclear weapons at the risk of the conflict escalating to an attack on the USA.

The decision to commit ground-launched cruise missiles and Pershing IIs to Europe was designed to calm European fears on this score. Current theory has it that a war in the European 'theatre' need not become global. The central flaw in this theory is the geographical asymmetry of the situation. For while Soviet long-range theatre nuclear weapons (LRTNW) cannot hit Washington or New York, American LRTNWs can hit Moscow and Leningrad and are targeted to do so – in 12 minutes from launch. The Soviet Union is hardly likely to respond to the destruction of half of Moscow or Kiev by an American-fired Pershing II with a second strike on, say, Manchester.

Rather, it will strike directly at the politico-military source of the attack – Washington, and not observe NATO's category of the European theatre as is its oft-publicized intention.

But the asymmetry is not only that between the USA and the USSR, it is also that between the USA and its NATO allies. Extended deterrence for the USA collapses into a limited nuclear war, or at least into a war the US wishes to see limited to Europe. But from a European perspective such a war is neither a deterrent nor limited; it is strategic: a war that would destroy the very prize being defended.

If war is to be deterred in Europe then most NATO governments subscribe to the view that everything must be done to ensure that the war would be nuclear and suicidal. This means taking risks. It also means that in practice theories of graduated response and escalation control would not have much purchase on events in Europe. US strategists, then, have a totally different perception of what a nuclear war in Europe would be: for them it is an intermediate war designed to gain battlefield advantage through the attrition of enemy forces. For the Europeans it is something that simply must not happen, but because it must not happen (in the curious logic of deterrence) it is also something that must be prepared for, believed in and made plausible by taking risks. There are broadly three ways in which the NATO threat is made realistic: decentralized and delegated control of nuclear weapons once they are put on alert, the ambiguity of command authority over the employment of nuclear weapons, and the complexity of wartime and crisis management. The very manipulation of the risks involved gives credibility to the NATO posture even if it ultimately contributes to a loss of political control.

see FORWARD BASED SYSTEMS, DETERRENCE, STRATEGIC DOCTRINE (WESTERN)

F-4 fighter The 'Phantom' is an all-weather supersonic versatile fighter in service with US forces in Europe and the USA as well as with Turkish, Greek and West German forces. During 1961–79 5,057 were produced, but it is now being replaced with a variety of other aircraft.
Specifications
Range: 2,200 km
Speed: Mach 2.2
Nuclear payload: three externally mounted gravity bombs offering a wide range of yields.
Number deployed: sources differ – *Military Balance*, 1983/84: 142 NATO 96 USA; *Nuclear Weapons Databook*, Vol. 1 1984: 1,098

F-16 fighter The 'Fighting Falcon' is a US and NATO nuclear-capable strike aircraft. Its development started in 1972 and the first US aircraft were operational in January 1979. During 1982–83 F-16s were deployed in West Germany.

Specifications
Range: 3,800 km
Speed: Mach 2
Nuclear payload: capable of delivering up to five bombs, but the usual armament is one B61 (four yield options 100–500 kt)
Number deployed: sources differ – *Military Balance, 1983/84*: 234 (of which 90 operated by NATO); *Nuclear Weapons Databook,* Vol. 1, 1984: 365

F-104 fighter The 'Starfighter' is a daylight interceptor/strike aircraft in wide use with NATO since the 1960s. It is to be replaced by the Tornado.
Specifications
Range: 2,400 km
Speed: Mach 2.2
Nuclear payload: one gravity bomb with a wide range of yield options
Number deployed: 261 NATO

F-111 fighter In service at RAF Lakenheath, RAF Heyford as well as Cannon Air Force Base, New Mexico and Mountain Home Air Force Base, Idaho, the F-111 is an all-weather long-range nuclear-armed strike aircraft. At their British bases, the F-111 are on QUICK REACTION ALERT (QRA) at all times. Its on-board terrain-following radar equips it for all-weather and night low-level bombing missions.
Specifications
Range: 4,700 km
Speed: Mach 2.5 maximum
Nuclear payload: up to 3 gravity bombs, two of which can be carried externally. Variable yields of each bomb (B43) up to 1 mt.
Number deployed: 240

fallout Fallout is the second form of radiation resulting from a nuclear explosion. The first form is called initial or 'prompt' radiation and is limited in range and time though very intense (see ENHANCED RADIATION WEAPON). Fallout is pulverized earth and other matter which gets sucked up into the fireball and becomes radioactive as a result of being bombarded by neutrons. The heavier pieces of matter would simply fall back to earth near the site of the explosion (GROUND ZERO). But the rest would be carried downwind, gradually returning to earth in the form of radioactive fallout. The amount of fallout for any given megatonnage depends on how near to the ground the warhead is at the moment of explosion. The nearer to the ground the greater will be the crater made by the explosion and the more fallout there will be. (The air bursts above Hiroshima and Nagasaki produced comparatively limited fallout.)

The first day of fallout will consist of dust and isotopes emitting gamma rays and some beta rays. Later it will consist of radioactive isotopes – caesium-137, strontium-90 or carbon-14 for example – which find their way into food and water.

In stable weather conditions fallout will affect a cigar-shaped area of the earth's surface downwind from ground zero. For example, a one megaton surface explosion would, in 24 hours and assuming a constant wind speed of 15 mph, deliver an accumulated dose of 200 rads 95 miles from ground zero spread across a belt of land 11.8 miles wide at its maximum and 5.4 miles wide at ground zero. Of course the accumulated radiation increases the nearer one is to ground zero. This is so for three reasons:

a) because places at or near ground zero will be exposed to radioactive fallout for a longer period of time than places further away;

b) because fission products decay quite rapidly (though some have a very long HALF-LIFE);

c) because rainy conditions or hilly terrain will absorb more and more of the fallout (see RADIATION).

see EFFECTS OF NUCLEAR EXPLOSION

fast-breeder reactor (FBR)

A nuclear reactor that produces more fissile material than it consumes. The reactor design is such that each fission generates more neutrons than are necessary for sustaining the chain reaction; some of the rest are absorbed by fertile nuclei, usually uranium-238 or thorium-232, which then decay to produce fissile fuels, namely plutonium-239 and U-233 respectively. Because the neutrons have to be 'fast', ie to travel at almost the speed at which they were ejected from the fissioning fuel, no moderator is used in a breeder reactor. The coolant has, therefore, to be very efficient, either sodium or sodium-potassium alloy, or, in the gas-cooled FBR, helium.

The attraction of an FBR is that after a period of years known as the 'doubling time' the reactor will have doubled its inventory of fissile material. Unfortunately, the doubling time is likely to be 40 or even 60 years, whereas when FBRs were first commissioned it was thought to be only a few years.

There are multiple technical problems in the construction and operation of FBRs, as there are with the reprocessing plants which are needed to provide plutonium fuel from the spent fuel of 'normal' burner reactors. FBRs and reprocessing plants increase the possibilities of PROLIFERATION.

see ATOMS FOR PEACE, NUCLEAR FUEL CYCLE, INTERNATIONAL ATOMIC ENERGY AGENCY, BOILING-WATER REACTOR

'Fat Man' atomic bomb

Weighing 10,800 lbs and measuring 12 ft long, the FISSION bomb 'fat man' was exploded 1,650 ft above Nagasaki on 9 August 1945 at 11.02 a.m. An IMPLOSION DEVICE was used (as against the gun device employed in the 'Little Boy' bomb dropped three days earlier at Hiroshima) to produce a yield of about 20 kt.

FB-111 bomber This, a variation of the F-111 fighter, is used by US Strategic Air Command as a medium range, low-altitude, high-penetration bomber. Due to its high speed, small size and low-level terrain-following capability, the FB-111 is seen as a much more effective weapon for attacking well-defended positions than the larger but more vulnerable B-52 bomber. It is due to be replaced by the ATB (ADVANCED TECHNOLOGY BOMBER) during the 1990s.

Specifications
Range: 4,700 km
Speed: Mach 2.5
Nuclear payload: 6 gravity bombs or 6 SRAM or a mix of 4 SRAM carried externally and 2 bombs internally
Number deployed: 56 stationed at Pease Air Force Base, New Hampshire and Plattsburgh Air Force Base, New York State.

fireball As soon as a nuclear bomb is exploded in the atmosphere, a huge spherical fireball is formed. This cools rapidly and expands to form the characteristic mushroom-shaped cloud.

firestorm The fire created by a nuclear or conventional explosion(s) which sucks in air from the surrounding area (and can also drag in people) and will not abate until everything combustible has been consumed. Its heat is such that it burns the oxygen in the air, causing death by asphyxiation to anyone in bomb-proof and fire-proof shelters in the vicinity. Conventional saturation bombing, as at Dresden in World War II, and the nuclear explosion at Hiroshima, both resulted in firestorms.
see EFFECTS OF NUCLEAR EXPLOSION

first-strike capability This is the ability to inflict a disarming or unanswerable first strike against a rival nation. The attack has to be able to destroy all strategic weapons attached to all three arms of an enemy's strategic triad (land-based missiles, sea-based missiles, and bombers). Counterforce targeting is essential to, but not equatable with, first-strike capability (see also FLEXIBLE RESPONSE).

At present, the USA is far ahead, both in the technology necessary for first strike capability (speed, reliability, accuracy, anti-submarine warfare capability, etc.), the numbers of missiles with such qualities either on station, about to be deployed, or being developed, and, perhaps also, in the strategic planning and co-ordination (C^3I) for such a capability to become operational.
see STRATEGIC DOCTRINE (AMERICAN), STRATEGIC DOCTRINE (SOVIET)

first use The initial employment of nuclear weapons in response to a conventional attack. First announced publicly as US policy on 30 May 1975 by James Schlesinger, Defense Secretary, it remains part of current NATO policy. In July 1982, at the UN Second Special Session devoted to Disarmament, the USSR pledged a unilateral commitment not to be the first to use nuclear weapons. Significantly, it stated that it expected other nuclear states to follow suit and that in the formulation of its policy it would take into account whether they did or not. NATO defends its position on the basis that it is essential to raise continued uncertainty among Warsaw Treaty Organization strategists as to NATO's range of responses to any attack. It is possible that first use, if it comes, would be at the TACTICAL level, using battlefield nuclear shells. It is probable that battlefield commanders at relatively junior levels are authorized to release such weapons under certain conditions. Their Soviet counterparts have similar authorization.

The Soviet pledge is important, but is by no means sure for all time. For many people, and not only those in the peace movements, a no-first-use pledge from all sides is the crucial next step in international arms negotiations.

see NON-NUCLEAR DEFENCE

fission Fission is the subdivision of a heavy atomic nucleus into two fragments of about equal mass. For this to happen the atom must be inherently unstable, that is, its nuclear binding forces must be inadequate to hold it together. Uranium-238 is stable in normal circumstances and can absorb low-energy neutrons without splitting, though under great heat it will undergo FUSION (see H-BOMB). Uranium-235, however, is unstable even in its natural state (it occurs as only 0.7 per cent of mined uranium) because it has three neutrons fewer than U-238, and neutrons are essential to the nuclear binding process. In fact, a few of its atoms disintegrate spontaneously at any one moment, emitting neutrons and pure energy in the form of gamma rays (ie it is radioactive). (For the way in which fission works as an explosive see ATOM BOMB)

Several other elements can produce or themselves constitute fissile material. Among them are plutonium, which is decayed uranium-239 (itself a result of U-238 absorbing neutrons inside nuclear reactors) and thorium-232, which decays into fissionable uranium-233.

Fission is used for nuclear power generation. A slow, controlled release of energy is obtained by using a mixture of uranium with about 3 per cent U-235. The most common way that the reaction can be controlled is by inserting or withdrawing graphite rods, which absorb radioactivity.

fission–fusion–fission reaction
see THERMONUCLEAR WEAPONS

flash (nuclear) This describes the intense pulse of heat and light emitted by a nuclear explosion (see EFFECTS OF NUCLEAR EXPLOSION). It is so bright that the flash effect of a 10 mt air burst could temporarily blind people more than 200 miles away on a clear night. The heat would set fire to everything within the fire zone – an area which varies in size with the height and strength of the explosion – and cause burns and start fires in a much wider area (see BURNS). The more powerful the weapon the longer the pulse of heat and light (three seconds for a 20 mt bomb, one fifth of a second for a 25 kt explosion).

flexible counterforce
see STRATEGIC DOCTRINE (AMERICAN)

flexible response
A nuclear strategy first adopted by NATO in 1977 and based on the principle of deterring aggression by enabling NATO to respond to any level of action initiated by an aggressor 'at the appropriate level'.

Document MC 14/3 of NATO's Military Committee commits NATO to:

a) 'meet initially any aggression short of general nuclear attack with a direct defence at the level chosen by the aggressor';

b) 'conduct a deliberate escalation if aggression cannot be contained and the situation restored by direct defence';

c) 'initiate an appropriate general nuclear response to a major nuclear attack'.

The assumption made in flexible response is that the opponent will respond gradually or even terminate hostilities before all-out nuclear war has begun (something that contradicts all published Soviet strategic nuclear doctrine). One of its effects, intended or not, is to make limited nuclear war a credible option without the destructive certainties associated with mutual assured destruction. However, even NATO Commander, General Bernard Rogers, has said, 'the use of theater nuclear weapons would in fact escalate to the strategic level, and very quickly.'

Presidential Directive 59 (see STRATEGIC DOCTRINE (AMERICAN)), signed by Jimmy Carter, took flexible response to its limit and opened the door to Reagan's 'strategy for protracted nuclear war'. It was preceded by an 18-month study ordered by the White House to:

a) determine the nuclear strategy that would eliminate the USSR as a functioning national entity;

b) investigate promoting separatism by destroying areas in the USSR which support the present government;

c) identify the targets that could 'paralyze, disrupt and dismember' the Soviet government by annihilating the ruling group.

flush
In nuclear terms, a 'flush' describes the dispersal of forces to comparative safety (eg the scrambling of aircraft or the dispersal of ships and submarines from their bases) under threat from an enemy nuclear strike.

footprint The explosion pattern of the warheads released from a multiple-warhead missile can be varied by changing the speed and timing by which they are released from their dispenser (POST-BOOST VEHICLE).

force de frappe
see FRANCE AS A NUCLEAR POWER

forward based systems (FBS) A term introduced by the USSR to refer to US nuclear systems that have less than intercontinental range but which, because of their location, could reach targets in the Soviet Union. The USSR regards these as strategic, and tried unsuccessfully to get them covered first in SALT I and then in negotiations on theatre nuclear forces. It sought 'compensation' for FBSs by being permitted to possess a larger number of central systems in her arsenal.

Around 1975–76 the question of FBSs became the touchstone in Europe for the USA's sympathy for its NATO allies during the SALT II negotiations. However, despite Helmut Schmidt's publicly stated belief that the 700 Soviet continental missiles posed a threat to Western Europe, the West European ministers decided against officially raising the issue of their presence. For to do so would have conceded the Soviet point about the strategic threat of US FBSs and might have given the USSR a lever with which to prise apart the US nuclear umbrella and the overall defence of Western Europe.

European realization of the suicidal nature of nuclear war has affected NATO's deployment strategy. West Germany has demanded a strategy of forward defence, with military operations conducted immediately on the border and has opposed waging a defence in depth which, in a war employing TACTICAL nuclear weapons, would only amount to suicide for the country (West Germany) being defended.

fractional orbital bombardment systems (FOBS) An attack system which launches a warhead into a very low (95 miles high) orbit above the earth. Before the completion of the first orbit a retro-rocket would slow the warhead down, causing it to drop on to its target. It would not become radar-visible until a mere 870 miles from target, providing only three minutes' warning.

Such a weapon is banned by the 1967 Outer Space Treaty. In 1968, the USA announced its belief that the USSR was developing a FOBS, although nothing has been heard of it since.

fractionation A missile may well carry more than one warhead. For example, the MIRV'd TRIDENT II D5 sea-launched ballistic missile is technically capable of carrying up to 17 warheads in each missile, and this division of a missile's total YIELD between separate warheads is known as fractionation.

France as a nuclear power France has invested heavily in nuclear weaponry at the expense of conventional troops and weapons – 13.8 per cent of the defence budget in 1982. Its nuclear armoury is indigenously designed and manufactured (unlike its British counterpart) making it genuinely independent. The *Force de dissuasion* is not large enough for extended deterrence but it does contain all three arms of a strategic triad as well as some tactical capability. It comprises:

1 *Groupement de Missiles Stratégiques,* on the PLATEAU D'ALBION, in southern France, made up of 18 SSBS (*Sol-Sol Balistique Stratégique*) S-3 1 mt missiles (range 3,500 km).

2 FOST (*Force Océanique Stratégique*) is made up of five submarines – SNLEs (*sous-marins nucléaire lanceurs d'engins*) – with 16 1 mt M-20 MSBS (*mer-sol balistique stratégique*) with a range of 3,000 km. A sixth submarine, *L'Inflexible,* to be deployed in 1985, will have 16 M-4 missiles each with six 150 kt warheads, and all but one of the other submarines will be converted to take this missile by 1992. Three more submarines have been commissioned.

3 FAS (*Force Aériennes Stratégique*) consisting of 24 Mirage IVA medium bombers carrying an AN-22 H-bomb; (there are 34 such planes in all); it will be partially superseded by a mobile missile, the S-X, though 15 will remain in service, armed with air-to-surface ASMP missiles. But the main replacement will be the Mirage 2000N low altitude, all-weather penetration bomber. Perhaps as many as 200 aircraft will be deployed.

4 *Force Aérienne Tactique*

● 45 Jaguar As (118 built in all) and 30 MIRAGE IIIEs (105 built in all) both carrying 125 kt AN-52 gravity bombs.

● 36 Super Etendards (64 built so far) on two aircraft carriers, the *Foch* and the *Clemenceau.*

All these aircraft have in-flight refuelling (IFR) capabilities (except the Mirage IIIE) which greatly increases their range.

● 42 PLUTON surface-to-surface missiles launched from a mobile platform. The Pluton has a range of up to 120 km and carries a single 15–25 kt warhead.

● HADES, to be deployed in the late 1980s, will have a highly mobile launch vehicle and is expected to have a range of 240 km and will be deployed with a variety of warhead configurations.

A hardened strategic command network (Ramses) is being constructed, and from 1987 four Transall aircraft will be converted for communication with submarines.

In May 1980 President Giscard d'Estaing announced, 'any nuclear attack upon French soil would be met automatically with a strategic nuclear retaliation.' The Mitterrand presidency has not changed this policy.

By the end of the next decade the combined Franco-British total of deliverable nuclear warheads could be 2,000 – substantially more than is required for a minimum basic deterrent. If ever the START negotiations were to succeed in reducing US and Soviet strategic warheads to, say, 5,000 each, this would represent 40 per cent of the Soviet strategic arsenal.

fratricide Fratricide occurs if the explosion of one incoming warhead has the effect of destroying one or more of the other incoming warheads. Flying debris and blast could be the immediate causes. Another would be the result of electromagnetic pulse (EMP).

EMP is an electromagnetic wave following upon the absorption of nuclear radiation by molecules in the air or ground. This single very-high voltage pulse of extremely short duration can destroy electrical or electronic systems. Fratricide would occur, therefore, if the EMP resulting from the first explosion fused the electronic circuitry of other incoming warheads.

Clearly fratricide could play havoc with estimates of the number of missiles needed to knock out the other side's silo systems or other targets, and fear of fratricide has produced targeting strategies that preclude more than two warheads per target (TWO-ON-ONE). Knowledge of the fratricide effect of a nuclear explosion lay behind the DENSE PACK design of the MX silos.

free rider argument
see BRITISH NUCLEAR DETERRENT

freeze (nuclear) The 'freeze' represented the response within the USA to President Reagan's ZERO OPTION. Although narrowly defeated in the US Congress in 1982 it still has massive support. It was aimed at preserving some kind of parity between the two superpowers (seen as a stabilizing deterrent factor) but preventing the deployment of a new generation of COUNTERFORCE weapons.

A freeze would:

a) ban the production of fission material for nuclear weapons;

b) ban the manufacture and testing of warheads;

c) ban the production and deployment of missiles;

d) ban the testing of new types of nuclear-capable aircraft and ban the further production of existing models with this capability;

e) monitor the storage and deployment of theatre nuclear weapons;

f) permit the regular replacement of certain items such as tritium modules (which act as a trigger for fusion reactions), gyroscopes and electrical systems for missiles on permanent alert, etc.

Effects if accepted:

1 *for the USA:*
No deployment of Pershing IIs, GLCMs; no more work on the MX Peacekeeper ICBM; no improvements to 300 Minuteman IIIs; no production of Trident D-5 (which would affect UK procurement plans); no production of the B-1 bomber and its 'stealth' version.

2 *for the USSR:*

No further deployment of SS-20s; no further deployment of SS-18s with ten MIRVed warheads, or of SS-19s with six warheads; no further deployment of SS-N-18s with seven MIRVs and no production of SS-N-20s with ten MIRVs; no more production or deployment of Tu-26 Backfire bomber and development to be halted on a new long-range bomber.

Result if accepted:

The USSR would have superiority in ICBMs; the US would have superiority in SLBMs and bombers.

Given that those who propose the freeze believe in the theory of DETERRENCE, and given that deterrence is the catch-all rationale for maintaining nuclear weapons in the first place, it is worrying for many people that the Reagan Administration (supported by its international allies) opposed the freeze. By so doing they have confirmed many in the view that the Administration's real aim has indeed been FIRST-STRIKE CAPABILITY, come what may.

In Britain in 1983, CND began to develop a position demanding a British freeze. This would have been a unilateral freeze on the testing, production and deployment of new nuclear weapons whether British or American, on British territory.

Frog 7 missile One of the USSR's 'Free Rocket Over Ground' missiles, it is fired from a wheeled launcher, three missiles per launcher. Originally deployed in 1965, the Frog 7 system is now being replaced by the SS-21 missile, though some 620 Frog 7 missiles are still in service (440 of them directed at NATO targets).

Specifications

Range: 70 km

Yield: 1×200 kt warhead

Accuracy: CEP 400 m.

functionally related observable differences (FROD)

Under the terms of the SALT II agreement (never ratified), there had to be some way of classifying an aircraft's nuclear role by associating external and observable features – perhaps pods or other fixtures which could only mean that the aircraft was nuclear-capable – in order to see if it came within the limitations of SALT agreements.

fusion The formation of an atomic nucleus by the union of two other nucleii of lighter mass. The most common substances employed are the hydrogen isotopes deuterium (one neutron plus one proton in the nucleus) and tritium (two neutrons plus the proton). These can be made to fuse at temperatures of over $1,000,000°$C to form helium and, in the process, convert a small quantity of their matter into energy – a vast amount of energy.

A hydrogen (fusion) bomb, also called a thermonuclear bomb,

works by exploding a small fission bomb to generate the heat ('thermo') necessary for the fusion process ('nuclear') to take place. The two hydrogen isotopes do not risk becoming critical, even when stored in large quantities, so the size of the bomb is theoretically limitless. The energy released is, anyway, more than three times that of an equivalent amount of fissionable material. But in practice there are other problems, and the so-called H-bomb is in fact a fission–fusion–fission explosion, the fusion part also serving as a trigger for a secondary fission reaction. The key to a viable thermonuclear bomb was not, as in the atomic bomb, what materials to employ and how to generate them. The key was design. The problem was how to arrange the hydrogen isotopes in relation to the atom bomb 'trigger' so that when the latter exploded it would produce, for two or three microseconds, millions of degrees of heat and thousands of atmospheres of pressure. The fission trigger had to drive the hydrogen isotopes into a tiny lump of matter of huge density. Only then could the 'thermonuclear burn wave' take place. If the design and timing were not perfect the isotopes would burn but no fusion explosion would take place.

At present there is no peaceful application for the fusion process because no container could withstand the heat required for its activation. But work is under way, and the most promising idea is to pass a very high temperature gas through a magnetic field and thus tap the release of energy without any solid materials touching it. The advantages over fission nuclear power are considerable: the reaction would be self-sustaining; the power generated would be huge; and there would be far fewer noxious waste products.

gadget nuclear device The Gadget was the first nuclear device to be exploded (Alamogordo, New Mexico, 16 July 1945). It used an IMPLOSION DEVICE to detonate 13.5 lbs of plutonium core with a surrounding layer of 5,000 lbs of high explosive. The yield was about 20 kt.

Galosh, Soviet ABM network Four anti-ballistic missile launch complexes, totalling 64 ABM-1B/Galosh interception missiles and associated radar, have been located near Moscow, as permitted by the 1972 Anti-Ballistic Missile Treaty and the 1974 Protocol. Half of the Galosh systems have now been dismantled, probably to be replaced by more modern interceptors.

Despite the relatively small defensive forces involved, the existence of an ABM system around Moscow has provided the excuse both for developing Mark-5 MARVing technology in the USA and for MRVing British Polaris warheads.

general nuclear response A term used to describe the final phase of a nuclear war in which the US President activates the SINGLE INTEGRATED OPERATIONAL PLAN.

Generals for Peace and Disarmament A group formed in 1981 of 13 retired senior NATO officers who, from time to time, publish statements on reducing the threat of nuclear war. In 1983 they published *Ten Questions Answered*, which says: 'No doubt it was painful for those who believed the world was flat to accept evidence that it was, after all, round. The time has come when we, too, must accept the painful fact that the nuclear deterrent, like the Emperor's new clothes, is a figment of the imagination.'

Three of the group's best known members are General-Major Gert Bastian, General-Major M. H. von Meyenfeldt and Brigadier Michael Harbottle. Its address is:

Generals for Peace and Disarmament, c/o Centre for International Peacebuilding Studies, Southbank House, Black Prince Road, Lambeth, London SE1

genie missile A short-range air-to-air dual-capable rocket used by the US Air Force for the interception of enemy strategic bombers. Of the thousands produced since 1957 (production ended in 1962) 200 nuclear-armed rockets with warheads in the 1.5 kt range were thought to be deployed in 1983.

see also ANTI-BALLISTIC MISSILES

Germany Germany has been at the very centre of the history of the nuclearized arms race between the two principal military blocs. On the one hand, the determination of the West never to repeat the disastrous policies of appeasement directed at Hitler has been 'transferred' into a series of axioms on how to deal with the USSR. On the other, the Soviet experience at the hands of Nazi Germany haunted it in the post-war years, dominated its politics in Europe, and ensured it would never agree to a unification of Germany unless the country were neutral. Again and again, negotiations over arms control, arms reduction and NUCLEAR FREE ZONES in Europe, have broken down over this issue, while the divided city of Berlin provided a persistent and overloaded symbol of the Cold War.

Within a month of Germany joining NATO in 1955, the WARSAW TREATY ORGANIZATION (WTO) had been formed as a defensive buffer. Before that, the creation of the Marshall Plan, which gave substantial aid to Western Europe, including West Germany, helped to precipitate the consolidating take-overs by the Red Army and local communist parties in Eastern Europe. West German insistence ensured the deployment posture of forward defence.

All nuclear warheads operated by West German forces are in US custody and, apart from the nuclear-capable artillery, aircraft and

Lance missiles operated by the US in West Germany (as well as British nuclear-capable forces), West German forces are nuclear-armed with:

- 216 Nike-Hercules missiles
- 72 Pershing IA missiles
- 586 M-109 howitzers
- 195 M-110 howitzers
- 108 F-104 aircraft
- 30 Panavia Tornado aircraft

graduated reciprocation in tension reduction (GRIT)
see BRITISH NUCLEAR DETERRENT

gravity bombs Of the 26,000 nuclear warheads in the US stockpile there are approximately 7,350 gravity bombs carried on strategic and tactical aircraft:

B-28
Approximately 1,200 in 1983
Yield: 70 kt, 350 kt, 1.1 mt, 1.45 mt.
Replaced by B-83 in 1984.
Deployed on B-52 and B1-B bombers, A-4, A-6, A-7, F-4, F-100 and F-104 tactical aircraft in the USA and NATO.

B-43
Approximately 2,000 in 1983
Yield: 1 mt
Deployed on B-52s, FB-111 medium-range bombers, F-4, F-16, F-111, A-4, A-6 and A-7 tactical aircraft both in the USA and NATO. It was originally designed to destroy high-value, urban-industrial targets and moderately hard military targets.

B-53
Approximately 150 in 1983
Yield: 9 mt
Deployed on B-52s in the USA only. It is to be replaced by B-83 and ALCMs.

B-57
Approximately 1,000 in 1983
Yield: 5–10 kt
Deployed on maritime patrol aircraft and helicopters both with US and NATO forces. The B-57 is a lightweight, multi-purpose nuclear depth charge/bomb for anti-submarine and land warfare.

B-61
Approximately 3,000 in 1983
Yield: 10–500 kt
Deployed on B-52s and a wide range of tactical aircraft both with US and NATO forces.

Greenham Common US airbase in Berkshire, UK, where 96 ground-launched cruise missiles (GLCMs) are to be based under the NATO dual track decision of December 1979. In the 1950s it was a base for US Strategic Air Command bombers but was handed back to the RAF in 1964. It is a collocated operating base, a status usually reserved for certain non-US bases which are geared up to being able to receive and service US aircraft.

The missiles, the first batch of which was flown in clandestinely at the end of 1983, are handled by the 501st Tactical Missile Wing with 1,700 personnel. The 96 missiles will be divided into six squadrons of 16 missiles each. At present (1984) there is one squadron on site. One squadron should always be on a QUICK REACTION ALERT if the base ever gets up to full strength. In times of tension it is supposed that the missiles, or at least the ones on quick reaction alert, will be moved away from the base 'to secret locations' in the country. They would be difficult to destroy without an estimated 1,000 megaton attack over the whole of southern England. What may be more likely is that the dispersal of Cruise could provoke a pre-emptive strategic nuclear attack on Britain.

The base has become famous for the peace camp outside it, which was begun in 1981 by a group of both sexes who marched to the base from Wales. Soon after it developed into a women-only peace camp (though it was always prepared to accept help from men). At the end of 1982 the women called on supporters to 'embrace the base'. Around 30,000 women surrounded the nine-mile-long perimeter fence. The peace-campers have suffered harassment from the local Newbury Council, from some local residents, and from the police. They have been arrested, intimidated, and vilified in the press, had their camp destroyed frequently and been forced off common land for trespassing. In early spring 1984 bailiffs ejected them again, ostensibly so that a road could be widened.

Greenham women's peace camp became a symbol both in Britain and abroad: for some, of drop-out, 'bolshy' radical feminism; for others, of women's stubborn and courageous resistance to Cruise and to all nuclear weapons.

ground-based electro-optical deep space surveillance (GEODDS)
see NORTH AMERICAN AEROSPACE DEFENSE COMMAND

ground burst The term is used to describe a nuclear explosion that occurs at ground level. Unlike AIR BURST explosions (which are detonated at some thousands of feet above the surface of the earth), ground bursts produce great quantities of radioactive debris from the pulverized material at the point of the explosion (see GROUND ZERO). The debris, sucked up into the mushroom cloud, will come down, perhaps hundreds of miles away, as radioactive FALLOUT.

ground-launched cruise missile (GLCM)

The Tomahawk GLCM (BGM-109) now deployed by the US in Europe grew out of the US Navy's development of a SEA-LAUNCHED CRUISE MISSILE (SLCM) in the mid-1970s. The first prototype GLCM was flown in December 1979 and on the 12 December 1979 NATO agreed to the deployment of 464 GLCMs at six bases:

> RAF Molesworth (64 missiles)
> RAF Greenham Common (96)
> Comiso, Sicily (112)
> Woensdrecht, Netherlands (48)
> Florennes, Belgium (48)
> Wueschein, W. Germany (96)

Each GLCM 'flight' consists of four transporter-erector-launchers (TELs – each armed with four GLCMs), two launch-control centres (LCCs), 16 support vehicles and 69 personnel. In time of emergency, the intention is to disperse the flights from their bases to pre-surveyed and prepared sites.

Each missile on QUICK REACTION ALERT (QRA) will be programmed for a series of target options which can be constantly updated. Re-targeting with previously programmed options is immediate, but will take longer if new targets have to be fed into the missile's on-board computer.

The extraordinary accuracy of GLCMs (see INERTIAL GUIDANCE and TERRAIN CONTOUR MATCHING) guarantees an almost 100 per cent probability of kill against targets hardened against nuclear attack – missile silos and C^3I posts, for example.

Although the flight speed of a GLCM is quite slow – about 550 mph – detection and interception is difficult. Continual changes of course can be pre-programmed, low exhaust heat reduces the infrared signature, and low altitude flying (about 30 m above flat ground) makes radar detection difficult. Once spotted, fighter aircraft such as the Soviet MIG-25 FOXBAT or ground-to-air missiles are capable of destroying in-coming GLCMs. The problem for a defender, however, is one of scale. A thoroughly reliable defence against a mass attack of armed and decoy GLCMs would be astronomically expensive – in the region of $100 billion, according to US Under-Secretary for Defense for Research and Development James Wade (October 1982). According to the International Institute of Strategic Studies there are no Soviet GLCMs presently deployed, although a medium-range version is being developed.

Specifications
Range: 2,500 km
Speed: 550 mph
Accuracy: CEP 30 m
Yield: 1×200 kt (though current reports suggest it may be equipped with a smaller W84 warhead with a variable yield of 10–50 kt)
Number planned: 565

Number deployed: 32+

see also CRUISE MISSILES, AIR-LAUNCHED and SEA-LAUNCHED CRUISE MISSILES.

ground zero A term applied to the epicentre of a nuclear explosion. It can be used in relation to both ground burst and air burst explosions even though the latter may occur 1,000+ ft above ground level.

gun device By firing one mass of uranium down a tube ('gun barrel') into another mass, a super-critical density can be achieved which results in a FISSION nuclear explosion. This technique was used in the bomb dropped at HIROSHIMA – 'Little Boy'.

Hades missile The backbone of the French tactical arsenal has been the PLUTON battlefield missile, but plans were passed in 1981 to develop a replacement – the Hades.

Unlike Pluton, which uses modified tanks for transport and launching, the Hades missile will have a specifically designed launch vehicle. It is expected that the Hades will have a much-improved range and accuracy over its predecessor, and will have a number of alternative warheads.

see also FRANCE AS A NUCLEAR POWER

half-life The half-life of any particular radioisotope is the length of time taken for half of its atomic nuclei to erupt and decay by transforming themselves into the nuclei of other atoms through the emission of radiation. After two half-lives, only one quarter of the atoms will remain radioactive, after three half-lives one-eighth, and so on. Some fission products have half-lives of just a few seconds; others of thousands of years. The former are the most dangerous soon after an explosion; the latter emit smaller amounts of radiation over a given period of time but, of course, continue to do so for a much longer period.

Some examples of half-lives:

aluminium-28	2.3 minutes
barium-140	12.8 days
carbon-14	5,730 years
caesium-137	30 years
chlorine-38	37 minutes
iodine-131	8 days
manganese-56	2.6 hours
oxygen-16	7 seconds
plutonium-239	24,000 years
silicon-31	2.6 hours
sodium-24	15 hours

| strontium-90 | 27.7 years |
| tritium | 12.3 years |

see also RADIATION

'Hard Rock' A home defence exercise which was planned in Britain for September–October 1982. The first stage involved a preparation phase followed by a response to the effects of a conventional attack on the civilian population. One major aim was to be 'to consider the implications of self-evacuation by the general public'. The second stage was to have included a simulated nuclear attack, a 31-hour post-attack 'survival' phase, and then a 'recovery' phase starting 28 days after the attack. This whole second stage would have had broad military involvement and have included local voluntary organizations in the exercises.

'Hard Rock' was cancelled by William Whitelaw, the Home Secretary, because 20 out of 54 county councils refused to participate, and as the main purpose was to exercise local authority personnel in conjunction with the military, it was pointless to proceed.

The postponement represented a victory for the NUCLEAR FREE ZONE movement, and for CND, who had planned their own riposte, entitled 'Hard Luck', which provided a cross-country computer breakdown, even to the village level, of likely dead and injured from a 200 megaton attack.

hard target The description applied to a target which has been protected against the blast and associated effects of nuclear weapons by means of structural reinforcement. An underground concrete-reinforced ICBM silo and a C^3I emplacement are examples of hardened targets.

To destroy a hard target, the incoming missile must be of great accuracy as well as having sufficient blast value. Hence the importance of a missile's CIRCULAR ERROR PROBABLE rating.

see LETHALITY, MISSILE ACCURACY

Harrisberg accident On 28 March 1979, the water pumps feeding water to the steam generators of Three Mile Island (TMI) unit 2 Light Water Reactor at Harrisberg, Pennsylvania stopped working. Deprived of steam, the coolant heated up and a valve opened (correctly) to release excess pressure. It remained open, however, releasing 32,000 gallons of radioactive water. Meanwhile 'scram' control rods dropped into the reactor core to stop the fission process. Unfortunately, temperature gauges were misread and this led to the uncovering of parts of the reactor rods, the material of which reacted with steam to produce a large hydrogen bubble. Two days later a plume of radioactive gas was released from TMI-2 and began to blow in the direction of Middletown. Before long the area had to be evacuated.

Everything conspired to mark out the Harrisberg accident as a turning point in the history of nuclear power and popular perception of it:

● certain safety features were unreliable and one was not even connected;

● training was inadequate so that for days no one knew how to proceed to rectify matters;

● Metropolitan-Edison, the operators, were castigated as not having enough experience to run the plant, for having failed to heed frequent warnings from a Nuclear Regulatory Commission (NRC) consultant, and for having not remedied certain faults which had been pointed out to them;

● the NRC itself came in for fundamental criticism from the Kemmeny Commission which reported on the accident for President Carter;

● the national media, who were denied proper information from evasive NRC and Met-Ed officials anxious to camouflage their shortcomings, wrote up the most sensational copy ('Race with Nuclear Disaster'), which simply fed a hysteria already primed by the very recent release of the film 'The China Syndrome'.

Public debate after the accident focused on the safety factors: in West Germany it was insisted upon that their reactors were built to far more rigorous safety requirements than in the USA; in Britain there was a certain smugness as it was pointed out that with gas-cooled reactors such an accident simply could not happen (which did not prevent the government ordering a Westinghouse LWR of virtually the same design as the one at TMI).

What was overlooked in Europe and America was the essential conclusion of the Kemmeny Commission Report: 'The most serious "mind-set" is the preoccupation of everyone with the safety of the equipment, resulting in the downplaying of the importance of the human element ... what the NRC and the industry have failed to recognize sufficiently is that the human beings who manage and operate the plants constitute an important safety system.'

heavy-water reactor Developed out of research carried on in Canada during World War II involving British, French and Canadian scientists, this reactor is sold as the Candu Reactor (short for Canadian deuterium uranium reactor). Pressurized heavy water (deuterium oxide) is used both as a moderator and coolant. A pressure of 85 atmospheres is used. Fuel is natural uranium dioxide pellets in zirconium alloy cans. Efficiency is just under 30 per cent. A higher burn-up of uranium is possible with heavy water than with graphite moderated reactors. Some of the energy output is produced by the fission of plutonium formed in the reactor.

Hiroshima At 8.15 am, 6 August 1945, the Japanese city of

Hiroshima was the victim of the first-ever war-time atomic bomb. The bomb, called 'Little Boy', had a yield of some 13 kt (very small by presentday standards) and was delivered from the *Enola Gay* just as most citizens were on their way to work. (See ATOM BOMB for historical and diplomatic aspects.)

The devastation caused by the *pikadon* (*pika* = flash; *don* = boom) is difficult to imagine let alone measure. The city suffered from blast, which flattened most of it, crushing thousands to death. A FIRE STORM developed, followed by a tornado. Then 'black rain' fell, over an area of 400 km², causing a chilling drop in the mid-summer temperature. The overall casualty rate was 56 per cent dead and injured. The Japanese estimated that by December 1945, 140,000 people had died as the result of the bomb.

Three factors differentiate Hiroshima from any other city devastated in warfare (apart from NAGASAKI):

1 The number of deaths caused by the delayed effects of radioactivity continue to this day. By 1980 this delayed total stood at 97,964. Total deaths from 'Little Boy' stand well above 200,000 (for comparison, the total US battle fatalities in World War II on all fronts was 290,000).

2 The survivors, the *hibakusha,* live distorted, listless and broken lives, shunned by the rest of society, finding it difficult to get employment and prone to early, painful death and wasting disease.

3 Those unborn in 1945, whose mothers were exposed to radiation, are prone to microcephaly, myopia, liver cirrhosis, tuberculosis and many other diseases and malformations to a much greater degree than is prevalent among their peers; they are also, on average, smaller in stature.

For a definitive study see *Hiroshima and Nagasaki: The Physical, Medical and Social Effects of the Atomic Bombings,* The Committee for the Compilation of Materials and Damage caused by the Atomic Bombs on Hiroshima and Nagasaki, Hutchinson, 1981.

see also EFFECTS OF NUCLEAR EXPLOSION

'Honest John' missile

'Honest John' missile This short-range (TACTICAL) ballistic missile has been replaced by the Lance missile in all NATO armies, except for those of Greece and Turkey. Although the missile has been modified to improve its performance and is now mounted on a self-propelled tracked carrier, it still needs to be pre-warmed to 77°F (24°C) for 24–48 hours before launching, to ensure an even solid-fuel burn.

Specifications
Range: 40 km
Yield: 1–20 kt range (with three options)
Accuracy: CEP 1.6 km
Speed: Mach 1.5
Number deployed: 54

'Hot Line' Agreement, 1963 This provided for a direct, private teletype link between the heads of state of the USA and the USSR. The Cuban missile crisis of 1962 had vividly displayed the perils implicit in modern nuclear-weapons systems and the need for prompt direct communication between the heads of state.

The 'Hot Line' Agreement has been well-exploited for public relations purposes as an example of the two nations' capability to reach agreement, but its real value in times of extreme crisis have yet to be proved. It has certainly been used to defuse tension in the Arab-Israeli war in 1967 and again in 1973. In 1971, the agreement was extended to include communication by satellite. In 1966 France established a direct link with the USSR, and in 1967 the UK followed suit.

However, the installation of LAUNCH-ON-WARNING systems to combat the short-range theatre weapons (eg Pershing II) which can reach strategic targets in under five minutes dramatically undermines the usefulness of the 'Hot Line' link.

hydrogen bomb The decision in the USA to build the H-bomb was at least publicly debated, unlike that in France, Britain or (certainly) the USSR. Two key American scientists took opposite views: Robert Oppenheimer, one of the creators of the atomic bomb, was against it. Edward Teller was for it and became the guiding intelligence behind it. The decision to go ahead came after the failure of the Baruch Plan (see ARMS CONTROL) and after the USSR had exploded an atomic bomb in 1949. Given the anti-Communist hysteria of the Cold War, not to mention the feelings generated by the Korean War, that the decision should have gone Teller's way was almost inevitable, even though in 1949 the General Advisory Committee of the American Atomic Energy Commission produced a report on the H-bomb which stated: 'We are all reluctant to see the United States take the initiative in precipitating this development .... We base our recommendation on our belief that the extreme dangers to mankind inherent in the proposal wholly outweigh any military advantage ... reasonable people the world over would realize that the existence of a weapon of this type whose power of destruction is essentially unlimited represents a threat to the future of the human race which is intolerable.'

The first test, 'George' shot, on 8 May 1951, showed that fusion was possible. The second, 'Mike' shot, on 1 November 1952, yielded 10 megatons – 700 Hiroshimas. However, it was not remotely a usable weapon. That changed on 1 March 1954 at Bikini Atoll: 'Bravo' shot, constructed from lithium dueteride, yielded a mammoth 14.8 megatons and also resulted in the first peace-time victim of radioactive fallout, a crew member of the Japanese fishing boat *Lucky Dragon*. The 'Bravo' shot was in fact a fission–fusion–fission bomb – the 'dirtiest' of nuclear devices because the outer casing of uranium-238 (which fissions under the impact of the very high-energy neutrons emitted by

the fusion explosion) produces highly radioactive fallout. The USSR exploded an H-bomb probably in 1955 and the arms race then switched to delivery systems.
see also FUSION

implosion device A uniform layer of high explosive surrounds a layer of uranium-238 which, in its turn, surrounds a subcritical mass of plutonium-239 at the core of the bomb. When the high explosive is detonated it creates a massive and uniform pressure (millions of pounds psi) which compresses the core material to a super critical mass. This FISSION technique was used on the very first atomic device – the Gadget – and on the bomb dropped at Nagasaki – Fat Man.

India India exploded a nuclear device in the Rajasthan Desert on 17 May 1974. Since then it has denied reports that it is developing a nuclear arsenal. However, with Pakistan apparently pressing ahead in that direction one must treat these denials with some scepticism.

India has 45 Canberra aircraft which could be nuclear capable. It has over 100 Hindustan Aeronautics HF-24 Maruts, now being replaced by MiG-23BN Flogger F ground attack aircraft. It is assembling 45 Jaguars from British components and will soon build the complete planes under licence.

Besides aircraft, India has an active space research programme with emphasis on indigenously built launchers and missiles (the SLV-3, the ASLV, and the Polar SLV which could place a 2,300 lb satellite into a 650-mile-high orbit) – all of which implies a medium-range nuclear-armed missile capability by the mid-1980s if required.

inertial guidance A guidance system designed to enhance greatly a missile's or aircraft's flight accuracy by pre-programmed, on-board computer adjustment of acceleration. As the system is entirely self-contained within the missile or aircraft, it is impervious to jamming or adverse atmospheric conditions in the launch area.
see also MISSILE ACCURACY

inertial navigation
see INERTIAL GUIDANCE

intercontinental ballistic missile (ICBM) A land-based missile, fixed (in silos) or mobile (on wheeled or tracked transporters) with a range in excess of 5,500 km. Once the ICBM has been boosted out of the earth's atmosphere it flies in a trajectory to re-enter the atmosphere and attack its target. An ICBM consists of a rocket booster propelled by either solid or liquid fuel (on the whole, older weapons use less stable liquid fuel which makes for longer launch preparation than solid fuel), and one or more RE-ENTRY VEHICLE carrying the warhead. These vehicles may be MULTIPLE RE-ENTRY VEHICLEs (MRVs), MULTIPLE INDEPENDENTLY-TARGETED RE-ENTRY VEHICLEs (MIRVS) or MANOEUVRING RE-ENTRY VEHICLEs (MARVs) and may also carry PENETRATION AIDs (decoys) and, in the case of MIRV'd missiles, a POST-BOOST VEHICLE (used to help power and orientate the re-entry vehicles as they descend towards their target).

During the decade 1972–82, the number of ICBM warheads in the US arsenal rose 200 per cent; their megatonnage increased by 30 per cent; their pin-point targeting and hard-target kill potential increased 200 per cent.

source: US Joint Chiefs of Staff, *US Military Posture for FY 1982*

Intermediate Nuclear Forces talks (INF)
see ARMS CONTROL AND ARMS LIMITATION

intermediate-range ballistic missile (IRBM) A class of land-based ballistic missiles with a range between 2,400–5,500 km. In the class, the USSR has the SS-5 (range 4,100 km) and the SS-20 (5,000 km). Although there are no comparable NATO or US missiles based in Western Europe (Pershing II is a MEDIUM-RANGE BALLISTIC MISSILE (MRBM – 900–2,400 km) and the other NATO missiles fall in the SHORT-RANGE BALLISTIC MISSILE (SRBM – 800 km or less class) it is to the cruise aircraft and Pershing II which form part of the LONG-RANGE THEATRE NUCLEAR FORCE (LRTNF) that we must look for an overall comparison of nuclear weapons of intermediate range.

International Atomic Energy Agency (IAEA) Formed on 26 October 1956 in the wake of the euphoria generated by Eisenhower's ATOMS FOR PEACE initiative, the IAEA is an autonomous intergovernmental organization dedicated to increasing the contribution of atomic energy to the world's peace and well-being and ensuring that the agency's assistance is not used for military purposes. Its activities have included research, funding, conferences and training programmes into the application of atomic energy to medicine, agriculture, water location and industry, and to providing technical assistance and information, especially to less-developed countries. Based in Vienna it has over 100 members.

Unfortunately its record has been well below the expectations of its founders. First, most of the peaceful applications have been either of limited value or non-starters. Secondly, peaceful nuclear power itself has proved expensive, wasteful when compared to other sources of power, and often inapplicable to many countries whose national grids were too small to cope with the vast input that even one reactor would generate.

Sometimes the IAEA pinpointed examples of bribery in the sale of reactors, and in 1978 it identified major problems with the site for a projected plant on the Bataan Peninsula, Philippines, which they discovered was a strong earthquake zone and contained several volcanoes.

Its worst failure is at the level of the relationship between the installation of nuclear reactors and the production, or recovery through reprocessing, of weapons-grade plutonium or uranium-235. Even after the explosion of the Indian bomb in 1974 it still refused to impose NON-PROLIFERATION TREATY safeguards on technology transfers. This forced a group of advanced industrialized countries to draw up a 'trigger list' of sensitive technology that they agreed should not be exported without suitable safeguards.

The key meeting of the IAEA was in 1978 where it was acknowledged that the 'critical time' between illegally extracting plutonium from a reactor and fashioning it into a metal was just 10 days, with a further two to put it into a nuclear device. They wanted to impose reactor inspections every 12 days but this was vetoed by Germany and Japan whose electricity production would have been fatally disrupted by such frequent shut-downs. To this day no 'critical time' inspections exist.

see also ATOMIC ENERGY COMMISSIONS

International Institute for Strategic Studies (IISS)

Established in 1958, its principal publication, *Military Balance,* has been published since the following year. *Military Balance* is an annual assessment of the military power and defence expenditure of countries throughout the world and is considered one of the foremost publications in its field, used by the media and governments alike. The information is far more extensive than most official publications and the data is treated as highly authoritative and 'neutral'.

However, of late this unquestioning attitude has changed. A study in 1980–81 by the US Center for Defense Information found 105 errors in the US section alone. 'Some figures have necessarily been estimated' admits the IISS in its preface – but which, is never stated.

Besides *Military Balance,* IISS publishes pamphlets and papers on strategic matters, among which is *Survival* (bi-monthly) and the Adelphi Papers (eight times a year). Its address is: IISS, 18 Adam Street, London WC2.

see also STOCKHOLM INTERNATIONAL PEACE RESEARCH INSTITUTE

isotope Each atom of an element has the same number of protons in its nucleus, but the number of neutrons in it can vary and each variant is called an isotope. Thus U-238 is the most common uranium isotope with 146 neutrons. U-235 has 143 neutrons. There exist or can exist other isotopes of uranium – U-233, U-239 and U-236 for example.

Hydrogen can have no neutrons (hydrogen), one neutron (deuterium) or two neutrons (tritium).

Chemically, all isotopes of the same element behave identically, but the different content of their nuclei affects their behaviour radically in nuclear reactions.

Israel as a nuclear power Unsubstantiated sources attribute as many as 100 nuclear weapons to Israel, though the current consensus of opinion is that its nuclear arsenal is in the region of 30 weapons. It already has the Jericho MD-660, analogous to the Lance short-range nuclear missile, with a range of nearly 480 km, and it is developing the MD-620 version of longer range. It is planning a cruise missile with a range of 1,920 km and nuclear-capable artillery. The Gabriel series of subsonic and future (Gabriel IV) supersonic missiles could, along with the other missiles mentioned, be produced in a nuclear-armed form.

The reported nuclear detonation in the South Atlantic in 1979 could well have been a result of collaboration with South Africa.

During the 1973 Yom Kippur war, Israel was hard-pressed on its Egyptian and Syrian flanks and, according to US reconnaissance, was preparing the assembly of nuclear warheads at Dimona nuclear research station for use in case of a Syrian breakthrough. Apparently Presidents Nixon and Brezhnev consulted and it was decided that Egypt be supplied with Soviet SCUD nuclear missiles; the two heads of state agreed that if nuclear weapons were indeed used then the superpowers would not themselves intervene.

Jaguar strike aircraft Of the 96 in service with the RAF in the UK and West Germany, 72 are nuclear capable (with yields probably below 100 kt). Their range is something less than 1,600 km with a full payload. Another 45 are in service with the French air force and 40 more with the Indian air force.

'Just War' theory The 'rules' by which a Christian may break the Commandment 'Thou shalt not kill' have been formulated throughout Christian history but are more specifically associated with St Augustine:

1   War is to be initiated only by leaders of states.
2   War must be waged for a just cause only.
3   War must be a last resort.
4   There must be a formal declaration of war.
5   There must be a reasonable chance of success.
6   The destruction caused in a war must not be disproportionate to the evil being fought.
7   Non-combatants must not be attacked directly.
8   Methods of fighting must be proportionate to the cause.

The use of nuclear weapons may then be contrary to the principles of a Just War, but as no-one is planning to use them or wishes to use them, can there be anything wrong with having them for deterrent purposes? There are alternative answers to this question, summarized thus by the Bishop of London:

> One type of theory will say that an act, if it is immoral in itself, cannot be done, however moral and just the motive with which it is done; but another tradition will place an act within the consequences and judge the ethics and morality of that act in terms not only of that act itself but also of the consequences to be achieved by that act .... So long as we keep the threat to a minimum that we can keep it to, we can take into account the end, namely, the preservation of peace, which the threat is intended to secure. It then becomes justifiable to do something which is unjust.

The US Bishop Thomas Gumbleston of Pax Christi expresses an opposite viewpoint:

> Deterrence can only be morally acceptable if it is interim to disarmament and only if the weaponry is minimal. Cruise violates all the conditions because when it is deployed on a large scale, it will be virtually undetectable and so remove all hopes of arms control. Pershing is even worse ... it is a first-strike weapon .... To kill is simply not there in the New Testament.

Kamchatka Peninsula A very sensitive military area in the Soviet Far East over which the ill-fated Korean flight 007 flew in a mysterious incident where the plane was over 200 miles off course, apparently unaware of its error. The plane was shot down by Soviet fighters, all civilians and crew on board were killed, and international outrage was provoked, tempered by a widely held suspicion that perhaps the plane was engaged on a decoy or spying mission.

There is a Soviet submarine base on the peninsula along the length of which there runs one of the American SOUND SURVEILLANCE SYSTEMS (SOSUS) chains for tracking submarine movements.

kiloton (kt) The yield of a nuclear warhead is expressed either in kilotons or megatons. A kiloton is the equivalent of 1,000 tons of TNT (a megaton = 1,000 kilotons).

The nuclear device dropped on Hiroshima was about 13 kt and the present nuclear weapons range from about 0.01 kt (personal-portable nuclear demolition charges, for example) to 20,000 kt (USSR's SS-18 ICBM).

Kola Peninsula Soviet submarine base near the north of Norway. Immediately Soviet submarines leave the base, they are tracked by SOUND SURVEILLANCE SYSTEMS (SOSUS). Various proposals to create a nuclear free zone in Scandinavia have foundered because they have been made conditional upon Soviet dismantlement of the Kola submarine base – which, with only two bases, the USSR has refused to do. In 1983 a series of explosions was reported.

see KAMCHATKA PENINSULA

Kyshtyn accident

Kyshtyn, in the Chelyabinsk region of the USSR, was the scene, in December 1957 or January 1958, of a major catastrophe involving nuclear fuel. No one knows what exactly caused the accident, and indeed for many years no one in the West even knew there had been one. However, in 1976 the Soviet dissident scientist Zhores Medvedev mentioned it in passing and said that it was probably a chemical explosion in radioactive waste (this suggestion unwittingly stirred up a hornets' nest as the British Atomic Energy Authority was under pressure at the time precisely over how to dispose of nuclear waste).

It was noticed that Soviet technical journals had devoted no less than 115 articles to the ecological effects of 'radiation experiments'. In one article the site of the 'experiments' – the Chelyabinsk region – was mentioned (having slipped past the censor) and it was known that a plutonium-producing reactor had been built in Kyshtyn in the late 1940s.

One can only speculate on how many people died. But reports from Soviet emigrants spoke of mass evacuations from the region, the burning of foodstuffs and advice against having children even ten years later. The road through Kyshtyn was closed for nine months and when it re-opened there were signs advising motorists not to stop for 20 miles and to drive at top speed with windows closed. A Soviet physicist who drove through the area in 1959 was aghast: 'The land was dead – no villages, no towns, only chimneys of destroyed homes, no cultivated fields or pastures, no herds, no people – nothing.'

Lance missile

A short-range, guided, surface-to-surface battlefield missile used by the armies of both the US and NATO as a replacement for the HONEST JOHN missile. The Lance is mounted on a highly mobile amphibious tracked launcher.

Sources differ on the number of missiles deployed:

Military Balance 1983/84:
deployed:

US	36
NATO	56

Nuclear Weapons Databook, volume 1, 1984:

Total active in 1983	945
On US Army's inventory	1450

Specifications
Range: 110 km
Yield: 1–100 kt (in addition, it has an ENHANCED RADIATION option of about 1 kt)

Accuracy: CEP: 225–375 m, depending on range
Speed: Mach 3

last resort theory A theory advanced as a reason why Britain should hold and retain an independently controlled nuclear deterrent. If Britain ever had to stand alone, for whatever reason, even though it could not ensure its own defence by the possession of nuclear weapons, it could deter any enemy with the threat of massive retaliation.

The contrary argument is that this theory would apply only when NATO and the US had proved unreliable. But to use or threaten to use nuclear weapons in such an unbalanced situation would be to invite national suicide, even if in the process several score Soviet towns were also obliterated.

The purchase of Trident, however, would alter the picture considerably. Theoretically the warheads from four British Trident submarines could hit about 960 separate targets – and based on a targeting policy controlled by the USA.

launchers The equipment used to support and hold a missile in position before firing. ICBM launchers are based on land and are either fixed or mobile. SLBM launchers are missile tubes in submarines. The submarine itself is called a launch platform, as is a surface ship, or a bomber.

launch-on-warning Politico-military decision to launch nuclear weapons upon warning of an enemy attack. As flight times get shorter and missiles more accurate, the fear has increased in both the USA and USSR that a surprise attack would find home missiles totally vulnerable in their silos; indeed, Soviet ICBMs could be destroyed by Pershing IIs just 12 minutes after they had been launched.

Launch-on-warning has major implications for strategic stability. It raises the question of who would have political control over the decision to launch nuclear weapons. It also brings home the terrifying prospect of accidental war. For the detection agencies which would give the warning are almost all man-made: radar, satellites, computer evaluation of signals, etc. There have been many instances of computers going wrong (computer chips not working, a training tape indicating a full-scale Soviet attack being inserted by mistake into the main computer). The warning systems also have definite perceptual limitations (they have confused reflections from the moon, or a flock of geese with a Soviet attack), A report by Senators Barry Goldwater and Gary Hart revealed 147 false alerts during the 18-month period following the installation of new NORAD computers.

lethality A term used to describe the ability of a missile to destroy a HARD TARGET. It can be quantified by a computation based on the megatonnage of the warhead and the accuracy of the missile.

see COUNTER MILITARY POTENTIAL, MISSILE ACCURACY, CIRCLE
OF ERROR PROBABLE, SINGLE SHOT PROBABILITY OF KILL, TIME
SENSITIVE TARGET, FIRST-STRIKE CAPABILITY

light-water reactor (LWR) A nuclear reactor in which
ordinary (light) water is used to transfer heat from the fuel to the
turbines. In its two forms – boiling water and pressurized water – it is
the most common reactor in the USA. LWRs were developed for use
in nuclear-powered submarines owing to their compactness, and
because, as they consume no oxygen, the submarine can remain
submerged for long periods. They are not particularly efficient as
energy producers and there is also concern that the emergency cooling
system might break down should the core fuel temperature rise
suddenly.

limited attack option
see SINGLE INTEGRATED OPERATIONAL PLAN

limited nuclear war (LNW) There are two central aspects to
LNW. First, as a strategy of FLEXIBLE RESPONSE. Secondly, the idea
of a nuclear war geographically limited to Europe with neither the
USA nor the USSR targeting each other. The two are, however,
linked. Limitation would result from deliberate restraint: by reducing
the number of weapons to be used, or by concentrating on short-range
weapons, or by the creation of sanctuaries (see SANCTUARY THEORY),
or by the exclusion of certain categories of target (eg cities and non-
military targets).

In 1974, James Schlesinger set out a plan for introducing US central
strategic nuclear weapons in situations short of general nuclear war. It
involved the pre-planning of 'packages' of nuclear weapons for use
against a variety of military and, increasingly, political targets. Over
the years the number of 'packages' and targets has increased
enormously (see SINGLE INTEGRATED OPERATIONAL PLAN –
SIOP). The operating idea and rationalization was 'to offer the US
President additional options for responding to a limited Soviet strike
against the USA apart from the single decision of ordering the mass
destruction of enemy civilians, in the face of the certainty that it would
be followed by the mass slaughter of Americans.'

In Europe the reception was mixed. Some agreed that DETERRENCE
is enhanced if the risks associated with the use of strategic weapons are
reduced (ie if the other side believes that you are more likely in certain
conditions to *use* them because their use would not be suicidal but
controlled). Others argued that 'the ability to wage war more flexibly
and efficiently … is often in conflict with the ability to deter its onset'.

A third group, notably West Germany and Holland, expressed the
concern that the new strategy raised the prospect of a nuclear war

confined to Europe, leaving the superpowers' homelands as 'sanctuaries'.

Many others are not sanguine that limited nuclear war is a genuine operational option. First they cite Soviet pronouncements that any nuclear attack would be met with an all-out nuclear response directed at the USA. Secondly, they are worried about the collapse of the 'firebreak' between tactical nuclear weapons and conventional weapons in Europe inherent in LNW strategy, especially given that NATO refuses to offer a pledge of no-first-use. Thirdly, they believe that in a nuclear war the C^3I would be largely destroyed and a free-for-all would replace the carefully graduated responses (and initiatives) of flexible response targeting and 'packaging' options.

Moreover, even if a war remained limited, either geographically or because of the refusal or inability of both sides to launch total war, its scale, if it involved nuclear exchanges, would, many maintain, be a world disaster.

linkage The linking of the ratification of an agreement on nuclear matters to an issue of a different order, eg the Soviet invasion of Afghanistan or human rights in the USSR. SALT II was not ratified because of the invasion of Afghanistan. It is significant that, sometimes to the horror of their allies, the USSR, and later China, have never linked talks on nuclear arms control to other matters. SALT I negotiations, for example, went on at the height of the US intervention in South-East Asia, which included the bombing of Hanoi and Haiphong, the undercover bombing of Cambodia, widespread use of defoliants and napalm, and the bombings of non-combatants – any one of which could have been 'linked' by the USSR to the SALT talks and been given as a reason for discontinuing them.

Behind Soviet refusal and US readiness to adopt linkage tactics lies the fact that at every stage of the arms race the USA has had an undisputed lead in numbers of warheads, delivery systems, accuracy and technology generally (only in sheer megatonnage has the USSR been ahead). It has therefore been more in the interests of the USSR to reach an agreement than it has the USA.

'Little Boy' atomic bomb On 6 August 1945 at 8.15 am, 'Little Boy' was exploded at 1,903 ft (580 m) over the centre of Hiroshima. It employed a gun assembly firing device to explode about 60 kg of uranium-235 to produce a yield in the 12–15 kt range.

London Suppliers Club
see URANIUM SUPPLY CONTROLS

long-range navigation (LORAN) A system for communicating with submarines. As normal radio waves cannot travel through water it is necessary to use low, very low, or extremely low frequency signals. The lower the frequency the further below the water surface the signal can reach. LORAN-C system provides a pulsing low frequency (LF) signal that can penetrate water 9–12 ft and can send a very slow one-way message. It can also provide a submarine with a fix in order for it to locate its position to within 160 m. One LORAN network is in the north-east Atlantic and another, 'Clarinet Pilgrim' in the central Pacific.

long-range theatre nuclear force (LRTNF)

Nuclear weapons with a range of between 1,000 and 5,500 km, sometimes called 'Eurostrategic' weapons. They were the subject of the Intermediate Nuclear Force talks in Geneva. (The USSR denotes weapons of this range as 'medium'.) Such US and NATO weapons can strike the Soviet Union, including its main C³I facilities. Equivalent Soviet missiles cannot hit any part of the USA except for Alaska. The USSR includes all US forward-based systems in this category.

The principal weapons involved are British Polaris SLBMs, French SLBMs and IRBMs, Soviet SS-20s and US GLCMs and Pershing IIs. Many hundreds of fighter planes and bombers (especially those with in-flight refuelling capability) should also be included as LRTNF. For reasons of space they are not included here; also because their capabilities are hotly disputed as to range, speed, nuclear capability and weight capacity.

M-109 howitzer

The M-109 is a heavy, tracked, tank-like, self-propelled gun, widely used by NATO countries (West Germany, Italy, The Netherlands, Belgium) and in South Korea by the US Army.

Specifications
Range: 30 km
Yield: W48 nuclear shell, 2 kt
Accuracy: na
Number deployed: US – 252, NATO – 1,488
see also M-110 HOWITZER, ARTILLERY, NUCLEAR

M-110 howitzer

A self-propelled, nuclear-capable field gun, the M-110 is deployed by NATO (in Belgium, Greece, Netherlands, Turkey, UK, West Germany) and by US forces in Europe, South Korea, Japan and within the USA.

The tracked, tank-like vehicle is capable of 9 mph over open countryside and 34 mph on roads. It can fire both conventional and nuclear shells at the rate of one every two minutes.

Specifications
Range: 35 km
Yield: W33 nuclear shell: 5–10 kt
       W79 nuclear shell: sub-kt–10 kt

Accuracy: CEP: 170 m.
Number deployed: US – 200 NATO – 387
see also M-109 HOWITZER, ARTILLERY, NUCLEAR

Magnox reactor Type of early British nuclear reactor. Heat extraction is by carbon dioxide gas under pressure (19 atmospheres at 245°C). The fuel is natural uranium metal rods clad in a magnesium alloy (Magnox). The reactor has a high reliability but a low efficiency (32.7 per cent) as natural uranium undergoes structural changes at high temperatures and melts at 1,130°C, while Magnox melts at 645°C. Also, refuelling has to be carried out frequently.

major attack option
see SINGLE INTEGRATED OPERATIONAL PLAN

Manhattan Project The top secret US wartime project to build an atomic bomb. The project was headed by General Leslie Groves who succeeded, with Vanneva Bush, in marrying together the civilian and military sections of the bomb project, and negotiating the sometimes stormy relations between the international team of physicists and the engineers who transformed their elegant theorems into reality. Groves kept overall power and information about the whole project firmly in his own hands, and was driven by the desire not only to see the project through to success, but, what for him was synonymous with this, to see the bomb used in wartime.

The project had several sites. The enrichment plants were built at Oak Ridge, Tennessee, the plutonium reactors at Hanford, Washington, while the construction of the bomb was carried out at Los Alamos, New Mexico, under the direction of ROBERT J OPPENHEIMER. The total cost of the project at World War II prices was $2 billion.

Even before the successful bomb test (using plutonium) at Alamogordo, scientists based in Chicago, headed by Szilard, began to oppose its use, in the knowledge that Germany was heading for certain defeat and had not, in any case, developed any nuclear bomb potential. However, with Roosevelt's death their protests were not heeded. As a response to Arthur Compton's suggestion that the bomb be dropped out at sea as a demonstration to Japan, a presidential committee finally agreed that 'the most desirable target would be a vital war plant employing a large number of workers and closely surrounded by workers' houses'. Groves, however, had already made up his mind: the bomb would be dropped on Hiroshima.

Curiously, none of the scientists who opposed the use of the new weapon communicated the one piece of information that might have swayed their superiors and which only they knew about: the deadly and long-term effects of radioactive poisoning. Otto Frisch and Rudolf Peierls had warned of this in their 1940 Memorandum. Between then and 1945 the brutalizing effects of the world war had coarsened the reactions even of a president to considerations of such a kind.

manoeuvring re-entry vehicle (MARV) A normal ballistic missile carries one warhead (re-entry vehicle) and can adjust direction only while the main rocket engine is still thrusting, during the first period of flight. After that, the missile or its warhead simply speeds like a bullet with no possibility of correction. A MARVed warhead (such as will be employed on the US's MX ICBM) is the most advanced of the new generations of multiple warheads. Several warheads are fixed to a 'bus' (see POST-BOOST VEHICLE) which releases them at different points in space, as appropriate for their different targets. However, MARVed warheads are themselves manoeuvrable as they re-enter the earth's atmosphere, both to achieve 'fine tuning' for greater accuracy, and to evade ballistic missile defence interceptor rockets.

see also RE-ENTRY VEHICLE, MULTIPLE INDEPENDENTLY-TARGETED RE-ENTRY VEHICLE (MIRV)

massive retaliation
see DETERRENCE THEORY

medium-range ballistic missile (MRBM) A class of land-based ballistic missiles with a range between approximately 900 km and 2,400 km. The USSR deploys the SS-4 and the US, Pershing II.

megaton (mt) The yield of larger nuclear warheads is expressed in megatons of high explosive (1 megaton = 1 million tons of TNT; 1,000 kilotons = 1 megaton).

Although the tendency – particularly in the US nuclear camp – has been to reduce megatonnage, yet, by increasing accuracy, improve the lethality of their missiles, there are still some very large ICBM warheads in both the US and USSR arsenals. For example, the USSR's SS-18 carries a 20 mt warhead (1,530 times more powerful than the bomb dropped on Hiroshima) and the US's Titan II ICBM carries 9 mt (690 times Hiroshima). The largest bomb ever tested was by the USSR – 55 mt. Khruschev boasted at the time that a larger device could have been tested, but it would have shattered every window in Moscow, 4,000 miles away.

see YIELD, KILOTON, EQUIVALENT MEGATONNAGE

Midgetman The difficulty in finding a suitable basing mode for the MX ICBM concentrated US strategic thinking on the small ICBM (SICBM). The deployment of thousands (3,350 are planned by the early 1990s) of these transportable ICBMs in silos hardened to withstand 7,000–8,000 psi and spaced 1,500–2,000 feet apart or on mobile launchers, would increase the likelihood of the missiles' survival in a nuclear attack. However, the high cost and technical

problems associated with the guidance system are major drawbacks. Each missile would carry one warhead of about 335 kt with a CEP of less than 133 m. $600 million in the 1984 defence budget was allocated for research and development of SICBMs.

see also SMALL INTERCONTINENTAL BALLISTIC MISSILE

MiG-21 Fishbed strike aircraft

Approximately 100 of these Soviet strike aircraft are still operational (first deployed in 1970).
Specifications
Speed: Mach 2.2
Weapons payload: 906 kg
Combat radius: 600 km

MiG-27 Flogger D/J strike aircraft

Approximately 650 of these strike aircraft are in service with the Soviet Air Force, according to *Military Balance*, 1983/84.
Specifications
Speed: Mach 1.7
Weapons payload: 3,397 kg
Combat radius: 800 km

minimum essential emergency communications network

see COMMAND, CONTROL, COMMUNICATIONS AND INTELLIGENCE

Minuteman II missile

Suspended in shock-resistant silos, hardened to withstand 1,200–2,200 psi overpressure, the US Minuteman II intercontinental ballistic missile is also protected against the ELECTROMAGNETIC PULSE (EMP) of incoming enemy missiles. The system was deployed in 1966 and is now showing signs of deterioration. By the mid-1980s it will have been replaced by the MX system or overhauled. There are 450 Minuteman IIs presently deployed.
Specifications
Range: 11,300 km
Yield: 1 × 1–2 mt warhead
Accuracy: CEP 370 m

Minuteman III missile

Boeing's improvement on the MINUTEMAN II intercontinental ballistic missile began its service in December 1970. There are 550 deployed at US Air Force bases at Malmstrom, Montana; Minot, Nevada; F. E. Warren, Wyoming and Grand Forks, Nevada, and more will replace Minuteman II missiles by the end of 1985.

An airborne launch control system (ALCS) reinforces the underground launch centres and a 'command data buffer' allows infinite retargeting of individual missiles in 25 minutes and the entire force in 10 hours.

Specifications
Range: 13,000 km
Yield: 250 with 3 × 170 kt MIRV'd W-62 warheads, 300 with 3 × 335–350 kt MIRV'd W-78 warheads
Accuracy: CEP 220–280 m.

Mirage IIIE strike aircraft
The French Air Force has 30 Mirage IIIEs in their strike force. Each has a weapons payload of 8,607 kg, including 1 (possibly 2) 15 kt gravity nuclear bomb(s), a speed of Mach 1.8, and a range of 2,400 km.

Mirage IVA strike aircraft
France has 34, each with a weapons payload of 7,248 kg, including a 60 kt nuclear gravity bomb. A nuclear air-to-surface missile of some 100 kt will be added to the armament in the late 1980s.
Speed: Mach 2.2; combat radius: 1,600 km.

Mirage 2000N strike aircraft
The successor to the French Mirage IVA strike aircraft. Due into service for the first time in 1986, some 200 of the aircraft are planned for deployment. They are equipped with far more sophisticated guidance systems than their predecessor, including a terrain-following radar system, similar to the TERCOM guidance of cruise missiles.

missiles
see BALLISTIC MISSILE, CRUISE MISSILE, INTERCONTINENTAL BALLISTIC MISSILE, MEDIUM-RANGE BALLISTIC MISSILE, SHORT-RANGE BALLISTIC MISSILE

missile accuracy
The increased accuracy of missiles and warheads is the single most important technological development since the 1960s. It has transformed the offensive strategic posture of FIRST-STRIKE CAPABILITY from the realm of the hypothetical to one of realistic possibility, especially with the new generation of US missiles (MX, Trident-D5, Pershing II, Cruise).

For COUNTERVALUE targeting keen accuracy is not an important factor. For COUNTERFORCE targeting it is a different matter entirely. The ability to destroy a HARD TARGET (military installations) depends on three factors: the accuracy of the warhead, its explosive yield, and the degree of overpressure that the target can withstand. Of these, accuracy is by far the most important. Doubling the megatonnage of a warhead increases its LETHALITY rating by only two thirds. Doubling its accuracy has the same effect as increasing its megatonnage eight times. Not surprisingly, given the American and, increasingly, the Soviet preference for counterforce targeting, missile technology has tended towards lighter warheads with a premium on accuracy.

To take an example: a Minuteman-II has a one megaton warhead and a CIRCULAR ERROR PROBABLE (CEP) of 370 m. Its lethality rating is 11. Converted to a Minuteman-III with three 170 kiloton MIRVs and a CEP of 220 m, total lethality (counting all three warheads) increases to 23. The hard target kill probability for the full payload has increased from 13 per cent to 24 per cent.

All corrections to the direction and speed of early missiles was done during the powered flight phase, using swivel nozzles and other forms of steering control. After the motors burned out no corrections could be made. Now, though, course corrections can be made, *after* the main motors have fallen away, to the 'bus' which carries warheads. The best-known missile navigational aid is Stellar Inertial Guidance (SIG), by which a missile's navigational computers obtain a reading from a star to allow them to correct the missile's position in space. Even greater accuracy can be obtained by corrections made during the warhead's re-entry into the earth's atmosphere (where meteorological conditions can greatly alter the intended flight path). Such a system is MANOEUVRING RE-ENTRY VEHICLE (MARV).

The generic name for systems which can guide a missile or warhead after the main motor has burnt out is a Correlation Guidance System. This can employ optical, radar, infra-red or microwave sensors to compare pictures of a route or target area with stored reference pictures in order to generate course corrections. TERCOM is one such system and is used in cruise missiles.

The MX guidance system is called the Advanced Inertial Reference Sphere; it can pinpoint the mid-course position for dropping off MIRV'd warheads to within 30.5 m, providing a CEP of less than 130 m.

Lastly, there is NAVSTAR, 'one of the most important and far-reaching programs in the Department of Defense'. If, as is probable, the MX uses Navstar fixes, accuracy will be improved to 300 feet. Finally, by employing MARV'd warheads the CEP could be reduced to less than 30 m (from a firing point 11,200 km away).

To summarize: increased accuracy paved the way for multiple warheads. Before, hard target kill probability was related to the EQUIVALENT MEGATONNAGE of the warhead, which would therefore have been as large as possible. The closer to the target that alterations can be made the more accurate will be the warhead. First we see the introduction of guidance systems to the 'bus' and later to the warheads themselves. In this sense, modern missiles are no longer 'ballistic' because their in-flight direction can be altered right up to the moment of impact. Each missile's accuracy is expressed in terms of its CIRCULAR ERROR PROBABLE (CEP). The CEP for any given missile is indicated under the heading for that missile. Soviet missile accuracy, though improving, is way behind the USA's. The much-feared SS-20, for example, has a CEP rating of some 400 m while that of Pershing II is 40 m. The American missiles, therefore, have a probability of hard target kill of 99 or 100 per cent.

Land-based strategic ballistic missiles are more accurate than the present generation of sea-launched missiles (although Trident II D5 SLBM will have a CEP of less than 100 m). The USSR has more of the former than the latter, and by American standards, they are not very accurate, but they provide the main counterforce Soviet arsenal. Sea-launched missiles used to be considered primarily as countervalue weapons. Five developments are taking place, however, which must be profoundly worrying to Soviet military and political leaders:

1 The USA is evening up the balance of ICBMs with the development of the highly accurate MX (CEP 130 m) which has MARV'd warheads;

2 SLBMs capable of using Navstar are being retrofitted into Poseidon submarines. The Trident II D5 warheads are accurate enough to count as silo-killing weapons. In other words a section of US SLBMs will become counterforce instead of countervalue weapons.

3 The USSR's own submarines can now be accurately tracked and targeted virtually all over the world. They could be destroyed as part of a first strike.

4 The 6,000 ground-, air- or sea-launched cruise missiles could swamp any air defence system, and their phenomenal accuracy ensures the destruction of any missiles in the silos they hit. The only reply to such a threat is to have a policy of LAUNCH-ON-WARNING so that at the first sign of a cruise attack Soviet missiles would be launched.

The combination of all these developments could be to leave the USSR, despite its massive arsenal, open to a disarming first strike. The key to them all is accuracy.

see also COUNTER MILITARY POTENTIAL, EQUIVALENT MEGA-TONNAGE, LETHALITY, SINGLE SHOT PROBABILITY OF KILL

missile gap A supposed gap between the numbers of inter-continental ballistic missiles held by the USA and the USSR – in favour of the latter. It was 'discovered' in the late 1950s in the wake of the shock administered to the US military by the launch of the Soviet Sputnik satellite. For USAF Intelligence, scrutinizing U-2 surveillance aircraft film, 'every fly speck on a film was a missile'. The SS-6 missile complex was eventually located at Plesetsk, but not before an ammunition shed, a Crimean War monument and a medieval tower had all been pronounced ICBMs. In fact Soviet technology was not very advanced and was concentrated on intermediate range missiles, and in that range, but only that, they had numerical superiority.

The missile gap figured prominently in Kennedy's pre-election attack on the Eisenhower administration. When it was found to be illusory the momentum was inexorable and the Minuteman and Poseidon programmes were allowed to continue.

Below is a table showing the astonishing difference between 'missile gap' paranoia and reality.

*The 'missile gap' in ICBMs**

	Date	United States	Soviet Union	Balance + = US superiority − = Soviet superiority
(a) Missile Gap projection	1960	30	100	− 70
	1961	70	500	− 430
	1962	130	1,000	− 870
	1963	130	1,500	−1,370
	1964	130	2,000	−1,870
(b) 'Actual figures'	1960	18	4	+ 14
	1961	63	20	+ 43
	1962	294	75+219	
	1963	424	100	+ 324
	1964	834	200	+ 634

*from *Defended to Death*, 1983, p. 91. Sources: note 12, p. 354 of same book.

The fault, as so often is the case when it comes to statistical matters, is partly the USSR's for failing to collect and release accurate data. Robert McNamara, Kennedy's Secretary of Defense, drew the lesson for both sides in 1967: 'But the blunt fact remains that if we had more accurate information about planned Soviet strategic forces we simply would not have needed to build as large a nuclear arsenal as we have today ... Furthermore, that decision in itself – as justified as it was – in the end could not have left unaffected the Soviet Union's future nuclear plans.' (18 Sept. 1967, 'The dynamics of nuclear strategy'; *Department of State Bulletin* 57, 9 Oct. 1967, p. 446.)

In 1982 he was more forthright: 'by 1962 the advantage in the US warhead inventory was so great *vis-à-vis* the Soviets that the Air Force was saying that they felt we had a first-strike capability and could, and should, continue to have one. If the Air Force thought that, imagine what the Soviets thought', (from an interview with McNamara by R Sheer, *Los Angeles Times*, 12 April 1982.)

Again and again (bomber gap, missile gap, WINDOW OF VULNERABILITY, Soviet tank superiority in Europe) the US and NATO high command has (perhaps genuinely) come to believe in a deficiency in one or another area of their forces compared to those of the Warsaw Treaty Organization. The result has always been to whip up a climate of opinion to enable or force a president to push through Congress the funding necessary for a new generation of weapons. In all cases the original fear has been groundless.

Moratorium on nuclear tests, 1958 The USSR, the USA and the UK drew up an interim agreement to stop all tests on nuclear weapons while negotiations for a comprehensive test ban treaty were in progress. Although such negotiations continued for four years, the countries failed to reach any significant agreement and testing was resumed in 1962.

MSBS M-20 missile This medium-range, submarine-launched missile is seen as playing a key role in the French nuclear deterrent force and, in many ways, it is similar in concept to the British Polaris missile system. It has a range of approximately 3,000 km and is equipped with one 1 mt nuclear warhead.

The MSBS force in Force Océanique Stratégique (FOST) is currently composed of five nuclear-powered submarines, each carrying 16 M-20 missiles. The submarines in service are *Le Redoubtable, Le Terrible, Le Foudroyant and L'Indomptable* and *Le Tonnant*. A sixth submarine, *L'Inflexible,* is due to go into service shortly (construction began in 1978). This last submarine will be armed with the next generation of MSBS missiles – the M-4.

MSBS M-4 missile Planned as a replacement for the French MSBS M-20 missiles, the M-4 is scheduled for deployment on the French Navy's latest submarine, *L'Inflexible,* which was originally scheduled for 1985.

The missile will carry a number of warheads (six or seven) each with a yield of around 150 kt, unlike its predecessor which carried only one warhead of 1 mt. It is believed that the M-4s' warheads will be MIRV'd, but this is not certain yet. Once the M-4 missile is operational, the rest of the MSBS fleet will be refitted.

A replacement for the M-4s – the M-5 – is already at the planning stage and the French hope to have nine submarines armed with M-5 missiles in operation by the 1990s.

multilateralism The belief that the best way to achieve arms reductions, whether conventional or nuclear, is through negotiations between all parties in possession of the arms the reduction of which is being sought. Reductions would be reciprocal and agreed by negotiation. Policing would be through a system of international or at least mutual inspection. Proponents of multilateralism specifically reject unilateralist measures as being counter-productive.

Thus David Owen says:

> 'unilateralists underestimate ... the extent to which large unilateral steps towards disarmament will actually impede progress in overall disarmament. Large steps ... remove the incentive from some countries to negotiate matching responses'.

In order to take part in multilateral talks one must have something to bargain with which one is prepared to lose. These are known as 'bargaining chips' and will be dealt with below. With a particular focus on British multilateralism one recognizes:

1 Multilateral negotiations have regrettably achieved very little to

date. This is an inescapable fact that ought to lead us, through a process of induction, to expect little from future negotiations. The MUTUAL AND BALANCED FORCE REDUCTIONS in Europe have, after 12 years, not yet agreed on basic definitions of weapons categories. SALT II was bilateral and took six years to conclude, only to be rejected by the US Congress and the new Reagan administration. It is significant that the British Government (of Edward Heath) did not want to be a party to the SALT talks for fear that British weapons might be negotiated away. It is not convincing, therefore, to hear some members of another Conservative government proclaim their eagerness to disarm provided the USSR will reciprocate.

2   Negotiations take a long time. This allows new systems to be developed and deployed. These are supposed to act as bargaining chips to force reductions on opponent's missiles. Polaris submarines will have to be withdrawn anyway in the 1990s because of their age. They have to be replaced if Britain is to be in a position to negotiate at such talks. Cruise missiles are a much stronger bargaining chip than Britain's Polaris because were they to be bargained away the US arsenal would still be substantial, whereas it is hard to see to what level the Russian arsenal must be reduced before British proponents of nuclear weapons would agree to trade off their limited arsenal.

The very concept of the 'bargaining chip' reveals multilateral negotiations to be about something other than disarmament. The whole point of such a 'chip' is that it is expendable. It is there *so that* the less expendable components of a nuclear arsenal will not be touched in the course of negotiations. But the hope is that by expending them, vital components of the opponent's arsenal will indeed be reduced. But the opponent will not agree to this from the very beginning, as has been shown by the fate of the Intermediate Nuclear Force talks. Only if vital forces on both sides are placed on the table for mutual reduction would multilateral talks have a hope of success. A bargaining chip mentality by one or both sides assures failure from the start (if only one side has bargaining chips then the talks will break down, as in the INF talks. If both sides possess bargaining chips, then their removal will not affect the central systems concerning which the talks were convened in the first place).

3   Bargaining chips have a habit of becoming essential. They acquire a constituency of industrialists, banks, sections of the military and politicians (and their equivalents in the USSR) who have an interest in ensuring that the weapon is not discarded. Cruise is a good example of this process. The 1972 PUGWASH conference summed up this process nicely and at the same time pointed to the way that arms negotiations (whether bilateral or multilateral) could actually become *part of* the process leading to the expansion and improvement of nuclear arsenals: 'If future negotiations should be used as an excuse or argument for new or expanded strategic arms programmes, so as to be able to negotiate from a position of strength, we question whether such negotiations

would be worthwhile. An effort to accumulate such "bargaining chips" for use during negotiations could result in a growth in strategic weapons so great as to offset any advantages that might result from eventual agreements.'

4   Multilateral negotiations do not take place in a vacuum. Even if Britain did want to sit at every 'top table' negotiation, and was seriously prepared to inject a sense of urgency into them, the prospect would not be good at present. The United States is in the middle of the most massive peacetime re-armament programme in its history. Between 1981 and 1986 there is to be allocated a sum of $1,500,000,000,000 to the defence budget. Its political leaders have been in no mood to negotiate reductions with the USSR (see ZERO OPTION), Caspar Weinberger has claimed that the USSR used the period of detente to accumulate more arms than in the period of the Cold War and added, 'if movement from Cold War to detente was progress, then let me say that we can't afford more progress'. Reagan himself has stated: 'No nation that placed its faith in parchment or paper while at the same time it gave up its protective hardware ever lasted long enough to write many pages in history .... The argument, if there is any, will be over which weapons, and not whether we should forsake weaponry for treaties and agreements.'

5   It is not certain that arms negotiations are best served by there being too many participants. Bilateral agreements are seldom reached as it is; but they can get hopelessly bogged down by one side playing on the existence of third or fourth parties, each with their specific interests to defend, each with their different vulnerabilities, in order to sidetrack the main talks.

6   Multilateralism is at odds with the strategic arguments employed for the need to maintain a nuclear presence (this is particularly so for Britain and France whose arsenals are limited; who, in other words, have little to bargain away).

It is said that nuclear weapons are required: to deter the Soviet Union from launching even a conventional attack on Western Europe; by Britain and France as weapons of last resort; so that there should be independent centres of decision to complicate matters for the USSR; in order, perhaps, to persuade the USA to join in a war in Europe by being able to launch missiles independently; in order that Britain should shoulder its NATO responsibilities and not become a 'free-rider' beneath the US nuclear umbrella; in order to prevent Soviet nuclear blackmail; to enhance Britain's or France's international status, obtain the ear of the US Administration and continue to be able to take a seat at the top table (see TOP-TABLE THEORY) in arms talks. All these reasons are adduced to prove the rationality and responsible statesmanship of maintaining a nuclear presence. But if these are indeed the reasons for keeping nuclear weapons then what, short of divesting itself of all nuclear capability, could the USSR do during multilateral negotiations which would cause the holders of these positions to agree to nuclear disarmament? There is a plain contradiction here.

see UNILATERALISM, BRITISH NUCLEAR DETERRENT, DETERRENCE THEORY

multiple independently targeted re-entry vehicle (MIRV)

RE-ENTRY VEHICLEs, synonymous with warheads, are released from ballistic missiles. Some missiles have many RVs (for example, the USA's submarine-launched Poseidon C-3 missile has 10, as has the USSR's SS-18 ICBM. The Trident II D5 submarine-launched missile will be able to carry as many as 17). MIRVs are carried in a POST-BOOST VEHICLE 'bus', the container element of the ICBM, and released at different intervals to proceed independently to separate targets. Below them in sophistication are MULTIPLE RE-ENTRY VEHICLES (MRVs) (such as those presently deployed on UK Polaris A-3 missiles) which are released together and fall on and around a target rather like a scatter bomb. Above them in sophistication are MANOEUVRING RE-ENTRY VEHICLES (MARVs) which are not only independently targeted but can also independently manoeuvre once they are released from the missile in order to evade defences.

multiple protective structure ('race track')

In 1979 President Carter announced the selection of a basing mode for the MX ICBM that involved a system of roadways, each about 25 miles in circumference, along which were to be positioned 23 missile shelters. A 'shield' vehicle, loaded randomly with either a real or a decoy missile, moves round the complete circuit, visiting each of the shelters in turn in a kind of 'find the lady' ploy to reduce the chance of surveillance and pre-emptive destruction. It was determined that such 'race tracks' should be established in Utah and Nevada, although MX basing is still not established and is a matter of heated debate.

The US Air Force promoted a more ambitious version of this style of ICBM basing. They suggested there should be 200 MX ICBMs being continuously moved around between 4,600 shelters spaced over an area of 5,000 square miles. The basing system would have cost $30–60 billion.

see DENSE PACK

mutual and balanced force reductions (MBFR)

Negotiations that have continued in Vienna since 1973 between Warsaw Treaty Organization and NATO countries on the limitation and reduction of all kinds of military forces in Central Europe. Complicated packages of troops, tanks, artillery and sometimes nuclear weapons have been tossed around for nine years in efforts to achieve troop ceilings of 700,000 on each side – to no avail. The only success registered has been, interestingly, a unilateral initiative from Brezhnev, who announced on 6 October 1979 the withdrawal of

20,000 troops and 1,000 tanks from East Germany. These were indeed withdrawn, as promised, on 1 August 1980.

Western leaders did not respond in kind, calling the gesture a 'ploy' in the INF talks. On the other hand, they too have had proposals of their own turned down by the other side. Sometimes missiles have been withdrawn on both sides, but they are invariably obsolete anyway or did not fit into modernized strategic patterns.

Mutual Assured Destruction (MAD) A concept of deterrence between the USA and the USSR based on the principle that if one side makes a nuclear strike against the other, the country attacked can cause reciprocal retaliatory damage on such a scale as to cause massive destruction.

see STRATEGIC DOCTRINE (AMERICAN), DETERRENCE

MX (missile experimental) 'Peacemaker' ICBM The US Air Forces's MX ICBM, presently being tested, is intended as the replacement for the Minuteman and Titan ICBM systems. The missiles have an automatic retargeting capability which reprogrammes targeting information in the event of the destruction or malfunctioning of other MX missiles, or the destruction of the original target. The Reagan Strategic Program announced in October 1981 that at least 100 operational missiles (with a further 126 missiles in reserve) would be fully deployed by 1990, 40 of which would be ready by 1986, housed in old Minuteman silos. The original intention was to superharden the silos to 5,000 lbs psi, but this idea has now been dropped. As yet, no definite decision seems to have been made about MX basing, though 23 options are currently being considered by a presidential commission set up in April 1983. The options under consideration include deep-rock silos, unmanned launchers travelling randomly in a covered trench, missiles attached to small submarines, and missiles launched from wide-bodied jets, from barges on the Great Lakes, and from railway carriages on public railways.

Specifications

Range: 13,000+ km

Yield: 10 MIRV × 300 kt W87 warheads

Accuracy: CEP less than 130 m.

see also RACE TRACK BASING SYSTEM, DEEP BASING and DENSE PACK.

Mya-4 Bison bomber This four-engined Soviet long-range bomber is similar in size to the US B-52, but carries only one-quarter of the B-52's payload. They were originally introduced in 1956, and 43 of the bombers are still in service. Most of them are equipped with 2 × 1 mt bombs.

Nagasaki On 9 August 1945, Nagasaki received the second nuclear bomb used in wartime. 'Fat Man' was a plutonium fission bomb, bigger than the weapon dropped on Hiroshima three days earlier. About 70,000 people died instantly. The death toll was less than those killed immediately at Hiroshima (140,000) because the city is in a valley, the hills of which absorbed much of the blast. However, the radioactive effects were similar.

Nagasaki has received less publicity than Hiroshima because it did not have the tragic fate of being the first city to be obliterated by a single bomb. But, being second, its destruction was even more wanton than Hiroshima's.

There appears to be no adequate reason why Nagasaki had to be bombed. Even the most cynical reason – that the bomb was of a different type from the Hiroshima uranium-235 fission bomb and the US military wanted to see if it worked – does not stand up; for the test at Alamogordo had employed the same plutonium fission device.
see HIROSHIMA, ATOMIC BOMB, IMPLOSION DEVICE

National Command Authority (US) The NCA comprises the President of the United States and the Secretary of Defense. In wartime they theoretically stand at the pinnacle of the US C³I command structure, capable, whether airborne or in a bunker, of receiving information, evaluating it and giving orders as to what action should be taken in response – what nuclear 'packages' should be used within a given 'time frame' and against what level and quantity of targets.
see SINGLE INTEGRATED OPERATIONAL PLAN

National Command Centers (US)
see COMMAND, CONTROL, COMMUNICATIONS AND INTELLIGENCE

National Military Command System (US)
see COMMAND, CONTROL, COMMUNICATIONS AND INTELLIGENCE

National Strategic Data Base
see NATIONAL STRATEGIC TARGET LIST

National Strategic Target List Also called the National Strategic Data Base, the frequently refined, updated and expanding list of targets, both in the USSR and on the territory of its allies as well as some neutrals, constitutes the nuclear target list embodied in the US SINGLE INTEGRATED OPERATIONAL PLAN (SIOP). At present the list has well over 40,000 targets. If this number seems excessive one should bear in mind that the number of potential targets in the Target Data Inventory stands at 500,000.

NATO
see NORTH ATLANTIC TREATY ORGANIZATION

Navstar A navigation system of 18–24 satellites which, by 1987, will provide global coverage to over 27,000 users from all four branches of the US military. It will be used by any ship, tank or aircraft to locate its exact position; it also has missile application of momentous significance.

Mode of operation

Navstar works on the following principle: if the velocity of two points and the time needed for a radio signal to travel between them are both known then the distance between the two points can be determined. If there are several satellites, the missile's distance from each can be calculated and from there its precise location relative to the earth's surface deduced. Now, if a missile, or a re-entry vehicle, were to take a regular position from Navstar, its trajectory and velocity could be plotted and corrected to realign it with its digitally stored flight-paths. Extraordinary accuracy is thus attainable.

The key to its success depends on the use of extremely accurate clocks to time the radio waves. The clocks must be robust enough to remain synchronized for long periods in space. After testing quartz, rubidium vapour and cesium clocks the final programme will use cesium clocks, or hydrogen laser clocks which are even more accurate but much heavier. In tests the system's navigational powers have been impressive but the clocks have not functioned well and have set the programme back to 1987.

Capability

When fully operational, Navstar will consist of 18 satellites in six orbital planes which will permit a signal to be received from four satellites 99.5 per cent of the time anywhere in the world. The satellites will provide position fixes accurate to within 10 m in all three dimensions, velocity to within 13 cm/second, and synchronization to a fraction of a microsecond. They will do this in any weather.

In 1980 President Carter noted that if Navstar receivers were added to missiles, 'then significant improvements in US missile accuracy could result; this development might warrant analysis of its potential arms control impact'. He added that there was no approved plan to add Navstar receivers to missiles. However, since then, it is known that MX ICBMs are to be so fitted (with possible retrofitting on other missiles).

Netherlands The Netherlands has signed the Non-Proliferation Treaty but remains a member of NATO, hosting the NATO HQ of allied forces in Central Europe and one of the HQs of Allied Command Channel.

Its position on the NATO decision to deploy long-range theatre nuclear weapons was that while the Defence Minister believed there was a need for a political and military answer to the USSR's SS-20 and Backfire bomber threats, he was 'unable to commit the Netherlands to the stationing of GLCMs on its territory'. Sections of the governing parties were opposed to the NATO decision and following a general election the new government has opted for an open-ended postponement.

The Netherlands has, per capita, the largest peace movement in the world, a coalition bringing together political, religious and ecological organizations.

neutron bomb
see ENHANCED RADIATION WEAPON

Nike-Hercules missile This medium-range surface-to-air nuclear-capable missile is used by the US Army in West Germany and is widely deployed by NATO forces in Greece, Italy and West Germany. Its main purpose is to supply an air defence system and, although it can be fitted with conventional warheads, its principal role is the destruction of enemy bombers by nuclear attack. The missile also has a surface-to-surface capability. It is estimated that more than 700 Nike-Hercules warheads are available for nuclear air defence, though the system is in the process of being replaced by the conventionally armed Improved Hawk missile and by future plans for the installation of the non-nuclear Patriot system.
Specifications
Range: 140 km
Yield: 1 kt
Speed: Mach 3.3

non-nuclear defence (NND) An anti-nuclear slogan, a subject of extensive research spanning a range of possibilities, and the way that most nation states actually deploy their forces (though not always necessarily defensively). The two terms of the phrase – 'non-nuclear' and 'defence' – are considered equally important.

Non-nuclear
Nuclear weapons and their associated control and surveillance systems are considered provocative, their possession the most likely reason for a nuclear attack on a country like Britain. Furthermore, they are regarded as a bluff; for to use them first would be to invite massive retribution and to use them in response to an enemy's first strike might perhaps be devastating for that enemy but would come too late to defend the territory in question. The example of Japan, when nuclear weapons were used against a non-nuclear country, is discounted because it came at the close of a bloody war which had opened in that theatre with an unprovoked attack on Pearl Harbor. If a nuclear power were to use its weapons against a non-nuclear state it would heap ignominy upon itself and might seriously demoralize its own armed forces. If it were seriously to threaten such use those in favour of NND

believe that occupation would be preferable to the results of a nuclear attack and would leave the door open to all sorts of other methods of resistance. A nuclear attack would also be self-defeating in that it would deny to the aggressors the fruits of their victory (industrial plant, workforce, raw materials).

Defence

The object of NND is to defend territory, people and democratic institutions. It aims to be non-provocative in its choice of weapons. Thus, obviously offensive weapons, be they bombers, tanks, aircraft carriers, air-to-ground and ground-to-ground missiles, would give way to anti-tank missiles, surface-to-air missiles, fighter aircraft and strengthened sea defences, for example. This would have its corollary in a non-provocative foreign policy designed to promote international peace and cooperation. The prime objective would be to aim for the de-nuclearization of Europe, starting with a band running along the border between East and West Germany, with the political thrust aimed at breaking down the military blocs which divide the continent.

Proponents of NND stress that defenders usually have a natural advantage in war – local support, better communications, knowledge of the terrain. They point to Sweden, Switzerland and Yugoslavia, all of which have defence policies involving the training of a large percentage of the population which can be mobilized at less than a day's notice. Britain, being urbanized and generally flat, is not suited for partisan-type actions should conventional weapons be unable to prevent the advance of an occupation force. But other tactics of non-cooperation, from strikes, boycotts and occupations down to smaller day-to-day gestures, are all possible components of NND. Proponents stress that, compared to a nuclear attack, NND, even if unsuccessful in the short term, is far less costly in lives.

On cost, the proponents of NND dispute that it would cost more than current expenditure mainly because very expensive weapons such as Tornado aircraft or aircraft carriers would not be part of the inventory. There is general agreement that new technology should be exploited in all sorts of ways, but not to the point of producing weapons which are almost as powerful as nuclear bombs but simply work in a different way. That would be pointless. They are against biological and chemical weapons. They do warn against reliance on very advanced techniques (such as the computerized battlefield suggested for Central Europe) because it produces its own leapfrogging technological arms race.

On NATO, proponents of NND usually agree with the British Government that if Britain were to go non-nuclear it would be inconsistent to remain indefinitely within a body which bases its strategy on the first use of nuclear weapons. They consider three options: to leave NATO altogether; to leave its military command structure, as has France; to stay in NATO provided certain conditions are met, starting with an insistence that NATO agree to a no-first-use policy.

Non-Proliferation Treaty, 1968 Regarded at the time as a major breakthrough in the regulation of nuclear arms, this treaty was signed by the UK, the USA, the USSR and a host of non-nuclear powers. (By 1983, the number of the latter had risen to 117.) The treaty has three main elements:

1 A commitment by those states who already have nuclear weapons not to make them available to those countries that do not have them.

2 A pledge by those non-nuclear countries involved in the treaty not to acquire nuclear weapons and to accept international safeguards, established and monitored by the INTERNATIONAL ATOMIC ENERGY AGENCY (IAEA), to ensure that their peaceful nuclear activities are not diverted to making such weapons; in return, there was an undertaking on behalf of those nations with advanced nuclear industries to assist the less technologically advanced countries in the development of their nuclear energy industries for peaceful purposes only.

3 An obligation on the part of those nations with nuclear-weapons systems to enter into genuine negotiations for arms control and nuclear disarmament.

However, the treaty was not signed by precisely those states whose nuclear weapons research programmes were nearing completion; for example, India (who exploded an atomic device in 1974), Israel (who was apparently assembling its own nuclear warheads in the 1973 war) and South Africa (who was ready to carry out a nuclear test in 1977, but was dissuaded from doing so by pressure from the USA and the USSR). China and France already had nuclear weapons and chose not to participate in the treaty.

non-violent direct action (NVDA) Any form of peaceful action which highlights the presence, the potential presence, and the dangers of nuclear weapons (and nuclear power installations) and military bases and draws attention to government policy on these. NVDA can be and is employed for the furtherance of any cause.

NVDA could comprise the following sorts of actions: peaceful occupation of a base or building site; the formation of a peace camp; demonstrations; vigils; torchlight processions; sit-downs; the temporary blocking of streets; impromptu meetings in public places; mass distribution of leaflets; lie-ins; packing the public gallery of parliament or a local council meeting – in fact anything that ingenuity can devise, including industrial action, mass non-cooperation, witholding of taxes or rents and other mass actions of such a kind.

NVDA aims to draw in participants in an organized and peaceful way while educating the public rather than antagonizing it, thus isolating the local or national authority over a particular question. It usually requires careful preparation. It is not seen by its proponents as the only or even the principal method of achieving its object – simply one of many tactics. It is prepared, sometimes, to go beyond legal limits if it is judged that any resulting arrests and trials would be tactically advantageous in what is, in effect, a protracted ideological battle for the 'hearts and minds' of the population as a whole.

see GREENHAM COMMON, CAMPAIGN FOR NUCLEAR DISARMAMENT

North American Aerospace Defense Command (NORAD)
NORAD is an integral part of the US C^3I structure. It is concerned mainly with intelligence but it also has a command role. Indeed in 1958 and again in 1976 it was revealed that its commander has the authority 'under severe restrictions and specific conditions of attack' to launch nuclear weapons.

Its HQ is situated 1,400 feet deep in granite caves within Cheyenne Mountain, Colorado, built with blast-proof doors and on helical springs to withstand a direct nuclear hit. There is an alternative command centre, Space Defense Center at Eglin Airforce Base, Florida, from which the Command can go airborne. It is linked to its own commands, to Strategic Air Command (SAC), the Pentagon, and to the White House. Its functions are as follows:

1 Bomber detection and warning
It has 83 radar sites including the distant early warning line ('Dewline'), along the 70th parallel (being updated to 'Seek First'), and the 'pine tree' line in mid-Canada. It has an over-the-horizon radar at Bingham, Maine, seven E-3A AWACS (airborne warning and control systems) aircraft and the Teal Ruby satellite network. In place of radar, the latter uses a passive sensor – a mosaic of tiny receptors, each one 'staring' in a fixed direction. Teal Ruby is excellent for detecting and tracking a flying object and is even sensitive to a vapour trail left some time before by an aircraft. Lastly, NORAD will have some 320 F-15 fighters, or their equivalent, at its disposal for fighting off a bomber (or a cruise missile) attack.

2 Ballistic missile early warning system (BMEWS)
BMEWS scans for Soviet ICBMs coming over the North Pole and has three radar sites (in Alaska, Greenland and Britain). Perimeter acquisition radar (PAR) in North Dakota uses phased array radars similar to Teal Ruby. It can spot missiles (including SLBMs) up to 4,600 km away, provided they are coming from a Polar direction; it can also detect MIRVs and compute their likely targets.

3 Detect submarine-launched ballistic missiles
This is now carried out by 'Pave Paws' phased-array radars, one site at Otis Air National Guard Base, Massachusetts, the other at Beale Air Force Base, California. Two more sites are planned. Each site has a

4,800 km range, 240° angle of scan, and their scope extends from the horizon to zenith. They also aid in NORAD's spacetracking work.

4 Space detection and tracking system (SADATS)

SADATS detects, identifies and tracks all objects in space and notes their orbital characteristics so they can be targeted if necessary. 'Spacetrack' is SADATS' backbone; it has radars around the globe, involving scientific observatories and amateur enthusiasts. It has two huge phased-array radars, one, south-facing, in Florida, the other, 'Cobra Dane' on Shemya Island in the Aleutian group. It is developing a satellite attack warning system that will provide a second-by-second display of all potentially hostile satellites. 'Cobra Dane' covers space to a depth of 4,800 km – not enough for the numerous high-altitude satellites now in orbit. To cover these to a depth of 32,000 km NORAD is developing ground-based electro-optical deep space surveillance (GEODDS) which will eventually use a Teal Amber optical system similar to Teal Ruby and be so sensitive on clear nights that it will be able to spot an object no bigger than a dinner plate 40,000 km away.

North Atlantic Council
see NORTH ATLANTIC TREATY ORGANIZATION

North Atlantic Treaty Organization (NATO) Original
signatories to the North Atlantic Treaty of 4 April 1949 were Belgium, Britain, Canada, Denmark, France, Iceland, Italy, Luxembourg, Netherlands, Norway, Portugal and the USA. Greece and Turkey joined in 1952, West Germany in 1955 and Spain in 1982. France withdrew from the military organization in 1966 but remained a member of the alliance.

Members agree to consult if the security of any one of them is threatened. An armed attack against one is regarded as an attack against them all and is to be met by action 'including the use of armed force to restore and maintain the security of the North Atlantic area'.

Civilian structure

1 The North Atlantic Council (NAC), composed of foreign ministers or permanent ambassadors at Brussels, chaired by the Secretary-General, meets twice yearly. Its most important sub-committee is the NUCLEAR PLANNING GROUP.

2 Defence Planning Committee (DPC), composed of defence ministers and ambassadors, meets before the NAC and is parallel rather than subordinate to it.

3 Eurogroup (excluding France and Iceland) meets to discuss European defence and, sometimes, to counter US domination of the alliance.

Military structure

The Military Committee is the top military authority and comprises the chiefs of staff of all member countries except France and Iceland (the latter has no armed forces to speak of). It makes recommendations to the Council and DPC. There are three NATO commands, as follows:

1   Allied Command Europe (ACE) which comprises Europe less Britain, France, Iceland and Portugal. SUPREME ALLIED COMMAND EUROPE (SACEUR) has its HQ at Mons, near Brussels, and has at its immediate disposal some 6,000 tactical nuclear weapons, 66 divisions and 3,500 tactical aircraft. It has four subordinate commands:

    a) Allied Forces Central Europe (HQ at Brunssum, Holland) is itself divided into the Northern Army Group and the Central Army Group;

    b) Allied Forces Northern Europe (HQ at Kolsaas, Norway);

    c) Allied Forces Southern Europe (HQ at Naples, Italy);

    d) Allied Command Europe Mobile Force (HQ at Seckenheim, W. Germany).

2   Allied Command Atlantic (ACLANT) covers the Atlantic area north of the Tropic of Cancer. Its West Atlantic HQ is at Norfolk, Virginia as is the Submarine Attack Command. The Eastern Atlantic HQ is at Northwood near London while the Iberian Atlantic Command is at Lisbon.

3   Allied Command Channel (ACCHAN) is designated the task of defending the English Channel and the southern North Sea. It has three subordinate HQs at Plymouth, Rosyth and Walcheren, the Netherlands. Its Maritime Air Command HQ is at Northwood.

NATO's intention is to meet a conventional attack with nuclear weapons and its refusal to renounce first use has for years been a stumbling block to East–West negotiations. There is serious doubt, even among many NATO senior officers, whether the use of nuclear weapons would be the best way to 'come to the defence' of a member that had been attacked – the whole raison d'être of NATO. It also raises the question of whether a country that renounces nuclear weapons (or decides against arming itself with them) should remain within the alliance (see CANADA).

For a brief comparison with WTO (Warsaw Pact) forces see WARSAW TREATY ORGANIZATION.

nuclear accidents These fall into different categories of seriousness:

1   Nucflash – an accident or unauthorized incident which would create the risk of nuclear war between the US and the USSR.

2   Broken Arrow – the accidental or unauthorized detonation or possible detonation of a nuclear weapon; the non-nuclear detonation or burning of a nuclear weapon; radioactive contamination; seizure, theft or loss of a nuclear weapon or component (including jetissoning); public hazard, actual or implied.

3 Bent Spear – nuclear weapons incidents other than nuclear weapons accidents or war risk detonation.
4 Dull Sword – any non-significant nuclear weapons incident.

In addition there are accidents connected with non-military nuclear reactors or the transport or treatment of nuclear waste at different stages of the nuclear fuel cycle and radioactive poisoning from nuclear tests in Southern Australia, the USA and the Pacific. SIPRI Yearbook 1977 lists some 113 accidents. Below are listed a few examples (two of the more serious accidents, KYSHTYN and THREE-MILE ISLAND (HARRISBERG) are described separately).

● *27 July 1956:* A B-47 crashed into a store containing three nuclear bombs at Lakenheath, Suffolk, setting it ablaze. A B-47 Stratojet was practising 'roller' landings when it slid out of control off the runway. Fuel was spilt on to an earth-covered storage igloo containing three B-6 atom bombs each with a yield of 60 kt. The fuel caught fire and there was a stampede out of the base by personnel and their families. The US fire chief had to decide whether to direct his hoses on to the burning igloo or the aircraft, in which four crew members were being burnt to death. Perhaps wisely, he chose the former. Although the storage configuration of the bombs was such that a nuclear explosion was not possible, nevertheless, a conventional explosion of the 10,000 lbs of TNT would have distributed the plutonium in the igloos over a wide area. The accident can hardly be squared with a statement in a Ministry of Defence brochure issued in 1980 that, 'nuclear weapons have been stored in this country for many years. There has never been any accident or radiation leakage'.

● *1958:* A B-47 accidentally dropped a one megaton bomb over Mars Bluff, South Carolina. The trigger went off.

● *1959:* A Bomark missile exploded following a fire at the McGuire Base, New Jersey; significant leakage of radioactivity.

● *5 October 1960:* NORAD HQ warned of a 'massive' Soviet missile attack after a radar malfunction at the ballistic missile early warning site at Thule, Greenland.

● *4 June 1962:* A one-megaton warhead destroyed over Johnston Island Pacific Test Range after Thor ICBM failed in a high-altitude thermonuclear weapon test. The same thing happened on 20 June.

● *April 1963:* US submarine, *Thresher,* lost off the US Atlantic coast. The enquiry ignored evidence that a fault in the nuclear-powered engine may have been the cause.

● *17 January 1966:* Two aircraft involved in a mid-air re-fuelling operation crashed off Palomares, Spain. One of them, a B-52, was carrying four 20–25 mt bombs, the detonation device for two of which exploded scattering plutonium and requiring a large clean-up operation. One bomb was recovered from the sea.

● *21 January 1968:* A B-52 crashed near Thule – four H-bombs were destroyed in the fire; radioactive contamination resulted.

● *20 February 1971:* NORAD HQ operator accidentally transmitted an emergency message ordering all US broadcasting stations off the air, by order of the President. Forty minutes elapsed before the code could be found permitting him to cancel the message.

● *27 February 1972:* Message sent to 22 Coast Guard units saying that President Nixon was assassinated on his visit to China and World War III declared. It was a hoax.

● *23 October 1975:* A 20 kt bomb in a canister fell down a test shaft at Nevada test site.

● *18 October 1975:* US early warning satellite 'dazzled' over Siberia. It was assumed to be Soviet jamming using a laser beam; in fact it was caused by accidental fire in gas pipeline.

● *9 November 1979:* NORAD computers indicated limited Soviet missile attack. Planes scrambled and missile stations put on alert (a training tape had been inserted into the computer system by mistake).

● *3 and 6 June 1980:* Another false alert by NORAD computers; 100 nuclear-armed B-52s alerted for take-off.

● *18 September 1980:* A technician dropped a wrench socket on to a fuel tank in a US Titan II silo. The explosion blew off the 740-ton door and sent the re-entry vehicle with its 9 mt warhead 600 feet into the air killing one man and injuring 21 others.

● *November 1981:* US Poseidon missile dropped 17 feet while being serviced at the Holy Loch submarine base, Scotland.

Drug abuse, irresponsible behaviour and psychiatric problems result in some 5,000 people being transferred from nuclear weapons duties in the US forces each year, including its forces in Europe.

Nuclear Activities Branch
see SUPREME ALLIED COMMAND, EUROPE (SACEUR)

Nuclear free zone (NFZ)

Regional diplomatic proposals
At various times proposals have been laid before the United Nations, or bilateral and multilateral approaches have been made between governments for whole regions to be considered as nuclear free zones. There have been four successful treaties to date: OUTER SPACE TREATY, SEABED TREATY, ANTARCTIC TREATY and TREATY OF TLATELOLCO. This entry looks at some of the other initiatives.

In 1957 the first Rapacki Plan 'provided for a NFZ covering Poland, Czechoslovakia, East and West Germany. In this area there would be no manufacture of nuclear weapons or secondary installations; the use of nuclear weapons against the area would be forbidden ... a broad system of ground and air control would be set up ... the policing apparatus would consist of NATO, the Warsaw Pact and non-aligned states ... unilateral declarations by the governments concerned, which would have the force of international undertakings, would be sufficient.'

Nuclear-free zone (NFZ)

The Plan was found unacceptable to the main Western powers (a) because it made no contribution to the reunification of Germany and (b) because it contained no limitation on conventional forces.

In 1958, Rapacki proposed a revised version in two stages:
a a freeze on nuclear armaments in the proposed zone;
b a reduction of conventional forces carried out simultaneously with the complete denuclearization of the zone, and with appropriate verification measures.

There was no official Western reply to these proposals.

In 1959, the Chinese People's Republic suggested that the Pacific Ocean and Asia be constituted a NFZ. Also in 1959 Khrushchev suggested the creation of a Nordic NFZ.

On 24 November 1961, 14 African states proposed at the United Nations a resolution which was passed by 55 to 0, with 44 abstentions. It called upon member states:

a To refrain from carrying out or continuing to carry out nuclear tests in Africa in any form;

b to refrain from using the territory, territorial waters or airspace of Africa for testing, storing or transporting nuclear weapons;

c to consider and respect the continent of Africa as a denuclearised zone.

(source *The United Nations and Disarmament, 1945–1970,* UN, New York, 1970, p. 331.)

In 1962 the third Rapacki Plan was presented to the EIGHTEEN NATION DISARMAMENT COMMITTEE. It was broadly similar to the second Rapacki Plan. This time the Western states rejected it not because of a supposed imbalance in conventional weapons but because the plan did not include nuclear weapons located in the Soviet Union.

In 1963, President Kekkonen of Finland proposed a Scandinavian NFZ. Norway called for parts of the USSR to be denuclearized; Sweden said the banning of all nuclear tests was a condition for the creation of such a zone.

In 1963, Khrushchev called for a nuclear-free Mediterranean.

In 1964 the Gomulka Plan was launched. It aimed solely to freeze nuclear armaments in Central Europe, specifically West and East Germany, Poland and Czechoslovakia. The plan called for a ban on the production of nuclear weapons in the area and a freeze on the stockpiles of weapons at their current levels, thus maintaining the existing balance of forces. The plan was rejected by NATO, most forcefully by West Germany.

During the following years Algeria held a conference which called for a Mediterranean NFZ; Khrushchev repeated his call for a NFZ in Scandinavia, adding that any denuclearization of Soviet territory would have to be reciprocated by other nuclear states; the Central European NFZ was raised in various forums, and an Iranian motion calling on the United Nations to establish a NFZ in the Middle East was lost in a welter of well-meaning phrases after Israel refused to sign.

The General Assembly decided in 1974 to make a comprehensive study of NFZs. The Stockholm International Peace Research Institute commented on the report, 'consensus was reached on but a few rather trivial, self-evident principles. The rest of the report is a compilation of contradictory views on matters most essential for the realisation of the nuclear weapon free zone concept'.

In 1975 the General Assembly approved a resolution to establish a South Pacific NFZ. China voted to accept the resolution. The other nuclear states abstained, claiming that the possible extension of the area to include points of the high seas or international straits could interfere with the rights of navigation.

In 1978 at a meeting of the Socialist International, Olaf Palme called for the creation of a nuclear free Europe, beginning with North and Central Europe. This was taken up by European Nuclear Disarmament in 1980.

In 1981 the Nordic NFZ was again discussed, this time by the Scandinavian foreign ministers. All four countries are in favour; however, as part of the proposal, the USSR would be required to remove its nuclear installations from the Kola Peninsula.

Local nuclear free zones

After it became clear that the first civil defence concern of the British government, in the event of a nuclear war, would be population control, including the use of armed police, special courts and concentration camps, many local authorities began to reappraise their own supposed role. Starting with Manchester City Council in 1980, around 200 local authorities in the UK have declared themselves 'nuclear free zones'. As such they oppose the manufacture, deployment and use of nuclear weapons within their boundaries and have rejected the role assigned to them in civil defence. Others also reject the transport of nuclear waste through their boundaries.

In 1982, 24 county councils refused to participate in HARD ROCK home defence exercise. Wales has a majority of nuclear free zone councils. At present, though, to have the status of a 'nuclear free zone' is somewhat gestural; it expresses an intent on the part of the local authority rather than any ability to implement it.

nuclear fuel cycle

During the nuclear cycle uranium passes from mining and milling, enrichment, fuel fabrication, reprocessing and back to enrichment for re-use as fuel or for military purposes, or, transformed partly into plutonium for use in fast breeder reactors or bombs.

Mining

Uranium is available usually only as 0.4 per cent of mined ore. The ore is crushed and milled into a fine sand and the uranium is leached out and finally concentrated as a mixture of oxides known as 'yellowcake', which is not very radioactive but is toxic. This is then purified and either enriched or not, depending on what sort of reactor it is destined for.

Enrichment

This is done using a very expensive gaseous diffusion process, good for the very high enrichment needed for bomb-grade material but not for the 2–3 per cent enrichment needed for most nuclear fuels. The gas centrifuge process is much cheaper and smaller scale; laser-enrichment is the most likely method of the future. Uranium is converted into uranium hexafluoride – hex – for enrichment. Hex is highly toxic and corrosive. If the doubling time (the number of years it takes a fast breeder to produce the same quantity of fuel that it was originally loaded with) of a fast breeder can be improved upon it may be possible to dispense with enrichment plants altogether.

Fuel fabrication

Fuel fabrication into pellets of uranium dioxide or plutonium dioxide is a very critical process demanding absolute purity of product and technical precision, for the cladding as much as for the fuel.

Loading and unloading

This can be done while the reactor is running for Magnox, Candu (heavy water) and advanced gas-cooled reactors (AGRs). The others have to be closed down. Spent fuel rods are extracted by remote control and dropped into vast cooling ponds.

Reprocessing

After 100 days in a cooling pond, fast-breeder fuel will still be giving out as much heat as Magnox fuel just after extraction. The radiating fuel rods are taken from the cooling ponds and dropped into nitric acid and eventually the plutonium and uranium are separated, in the form of nitrate solutions from the other fission products and the fuel-rod cladding material. The reprocessing plant is the likeliest place for plutonium thefts, or plutonium side-tracking for military purposes to take place. At present, international inspections are neither strict, accurate, nor frequent enough to ensure against these possibilities.

Radioactive waste

The hot, acid solution, full of actinides, that remains from the reprocessing of uranium fuel is radioactive for hundreds of thousands of years. At present it is stored in very complex and expensive stainless steel tanks set in interconnecting rows and sealed in steel-lined concrete buildings. There it remains until other methods are devised for its disposal. Some proposed solutions for this are: shooting the waste out into space; burying it in the earth's core through the edges of the tectonic plates on the ocean bed; burying it under Antarctic ice or beneath seismically stable geological formations within hardened glass structures.

So far the fuel cycle has been described but the source of the waste products has not been identified. Most public comment has sought to link nuclear wastes with the civilian nuclear power programmes of different countries. The astonishing fact is that in 1981 no less than 98.8 per cent of high-level radioactive waste in the USA resulted from military activities. And 75 per cent of low-level wastes was derived from the same activities. The US Department of Energy and its predecessors, the Manhattan Engineer District, the Atomic Energy Commission and the Energy Research and Development Administration have been turning out nuclear wastes from military programmes for 35 years. For example, out of the 140 million tons of US waste that needs to be isolated, about 79 million tons can be traced back to military programmes. Below is a comparison of waste totals from military and civilian activities:

	military	*civilian*
High-level waste from reprocessing plants	10,196,000 cubic ft	29,000 cubic ft
Unprocessed spent fuel rods from nuclear reactors	Dept of Energy spent rods (not yet counted as waste)	97,500 cubic ft
Transuranic wastes to be treated as high-level waste	13,200,000 cubic ft	12,800,000 cubic ft
Low-level waste	62,100,000 cubic ft	23,600,000 cubic ft

In addition, 83 Department of Energy nuclear reactors have been de-commissioned and a further 32 will have to be at some time. The Navy has seven de-commissioned reactors and 131 more which will have to be.
see NUCLEAR POWER, NUCLEAR REACTORS, RADIOACTIVE WASTES

Nuclear Planning Group (NPG) A committee of the North Atlantic Council. All members are represented on it except France, which is not a member of the NATO military organization, and Iceland, which has no armed forces. It was set up to strengthen ties between the USA and its NATO allies in Europe by allowing the latter to be privy to, and even to be involved in, US nuclear targeting plans in the European sector.
see NORTH ATLANTIC TREATY ORGANIZATION

nuclear power The production of electricity using fissionable fuel instead of fossil fuel. There are over 50 countries running nuclear reactors to produce electricity. The first reactors were built exclusively for the plutonium byproduct used in the construction of bombs. The heat produced was a waste element. Unfortunately, although the heat is now used, plutonium remains an inevitable byproduct because of the way uranium-238 tends to absorb slow

neutrons to become uranium-239 which then decays into plutonium-239, which is fissile.

Herein lies the principal danger of nuclear power, greater even than the effects of leakages and meltdowns: for it provides a state with the most important (artificial) ingredient in the construction of a nuclear bomb.

The attraction of nuclear power to countries with no ready source of fossil fuel is understandable. However, in too many countries such fuel is available but has not been sufficiently exploited because the nuclear option has been chosen, at least in part. However, it should be noted that the vast bulk of nuclear power capacity is concentrated in OECD countries (about 230,000 megawatts out of a total of maybe 250,000 megawatts) and most of the rest is situated in Eastern Europe and the USSR.

One danger not to be underestimated is that nuclear reactors make prime targets in any nuclear targeting scenario. Should one be hit, the entire reactor core would be vapourized and the resulting fallout could be hugely more lethal, over a wider area and for a longer duration, than a nuclear air or ground burst.

see NUCLEAR FUEL CYCLE, NUCLEAR REACTOR

nuclear powered ballistic missile submarine (SSBN)

Perhaps the most potent part of the nuclear strategic triad (ICBMs and nuclear-armed bombers being the other two elements), SSBNs are the most difficult for an enemy to detect and destroy.

USA

Total 34 SSBNs, 31 of which are of the Lafayette and Franklin classes; 12 boats are armed with 16 Poseidon C-3 missiles and 16 with Trident I C-4 missiles; 3 larger Ohio class vessels are now in service (with 17 more to be commissioned by 1990). Each is armed with 24 Trident I C-4 (each missile = 8×100 kt MIRV warheads). The ninth boat will be armed with Trident II D-5 missiles and the first 8 vessels will then be converted to D-5 (about December 1988).

Britain

Total 4 SSBNs (HMS *Resolution, Revenge, Renown,* and *Repulse*). Each is armed with 16 Polaris A-3 missiles (each missile = 3×200 kt MRV warheads; one Polaris submarine could deliver more explosive than all that used by all combatants during World War II). During the 1970s the Chevaline 'front end' improvements to the Polaris A-3 missile was started in secret. The missile will now consist of 6×50 kt MRV of greater accuracy than the old A-3.

France

The FOST (Force Oceanique Strategique) operates 5 SSBNs, each armed with 16 MSBS M-20 missiles. A sixth boat, *L'Inflexible,* is due to be deployed in 1985 and will be fitted with a new missile (M-4:

Range 4,000 km, 6–7 warheads per missile, each 150 kt). A seventh SSBN is due by the mid-1990s, when the whole fleet will be armed with the M-5 MIRV missile.

USSR

Has 35 Delta class and 26 Yankee class armed with a total of 921 SLBMs. This total has been increased by a new Typhoon class boat armed with 20 SLBMs (each missile has up to 12 warheads of unknown yield). At 170 m long the Typhoon-class SSBN is about 30 per cent larger than its US equivalent, the Ohio-class. However, the Ohio is armed with 192 warheads as against the Typhoon's 180.

nuclear reactor A device in which a nuclear fission chain reaction can be controlled. Built originally for the production of weapons-grade plutonium, reactors have peaceful applications too, most notably for the production of electricity (but see NUCLEAR FUEL CYCLE and PLUTONIUM). The nuclear reactor is equivalent to the boiler in a conventional, fossil-fuelled thermal power station, but is less flexible at reducing or accelerating heat production, so is used to supply base-load requirements for a grid. Its efficiency is on a par with conventional boilers, around 30 per cent.

The fuel, usually uranium (with varying degrees of enrichment, or none at all, and sometimes with an addition of plutonium) is bombarded by neutrons which are usually slowed down by a moderator – heavy water, graphite, or light water – so as to produce further fissions to sustain a chain reaction. The chain is regulated using control rods made of boron or cadmium which are neutron-absorbing. By inserting or retracting the rods from the reactor core the rate of fission and, therefore, the heat output, can be controlled. Lastly, reactors require a coolant: helium, carbon dioxide, heavy water, light water, and molten metal such as sodium, can all be used.

Great care has to be taken with construction, day-to-day operation, the handling of fuels at all stages, especially loading and unloading, maintenance, water disposal and emergency drills. This is especially true of fast-breeder reactors, though there have been many accidents and mishaps in other reactors. Fusion nuclear reactors are at an early stage of development.
see FISSION, FAST-BREEDER REACTORS

nuclear umbrella As with COUPLING, the nuclear umbrella is a term associated with DETERRENCE theory. It is meant to imply the protection of Western Europe by US nuclear forces – both those stationed in Europe and those strategic weapons based either in the USA or aboard US SSBNs.
see also FORWARD BASED SYSTEMS

'nuclear winter' In October 1983, 500 people attended a top-level conference, held in Washington DC, on the long-term worldwide ecological consequences of nuclear war. At its conclusion it linked up by live satellite TV with 100 experts from the Soviet Academy of Sciences.

The most important conclusion of the conference was as follows: a significant nuclear exchange would cause gigantic and long-lasting fires which would produce enormous quantities of smoke. The smoke would rise into the atmosphere and block out the sun's rays. Temperature would fall to between $-30°C$ and $-40°C$ and remain there for nearly a year – the 'nuclear winter'.

It would affect the whole Northern Hemisphere, would kill plants, crops, forests and animals. Water would freeze. Millions who had survived the nuclear exchange would die of cold, hunger, thirst and disease. Most disturbing were the following:

1 An explosion of 100 megatons (half the amount postulated to drop on Britain alone in home defence exercises 'Hard Rock' and 'Square Leg') over cities could produce a two-month period with temperatures of around $-23°C$.

2 Radioactive fallout would be worse than formerly predicted because 'intermediate fallout' would be bounced back to earth by the dust and smoke in the atmosphere.

3 The Southern Hemisphere would not be spared, as many had previously believed. The smoke would not spread there in such abundance as to the North, but spread it would. The tropical rain forests, essential for the world's ecological balance, would perish with even a small drop in temperature and sunlight. Moreover, people in many countries that rely heavily on food imports from the North would starve.

4 Once the smoke had cleared, the ecosystem would be permanently damaged. For one effect of a large-scale nuclear exchange is the destruction, by nitrogen oxides formed in the explosion, of parts of the ozone layer. This layer acts as a blanket which absorbs most of the sun's harmful ultraviolet rays. At first, the smoke would protect life on earth from these rays, but once it had cleared the increase in ultra-violet radiation could prove highly destructive to plant and animal life, including humans.

One biologist summed up the peril of nuclear winter thus: 'In almost any realistic case involving nuclear exchanges between the superpowers, global environmental changes sufficient to cause an extinction equivalent to or more severe than that at the close of the Cretacious are likely.'

OPANAL The Agency for the Prohibition of Nuclear Weapons in Latin America with its HQ in Mexico. Responsible for supervising compliance with the TREATY OF TLATELOLCO, 1967, OPANAL holds biannual consultations among member states, has a General

Conference, a Council and a Secretariat. The Council is composed of five members elected at the Conference. It functions continuously.

Oppenheimer, J. Robert

The nuclear physicist given responsibility by General Groves for the Los Alamos bomb-construction part of the Manhattan Project. He was given the job, despite FBI opposition, because of his left-wing sympathies during the Spanish Civil War and the fact that some relatives were members of the US Communist Party. A brilliant physicist, a superb communicator, a well-rounded humane intellectual he turned out a very able administrator with few qualms about seeing the project through to its conclusion even to the point of dropping the bomb on Japan. Years later he commented, 'When you see something that is technically sweet you go ahead and do it and you argue what to do about it only after you have had your technical success. That is the way it was with the atomic bomb.' At the Alamogordo bomb test his utterance from the *Bhagavad Ghita* later became famous:

'If the radiance of a thousand suns
were to burst at once into the sky,
that would be like the splendour of the mighty one ...
I am become death,
the shatterer of worlds.'

He correctly predicted to a disdainful President Truman that the USSR would develop an atomic bomb within five years of the US explosions. He sat on the consultative committee that proposed (the Acheson-Lilienthal Plan) the establishment of an International Atomic Development Agency that would own all uranium mines worldwide and would manufacture all nuclear devices except those useful for peaceful research. He also suggested 'denaturing' uranium until it was needed. Vannevar Bush forced the panel to modify this idea in a direction that could only imply distrust for the USSR. The last hope that the remnants of the Acheson-Lilienthal Plan could serve as a basis for negotiations with the USSR was killed by the choice of Bernard Baruch to present it to the United Nations. Oppenheimer refused to sit on Baruch's committee.

Despite private qualms about the bomb ('I feel I have blood on my hands'; 'The physicists have known sin; and this is a knowledge which they cannot lose', and, of the H-bomb, which he opposed, 'This is a weapon which has no military significance. It will make a big bang – a very big bang – but it is not a weapon which is useful in war.'), Oppenheimer was prepared to advocate tactical nuclear weapons, the construction of an anti-bomber defence line, and the building of missiles rather than bombers as a delivery system. He simply spoke his mind, but in doing so antagonized Strategic Air Command at the height of the McArthyite witch-hunts. He had earlier incensed Louis Strauss by arguing successfully for permission to be given for the export of radioactive isotopes, despite the stringent conditions of the

Atomic Energy Act. With offhanded self-assurance he remarked, 'My own rating of the importance of isotopes is that they are far less important than electronic devices, but far more important than, let us say, vitamins. Somewhere in between.' Strauss neither forgot nor forgave. Using an insignificant incident from before the war, when Oppenheimer had been approached by a friend who had a Soviet contact, Strauss, now chairman of the Atomic Energy Commission, and the FBI pressed charges against Oppenheimer. He was supported by many scientists, but not by Edward Teller, and was found unfit to continue in his present posts. On 3 December 1953 President Eisenhower ordered a 'blank wall' between America's most famous living scientist and any access to sensitive information.

see MANHATTAN PROJECT

Outer Space Treaty, 1967

The two principal points of this, the second of the so-called 'nonarmament' treaties, are:

1   No weapons of mass destruction, nuclear or otherwise, should be placed in orbit round the earth, or installed on the moon or any other planet.

2   The moon and other planets should be used exclusively for peaceful purposes and all bases, testing and manoeuvres of a military nature are prohibited. So far 89 countries have signed the treaty.

The USA had, in fact, exploded a nuclear device in outer space in 1962 and discovered that many satellites were severely damaged by the resulting ELECTROMAGNETIC PULSE, so in many ways the treaty merely codifies what had already been demonstrated as unfeasible. Also, as the treaty refers specifically to weapons of 'mass destruction', a loophole is left for weapons of concentrated lethality such as lasers.

overkill

The ability to exterminate a population more than once. Both the USA and the USSR possess this ability many times over. The quest for strategic superiority is somewhat grisly in this context, amounting, in effect, to having more overkill than one's opponent.

It is true that, as many proponents of nuclear weapons point out, the graph relating 'megatonnage dropped' to 'immediate damage caused' and 'prompt' deaths, rises steeply at first and then flattens out. But the point at which it begins to flatten out was reached around 1964, when the USA had just 400 equivalent megatons for each leg of its strategic triad. As Henry Kissinger said in 1975, 'One of the questions we have to ask as a country is what in the name of God is strategic superiority? What do you do with it?'

As missiles become more accurate and reliable, so an opponent's fear that it would not have second-strike capability leads it to increase its nuclear inventory. The other side's fears mount in turn and their inventory expands to meet the supposed threat. Total overkill grows but can never reach a limit so long as either side fears that the other may be about to possess disarming first-strike capability.

overpressure Enormous pressure builds up at the point of nuclear explosion and produces a blast wave extending outward at about the speed of sound. Normal atmospheric pressure is 14.7 psi. Overpressure is the amount of psi by which pressure exceeds this norm. Buildings collapse at around 6 psi overpressure. Humans are far more flexible than buildings and can, theoretically, withstand up to 30 psi overpressure and live – although other factors would almost certainly kill them. Much lower levels, above 5 psi overpressure, can rupture eardrums and cause internal haemorrhaging.

The British Home Office and the US Office of Technological Assessment use different techniques for estimating the blast effects (as, indeed, all other effects) of a nuclear explosion. The Home Office figures are the lower of the two. For the Home Office an 'A ring' is an area surrounding ground zero where the overpressure is 11 psi or more and they estimate an 85 per cent fatality level without blast shelter protection. A 'B ring' has between 6 and 11 psi overpressure and fatality estimates within it are at least 40 per cent without blast shelters. In the 'C ring' (1.5 to 6 psi) 'blast could cause lethal flying missiles'. The degree of hardness of a target is expressed in psi overpressure capability and missile silos are often hardened to withstand as much as 3,000 psi overpressure.

The Home Office will almost certainly have to revise its method of calculating the effects of nuclear explosions following the publication of the British Medical Association's *The Medical Effects of Nuclear War,* which employed statistics produced by Scientists Against Nuclear Arms.

see also CIVIL DEFENCE; S Openshaw, P Steadman and O Greene, *Doomsday, Britain after Nuclear Attack,* Blackwell, 1983

Palomares accident In 1966 a B-52 collided with a re-fuelling tanker in mid-air, over Palomares, Spain in probably the most serious 'broken arrow' (see NUCLEAR ACCIDENTS). It was carrying four bombs, believed to be in the 20–25 megaton range. The detonation devices of two of the bombs went off, scattering plutonium, and 1,400 tons of radioactive soil had to be removed. All four bombs were recovered, one from the sea.

Partial (or Limited) Test Ban Treaty, 1963 This was more an anti-pollution measure than a genuine attempt to limit arms development. From the mid-1950s, concern had been growing about the wide-reaching effects of radioactive fallout from nuclear tests and the possibility of environmental contamination and subsequent genetic damage. In 1963 the USSR, the UK and the USA finally agreed, after lengthy negotiations, to sign a treaty prohibiting the testing of nuclear weapons in the atmosphere, in outer space, and under water (thus effectively limiting testing to underground sites). Since 1963 the Partial Test Ban Treaty has been signed by over 100 countries (obviously not all of these have any nuclear weapons to test), though France and the People's Republic of China refused to sign and continued atmospheric tests.

Although of real value as an anti-pollution move, the treaty has done little to check the development and testing of nuclear weapons. In fact, more tests have been conducted underground since signature of the treaty than had previously taken place in the atmosphere; the (officially admitted) rate of tests before the treaty was two per month, rising to at least three per month after the treaty. Some of this increase can be accounted for by the growth of China and France as nuclear powers, but most of the difference is a consequence of the development of the nuclear weapon programmes of the USA and the USSR.

Pave Paws phased array radar
see NORTH AMERICAN AEROSPACE DEFENSE COMMAND

payload In nuclear terms, payload represents the amount of explosive (usually expressed in thousands of pounds weight) carried in the RE-ENTRY VEHICLE of a BALLISTIC MISSILE or, with aircraft, in their combination of bombs, SHORT-RANGE ATTACK MISSILES (SRAM) or AIR-LAUNCHED CRUISE MISSILES (ALCM).

Peaceful Nuclear Explosion Treaty (1976) In May 1976
the US and USSR signed an agreement limiting peaceful nuclear explosions to complement the 1974 Threshold Test Ban Treaty.

The treaty limits individual explosions to 150 kt and multiple explosions to 1,500 kt. Verification is by national means. It lasts five years and is automatically extended. However, both this treaty and the Threshold Test Ban Treaty were not ratified by President Carter and both await action from the Senate. Nevertheless, the two countries have agreed to observe the terms of both treaties.

penetration aid A device within offensive weapons systems to increase the probability of warheads penetrating enemy air defences. They can simulate or mask a missile warhead or an aircraft in order to mislead enemy radar and divert defensive anti-aircraft or anti-missile fire away from the real warheads.

perimeter acquisition radar
see NORTH AMERICAN AEROSPACE DEFENSE COMMAND

permissive action links (PAL) Devices that prevent the unauthorized arming and firing of a nuclear weapon without the insertion of a prescribed code or combination (which would be frequently changed). Such devices can include equipment which will

destroy the weapon if unauthorized arming and firing is attempted.
see also DUAL KEY, COMMAND DISABLE SYSTEM

Pershing 1A missile

A medium-range mobile nuclear ballistic missile in service in West Germany – 108 missiles with the US Army and 72 missiles with the West German Air Force. Those in the US inventory are currently being replaced by the more accurate, faster and more powerful Pershing II. The change-over began in December 1983 and should be completed by 1985. The Pershing 1A missiles were first deployed in Europe in 1964. Various sophistications to the missiles have been introduced since then, including the application of an automatic reference system that enables the launching of the missiles from previously unsurveyed sites.

Specifications
Range: up to 740 km
Yield: three options of 60, 200 and 400 kt
Accuracy: CEP approximately 400 m at maximum range
Speed: Mach 8

Pershing II missile

A medium-range, mobile, ballistic missile, Pershing II is destined to replace the now ageing Pershing IA ballistic missile deployed in West Germany by the US Army and the West German Air Force. It will provide a significant improvement in accuracy over Pershing IA (Pershing IA CEP = 400 m; Pershing II CEP = 40 m). This dramatic improvement is achieved by means of the radar area correlation guidance (RADAG) which compares the target area with information stored in on-board computers and makes continuous flight-path adjustments.

Although the yield of Pershing II seems, at first sight, to amount to a reduction of firepower in comparison with Pershing IA (Pershing IA = up to 400 kt; Pershing II = up to 50 kt) the increase in accuracy improves the new weapons's lethality. The relationship between accuracy and lethality is, simply expressed, a cube-root relationship. If the CEP of a missile is halved, eg reduced from 100 to 50 m, the lethality of the missile increases by a factor of eight. This is particularly important when considering a missile's ability to knock out a 'hardened' military position, a missile silo or command post. If the accuracy of a missile gives an attacker a high chance of destroying missiles in their silos then it offers the attacker a strategic opportunity denied to his less accurate opponent. The attacker now has a first-strike capability. Far from a reduction of threat, some commentators have seen Pershing II as a radical escalation:'one of the most capable counterforce weapons in the US arsenal ... the RADAG system allows it to home on to virtually any kind of fixed target; no effective defence against it exists' (Stockholm International Peace Research Institute, *Yearbook,* 1982).

It is planned to deploy 380 Pershing IIs, 108 of which are to be in West Germany. By mid-1984 nine were in service.

Specifications
Range: 1,800 km
Yield: 5–50 kt range
Accuracy: CEP 40 m
Speed: Mach 8

Plateau d'Albion The site of the smallest leg of France's strategic triad, le groupement de Missiles Stratégiques (GMS), near Avignon, Provence. GMS comprises 18 intermediate-range MSBS S-3 missiles each armed with one megaton warheads and having a range of 3,000 km. Although, indeed, because they are vulnerable to the more accurate Soviet missiles, French strategic thinking suggests that they put every potential aggressor before a dilemma: 'either the aggressor threatens France's territory without having first destroyed those missiles and therefore risks the destruction of some of its population and economic centres; or he destroys those missiles at the same time he launches his overall offensive, but in so doing he reveals his determination, thus justifying reprisals by French SLBMs'.

pluton missile This is a French mobile battlefield missile which is installed and fired from the AMX-30 tank chassis, the missile container being used as a launching ramp. The missile was developed by the French as a replacement for the 'Honest John' missiles that had to be surrendered when France pulled out of a direct military commitment to NATO. The missile has the capability for two alternative warheads: the AN-51 warhead of 25 kt (this is the same nuclear charge as on the AN-52 bombs carried by the French Air Force's Mirage and Jaguar aircraft), and a warhead with a 15 kt payload. Its range is between 10 and 120 km, and it has a CEP of 150–300 m, depending on range.

It is planned for the Pluton missile to be replaced by the more advanced 'Hades' missile by 1992.

plutonium An entirely artificial substance formed by the decay of uranium-238 which has previously acquired an extra neutron by absorption in a nuclear reactor. Plutonium-239 is fissile, has a critical weight of just five kilogrammes, and is employed either in nuclear fission bombs or in fast-breeder reactors, where it constitutes some 6 per cent of the fuel. It has a HALF-LIFE of 24,000 years. As uranium-235 is very expensive to obtain in sufficient quantity for bomb construction, plutonium, an inevitable byproduct of all nuclear reactor systems, is the preferred fissile material for fission bombs. The relative ease with which it can be produced makes proliferation of nuclear weapons a dangerous probability.

Polaris A-3 missile Before the introduction of Poseidon C-3 sea-launched ballistic missiles in 1969, the Polaris was the main strategic weapon of the US and British navies. The first test flight of the Polaris missile was in 1958, and the first Polaris submarine, USS *Daniel Webster,* went on patrol in 1964.

The British Navy is still armed with Polaris weapons, although these have been upgraded under the Chevaline front-end improvement programme, with the result that the total warhead count has risen from 192 to potentially 384. The US Navy has replaced Polaris with Poseidon and Trident C-4s. The relative inaccuracy of Polaris (CEP 900 m) would only make it suitable as a countervalue weapon, for use against soft targets, such as cities, military and industrial centres.

Specifications
Range: 4,600 m
Yield: 3 MRV × 200 kt (Chevaline = 6 MRV)
Accuracy: CEP 900 m
Number deployed: 64 (GB = 4 Polaris submarines, each with 16 missiles)

Poseidon C-3 missile The Poseidon C-3 sea-launched ballistic missile is the main strategic nuclear weapon of the US Navy. Tests began in 1968 and by the end of 1969, Poseidon began to replace the older and much less accurate Polaris A-3 SLBM. At present the Poseidon fleet of submarines is composed of 31 vessels, 19 of which are armed with Poseidon C-3s (16 to each boat), and 12 with the newer Trident C-4 SLBM. The 19 boats armed with Poseidon missiles account for something over 3,000 warheads; each missile can have as many as 14 MIRV'd warheads, but it is generally assumed to carry 10. The missile's relative inaccuracy means that it is most effective against soft targets – military bases, airfields, ports and cities.

Specifications
Range: 6,000 km
Yield: 10 MIRV'd × 50 kt (14 MIRV'd with reduced range)
Accuracy: CEP 450 m
Number deployed: 304

post-boost vehicle (PBV) Once the initial launch has set a missile on its ballistic trajectory, the PBV – or 'bus' – detaches itself from the main booster rocket and can alter its flight path by means of smaller booster jets in order to release the re-entry vehicles (which carry the nuclear warheads in their targeting sequence. If a missile has only one re-entry vehicle, a PBV may still be used to increase accuracy by a series of adjusting boosts which will tailor the re-entry vehicle's trajectory.

precision-guided weapons (PGW) Weapons ideal for warding off an attack, and are especially effective against tanks. They can be linked up with computers and could be aimed and fired by remote control. Such weapons carry conventional warheads but are of such accuracy that a section of NATO thinking is beginning to perceive their attraction, together with other conventional weapons systems, as compared with tactical nuclear weapons.

Presidential Directive 59
see STRATEGIC DOCTRINE (AMERICAN); FLEXIBLE RESPONSE

pressurized water reactor (PWR)
A type of light-water reactor. Water acts as both coolant, moderator and heat-transfer agent. But the steam is not, as in the boiling-water reactor, produced in the reactor core. Instead, heat is transferred to a secondary circuit where a heat-exchanger produces the steam (at low temperature and pressure) to drive the generators.

Efficiency is poor at about 32 per cent. Fuel is uranium-dioxide pellets 3 per cent enriched and clad in zirconium alloy. Construction has to be very strong from a safety angle to withstand the high pressures (up to 150 atmospheres). There are more PWRs than any other type of reactor. Worries over safety centre upon the viability of the emergency core cooling system.

Prevention of Nuclear War Agreement, 1973
Signed in Washington on 22 June 1973, by President Nixon for the US and General-Secretary Brezhnev for the USSR, the agreement stated that the major objective of the policies of both countries was 'to remove the danger of nuclear war and the use of nuclear weapons'. This was to be achieved by showing restraint and a dedication to a general policy of stability and peace in their relations with each other and, should the danger of a nuclear conflict arise, a commitment to 'enter into urgent consultations with each other and make every effort to avert this risk'.

primary alerting system
see COMMAND, CONTROL, COMMUNICATIONS AND INTELLIGENCE

proliferation
The spread of nuclear weapons capability and the possession of nuclear weapons to more and more states. The 1968 NON-PROLIFERATION TREATY (NPT) has been signed by some 110 countries but, significantly, not by several countries with the economic muscle and technical expertise to achieve nuclear capability – Argentina, Brazil, China, France, Israel, India, Pakistan and South Africa among them. Of these, France and China, before 1968, and India, Israel and South Africa after that year have tested or developed nuclear weapons, the first two, of course, to a considerable extent.

The danger of proliferation is exacerbated by two factors, one technical, the other political. The spread of nuclear technology and of actual reactors, especially following the ATOMS FOR PEACE initiative of President Eisenhower, enormously increased the danger that a state could divert plutonium from a 'peaceful' reactor to a bomb construction programme. Fear of this lay behind Israel's bombing of the Iraqi nuclear reactor in 1981. And, indeed, such diversion did take place in India in 1974 when plutonium produced by a Candu Canadian reactor was used to build an atomic device which was tested in that year. Since then the USA and Canada especially have fought to increase restrictions, first on the sale of uranium and then the export of nuclear technologies without adequate safeguards. But the inability of the International Atomic Energy Agency to impose 'critical time' inspections on all reactors and reprocessing plants because of German and Japanese opposition leaves the way open for plutonium diversion of the kind that took place in India.

The second – political – factor is simply this: one of the conditions of the NPT was that the nuclear weapons states would pursue negotiations on effective measures for the cessation of the arms race 'at an early date', proceeding to nuclear disarmament and eventually to general and complete disarmament, supervised and controlled internationally. In fact nothing of the sort has happened and this leaves the way open for signatories of the NPT to revoke on its terms on the basis that the nuclear weapons states have not observed them either.

Britain and proliferation

Britain was involved at the start of the development of the atomic bomb. Work in this field in the 1930s at Cambridge and, during the war, in Canada under British supervision, ensured that several British scientists participated in the MANHATTAN PROJECT. The bombs that dropped on Hiroshima and Nagasaki, however, were indisputably American; and they contained, as their corollary almost, the seeds of their own counterparts in the USSR. Britain, as a close ally of the USA, though wounded by the excluding clauses of the Atomic Energy Act, need never have taken the decision to build an atom bomb. Yet Prime Minister Attlee was led deftly towards that decision by Lord Bridges, Secretary to the Cabinet.

The explosion of the British A-bomb was, in a very deliberate sense, the first example of nuclear proliferation. It is easy today to imagine Britain as 'always' having had the bomb – along with the USA and the USSR. This was not so; Britain was third, in 1952, three years after the Soviet Union and seven years after the USA. Development of the bomb was opposed in Britain by several senior scientists and even by the chiefs of staff who realized, too late, that it would eat up funds for the development of other weapons (not least the aircraft and missiles capable of delivering it). One of the scientists, Henry Tizard, wrote, 'We persist in regarding ourselves as a Great Power, capable of anything and only temporarily handicapped by economic difficulties. We are not a Great Power and never will be again. We are a great nation, but if we continue to behave like a Great Power we shall soon cease to be a great nation.'

Protect and Survive A pamphlet issued by the Home Office advising British citizens how they should prepare in the event of an imminent nuclear attack. People were to build fallout shelters either in their gardens or in one of the rooms of their houses. Any attempt at evacuation would be met with stern measures (not excluding shooting). The pamphlet seemed to assume that people lived in well-built houses, possessed gardens and had sufficient funds to lay out on 14 days' supply of food, medicine etc.

Compared with the truly horrific effects of a mock nuclear attack, depicted in the government's own operation 'Square Leg', the preparations outlined in the pamphlet were truly pathetic. The pamphlet was met with a storm of derisive comment from the media, including a particularly scathing riposte from E P Thompson called *Protest and Survive*. The heat generated did, however, bring home to millions of people just what nuclear war implied and, in that sense, was probably the greatest conceivable boost to those organizations opposing nuclear weapons.

Pugwash Movement Founded in 1957 in response to the Russell-Einstein Manifesto to bring together scientists from East and West for discussions, conferences, etc. The Pugwash Council and Executive Committee issues occasional official statements. It is based in Geneva.

In August 1980, at the Pugwash Conference on Science and World Affairs, medical doctors from many countries, including the UK, USA and USSR, issued a warning about the dangers of nuclear war which concluded: 'Medical disaster planning for nuclear war is futile. A nuclear war would result in human death, injury and disease on a scale that has no precedent in history, dwarfing all previous plagues and wars. There is no possible effective medical response after a nuclear attack.'

quick reaction alert (QRA) A description of the state of certain weapons systems which are kept on alert, ready at short notice to be fired at designated targets. Certain NATO aircraft, including some F-111s on station in the UK, as well as Pershing IA missiles, are kept in this state.

All forces, nuclear or otherwise, are kept at different states of readiness, described as their 'defence condition' or 'Defcon'. At certain times of crisis the Defcon is raised for all or certain categories. For example, in 1973, President Nixon raised the Defcon of US forces worldwide at the time of the Arab-Israeli war (this included those forces stationed in Britain, without any consultation with the British Government).

When President Reagan was shot, Caspar Weinberger, Secretary of Defense, announced to a hastily gathered meeting of Cabinet personnel, 'I have raised the alert status of our forces'. Alexander Haig, in his memoirs, recounts how he was shocked by this statement because 'it would be detected promptly by the Soviet Union. In response, the Russians might raise their own alert status.' He asked Weinberger, 'Have you changed the Defcon of our forces?' Weinberger clearly did not know what the word meant but eventually said that he had ordered the pilots of Strategic Air Command (SAC) to their bases. Haig concluded that he had, by this act, raised the Defcon. Weinberger disagreed. When asked to describe what exactly he had ordered, Weinberger replied, 'I'll go find out' and left the room. It transpired that he had not raised the alert status (Defcon) of the forces after all.

'Race Track' basing system
see MULTIPLE PROTECTIVE STRUCTURE

Rad Short for 'radiation absorbed dose', the rad is used to measure the effect of RADIATION on living soft tissue. It measures the absorbed dose of ionizing radiation equal to the amount of radiation that releases an energy of 100 ergs per gram of matter.

radiation The word covers *either* the process of emitting electromagnetic energy (heat light, gamma rays, X-rays, etc) or sub-atomic particles (electrons, neutrons, protons, alpha particles, etc), *or* the energy of particles thus emitted. Radiation is undetectable by any of the human senses but it is or can be lethal.

Certain types of matter, the atomic structure of which is unstable, spontaneously emit energy and sub-atomic particles; they are, in other words, radioactive, ie they emit radiation. Some of these, uranium (especially uranium-235), thorium and actinium, occur naturally in the earth. Others, such as plutonium-239, can be artificially produced.

Here we are concerned not with radiation occurring naturally on earth, or in the background radiation which permeates space, but with radiation resulting from nuclear explosions or controlled nuclear fission in a nuclear reactor, and that associated more generally with the fuel cycle.

Radiation from nuclear explosions
Radiation from a fission or a fission–fusion–fission (FFF) bomb takes two forms:
1 Initial or 'prompt' radiation is the flash of energy (heat, light, neutrons and gamma rays) emitted at the moment of explosion. It is very harmful, although not over a very extended area because neutrons and gamma rays become weakened as they spread out and are absorbed into the atmosphere. Gamma rays are the most dangerous because

they can penetrate the body with ease. Most people within lethal range of initial radiation from, say, a 500 kt bomb would die of other causes such as blast; but smaller bombs, especially enhanced radiation weapons, could kill by initial radiation.

2 Delayed radiation is better known as FALLOUT. It is less immediately serious if the explosion is an air burst although the neutron bombardment of nitrogen in the air produces carbon-14, which has a HALF-LIFE of 5,670 years, and nitrogen oxides which destroy the ozone layer (see NUCLEAR WINTER). Atmospheric tests and high-altitude air bursts produce radioactive dust which floats too high to be cleansed by rain water. This dust can stay in the atmosphere for years, slowly drifting to earth all round the globe.

A ground burst sucks up large quantities of earth and other surface material into the mushroom cloud where it, too, becomes radioactive and falls, along with the bomb material and other radioisotopes, in a cigar-like configuration downwind from the explosion.

Dosage and medical effects of radiation

Radiation absorption is measured in RADS and the dose rate in rads per hour. What is important is not just the rate per hour but the accumulated dose. There has been little experience of the medical effects of radiation from the effects of nuclear weapons, and consequently there is much uncertainty as to the death rate for a given dose of rads. This is because the air bursts over Hiroshima and Nagasaki caused prompt radiation and, in the former, radioactive rain, but very little fallout. The unfortunate crew of the *Lucky Dragon* did receive fallout from the first fission–fusion–fission bomb test on Bikini Atoll, 85 miles away from their boat; an unknown number of people was affected by fallout from other tests.

Patricia Lindop and Joseph Rotblat have made the following estimates:

Dose (rads)	Short term average deaths	Cause
0–200	nil	
200–600	0–90%	internal bleeding or infection (2 to 12 weeks)
600–1000	98–100%	internal bleeding
1000–1,500	100%	collapse of circulation (within 14 days)
5,000 +	100%	failure of breathing or brain damage (within 48 hours)

They estimate that a one megaton bomb would produce an accumulated dose of 600 rads over an area of 660 square miles; for people living 60 miles downwind from such an explosion, and assuming a wind speed of 15 mph, an accumulated dose of 780 rads could be expected.

The ionizing radiation from a nuclear explosion (or a major leakage from a nuclear reactor) injects excessive energy into human and animal body cells. Cells in the intestine are most vulnerable because of their capacity to subdivide easily and to reproduce themselves rapidly. Intestine walls give way with the contents seeping into the bloodstream. Bone marrow is very vulnerable and, if attacked, can no longer produce platelets to clot the blood. Thus haemorrhages are a common result of radiation exposure.

Children are more vulnerable to radiation than adults because, their bodies being smaller, gamma rays and even beta rays can more easily penetrate their skin and reach their intestines and bone marrow.

Radiation sickness is noticeable after a few hours, when the victim will suffer from vomiting. Later will come diarrhoea, listlessness and depression. The victim's hair will fall out and bleeding may begin from the nose, mouth and bowels. Smaller doses carry a high risk of leukaemia and other cancers in later life.

Radiation does not end with fallout. Radioactive particles enter the food and water cycle (for example by cows eating grass which contains radioactive fallout). Some of these particles have very long half-lives. Four radioisotopes are particularly dangerous because they are so easily absorbed by the body: strontium-90, iodine-131, caesium-137 and carbon-14.

Strontium-90 is chemically similar to calcium so is absorbed into bones and blood, especially through drinking milk. Young children who drank milk from 1955 to 1965 have more strontium-90 in their bones than older or younger people, due to the large number of atmospheric nuclear tests at the time. Iodine-131 can stunt physical and mental growth. Caesium-137 can reach the reproductive organs and thus present a genetic hazard. Carbon-14 causes abnormalities in unborn children.

Radiation is perhaps the most insidious, dangerous and morally repugnant aspect of nuclear weapons. For it attacks innocent citizens, animals, nature itself. And it endures, entering food and ecological chains to affect total innocents, either unborn or possibly in another continent altogether (see EFFECTS OF NUCLEAR EXPLOSION).

Nuclear reactors and radiation

Workers in nuclear plants suffer higher doses of radiation than the rest of the population. This is so everywhere in the world. Radiation checks and safety procedures are not always respected either by management, those who are meant to supervise them, or even the workers themselves. Radiation leaks are most likely to occur:

a when the fuel rods are being changed in a reactor;

b as a result of coolant not reaching the core, which overheats as a consequence, with potentially dire results;

c when nuclear waste and spent fuel is in transit;

d in fast breeder reactors, where the fission process is not moderated and fast neutrons are in abundance;

e in reprocessing plants, where plutonium, which is very fissile and has a low critical mass, is plentiful; also the residues left over after reprocessing are very dangerous indeed;

f irradiated water can be dumped into the sea either in larger quantities or in a more radioactive condition than prescribed, as at Sellafield so it appears;

g during or after the disposal of nuclear waste, especially from reprocessing plants. This sort of waste poses a long-term (really long-term, ie tens of thousands of years) radiation hazard (see NUCLEAR FUEL CYCLE and RADIOACTIVE WASTES.)

radioactive decay When radioactive matter emits radiation in the form of energy and particles, it simultaneously decays into another isotope of the same or different element, which may disintegrate further until a stable isotopic state is reached.

Each radioisotope emits its energy over a specific period. Thus half the nuclei of strontium-90, for example, will decay within a period of 27.7 years. Which nuclei actually do decay within that time, and which hold together to release their radioactivity later is entirely random. see HALF-LIFE, SEVEN-TENTHS RULE

radioactive wastes All processes in the NUCLEAR FUEL CYCLE have gaseous, liquid or solid byproducts which emit ionizing radiation, damaging to all living organisms. They are classified by the International Atomic Energy Agency as low-level, intermediate-level and high-level waste. This is based on a comparison with the background radiation coming mainly from the sun, estimated at 0.1 REM a year. At each stage of the fuel cycle waste is produced:

1 *Mining.* One of the products of uranium decay is radium-226 which remains in the ore after uranium has been extracted and remains radioactive for thousands of years. It produces radon-222 gas which decays into polonium-218 which, being electrically charged, clings to dust particles. In poorly ventilated mines radioactive dust can cause lung cancer in miners.

2 *Milling.* A large amount of liquid waste is left over after the production of uranium yellow cake. It is chemically toxic as well as radioactive.

3 *Enrichment.* The waste here is chemically rather than radioactively toxic and can be buried safely below ground.

4 *Nuclear reactors.* One of the principal discharges from reactors is argon-41: air which is blown round the concrete biological shield to protect it from the heat of the reactor core. It is discharged into the atmosphere in large quantities; however, as it has a HALF-LIFE of only 110 minutes it has decayed by the time it reaches ground level. Carbon-14 is discharged in the form of carbon dioxide by gas-cooled reactors and tritium is discharged by heavy-water reactors. Sodium coolant becomes highly gamma-active sodium-24 and has to be kept carefully shielded; it is produced in fast-breeder reactors. Iodine-131, with a half-life of eight days, can be produced when the rod cladding develops flaws and leaks fission products into the coolant. Iodine-129, with a half-life of sixteen million years, may also be produced. Washing water or water from cooling ponds is classified by the International Atomic Energy Authority as low-level waste and is dumped into the sea, with limits set on the discharge amount (limits which are not always observed).

Intermediate level waste includes metallic components from the reactor core and the cladding stripped from fuel elements during reprocessing. It is stored in concrete vaults.

5 *Reprocessing*. At this stage high-level waste is produced. The acid solution left over after the removal of uranium and plutonium contains fission products which in the case of actinides remain intensively radioactive for hundreds of thousands of years. They also generate dangerous levels of heat as they decay. At present they are stored in especially cooled, double-construction stainless-steel tanks fitted with filters, leak detectors and agitators to prevent any solids from setting into a critical mass. The whole lot is sealed into steel-lined concrete vaults.

One suggestion for solving the waste-disposal problem is to fabricate it into glass blocks (after allowing for a cooling time to prevent the glass melting). The removal of the actinides would aid this method but even then the blocks of glass could not be placed, for example, in uranium mines for almost 1,000 years. With or without vitrification, ultimate disposal could take the following forms: shooting waste into the sun; melting it into the ice cap; inserting it between the tectonic plates of the earth's surface into the earth's core; or burying it in stable geological formations on land or under the sea.

radiological weapon (RW)

A weapon other than a nuclear explosive device designed to cause destruction, damage, death or injury by disseminating radioactive material. The enhanced radiation weapon is moving in this direction but still causes an explosion which releases heat and blast in addition to neutrons.

It is curious that RW are permitted while chemical and biological weapons are outlawed. But, of course, to outlaw radiological weapons would beg the question of the international legality of nuclear weapons themselves which kill not only by the effect of fast neutrons and fallout but also by heat and blast as well.

RAND Corporation

Founded at the close of World War II as Air Force Project RAND, it later assumed its present title. It is the American 'think tank' par excellence. Although it produces studies in the fields of economics and the other social sciences its central role has been to generate US strategic nuclear doctrines.

Bernard Brodie was the leading figure at RAND in the early

days – the first nuclear strategist. According to him, deterring, not fighting, wars was the military's main function in the nuclear age; but this meant keeping the nuclear arsenal invulnerable to attack while threatening a potential aggressor with 'retaliation in kind'. Later he began to consider how the bomb could be rationally used in war, and RAND theorists have been preoccupied with that question ever since. Towards the end of his life he questioned the notions of nuclear warfighting that he had helped to create and died a pariah amongst the RAND 'defense intellectuals'.

John von Neumann was the inventor of 'games theory' which for many at RAND appeared to be a scientific method for analysing nuclear war and the Cold War.

Albert Wohlstetter, another mathematician, used Paxton's theory of 'systems analysis' to detect what he saw as the vulnerability of Strategic Air Command's forces in the event of a Pearl Harbor-type attack – his wife Roberta, also at RAND, had made a study of Pearl Harbor. Albert detected the 'missile gap' of the late 1950s (which turned out to be fictitious).

In World War II 'Operational Research' had to answer the question: 'What is the best that can be done given the following weapons with the following characteristics?' A systems analyst would ask and try to answer a different question: 'What kind of equipment with what characteristics would best accomplish such and such a mission?'

While John Foster Dulles was proclaiming the policy of 'massive retaliation', William Kaufmann formulated a theory of 'LIMITED NUCLEAR WAR' in opposition to it; it was he who, in the early 1960s, advocated a strategy of 'COUNTERFORCE, no-cities targeting' which was taken up by Robert McNamara when he became US Defense Secretary. Around the same time the more belligerent Herman Kahn, the best self-publicist at RAND, argued the case for a credible FIRST-STRIKE CAPABILITY, throwing in limited nuclear war options and a massive fallout-shelter programme as well.

Kennedy was very much RAND's man at the White House although his Assistant Secretary of Defense, Paul Nitze, was not from the Corporation though much influenced by its theories. (This Cold War defence intellectual later defected from the Democrats to found the Committee on the Present Danger, which torpedoed SALT II and went on to take over many positions in the Reagan White House.)

McNamara was fascinated with RAND's theories and at first accepted them as official policy; later he became disenchanted, believing that limited options were impractical and that they provided the joint chiefs of staff with excuses to request more nuclear weapons and more targets – which was indeed the case. Nevertheless, he, like Harold Brown under the Carter Administration, still believed in 'sending signals through force', the underpinning of counterforce limited nuclear warfare, and neither of them could escape its logic.

James Schlesinger was himself a RAND intellectual who later became President Nixon's Secretary for Defense. His study on limited nuclear options (NU-OPTS) became official policy as NSDM-242. But its novelty consisted only in the existence of new MIRVing technology to carry it out and the fact that most politicians and the general public had believed that US guiding strategic policy was Mutual Assured Destruction (see STRATEGIC DOCTRINE (AMERICAN)) when in fact it was counterforce targeting.

Despite their undoubted brilliance the RAND theorists have been severely hampered by a number of factors.

First of all they are theorists for a future war which has no precedents. They cannot re-adapt their theories according to practice, as Operations Research did in World War II. They can only alter them if the theories themselves are shown to be mistaken or for political considerations. Their theories are so removed from reality that they are often wrong when time allows them to be compared to reality (eg the 'missiles gap'). Sometimes they simply do not have the correct information to start with so their assumptions are wrong (eg Brodie thought there was a uranium shortage and that very few bombs could be constructed, so that any superiority in bombs would be much more important strategically than if both sides possessed overkill many times over).

RAND set the terms of the nuclear debate, inventing the terminology, stressing what was important and what was not. Some of this has backfired, as when politicians and military men still stress factors such as THROW-WEIGHT or EQUIVALENT MEGATONNAGE when MISSILE ACCURACY is now the key variable. Ideologically over-determined by the Cold War, they are locked into a vision of the USSR which makes arms negotiations virtually impossible. Wedded to the weapon that has spawned them, they cannot conceive of hostilities in terms other than nuclear – even if limited – war; and any alternative world order which supersedes the present system of competing nation states set into two politico-military blocs is quite beyond their purview.

With the advent of the Reagan Administration the Corporation found a political leadership fertile for RAND ideas. These theories stretched back to the 1950s, were documented and implemented through PD59, NSDM-242, the Foster Panel's work, NU-OPTS, McNamara's SIOP-63 guidance and all the work at RAND itself by Schlesinger, Kaufmann, Marshall, Kahn, Digby, Paxton, Neumann, Wohlstetter and Brodie. The ideas had been around for so long that it was easy to forget that there was nothing more to substantiate them in 1982 than there had been 30 years earlier. Their method, based on mathematical calculation, had become first a catechism and then a dogma.

The key problems still remained; it seemed logical to keep a nuclear war limited; yet nobody could define limited options which were practical. And no one could say what would happen if the USSR refused to play the game, ie refused the notion of limited nuclear war, and *ignored the signals,* as the Vietnamese had done in Vietnam. How would such a war be ended even were it to remain limited?

Fred Kaplan ends his book on the RAND Corporation, *The Wizards of Armageddon* (New York, 1983, pp. 390–91) thus:

> It was a compelling illusion .... They continued to play the game because there was no other. They performed their calculations and spoke in their own strange and esoteric tongues because to do otherwise would be to recognise ... the ghastliness of their contemplations. They continued their options because without them the bomb would appear too starkly the thing that they had tried to prevent it being but that it ultimately would become if ever it were used – a device of sheer mayhem, a weapon whose cataclysmic powers no one really had the faintest idea of how to control. The nuclear strategists had come to compose order – but in the end, chaos still prevailed.

Rapacki Plan
see NUCLEAR FREE ZONES

rapidly deployable sensor system
see SOUND SURVEILLANCE SYSTEM

re-entry vehicle (RV)
That part of a ballistic missile designed to carry a nuclear warhead and to re-enter the earth's atmosphere after completing a ballistic trajectory which has taken it out into space. the term covers single warheads, multiple re-entry vehicles (MRVs), multiple independently targetable re-entry vehicles (MIRVs) and manoeuvring re-entry vehicles (MARVs). In the case of MARVed warheads, the re-entry vehicle will also carry a guidance system, fuel and small rockets used for directional correction.
see also POST-BOOST VEHICLE, PENETRATION AIDS

regional nuclear plan
see SINGLE INTEGRATED OPERATIONAL PLAN

rem
A unit of dosage of ionizing radiation applied to humans. It is defined as the dosage that will cause the same amount of biological injury as one roentgen of X-rays or gamma rays. It is short for 'roentgen equivalent man' and although it is rather poorly defined it is helpful in setting radiation exposure limits.
see RAD, RADIATION, EFFECTS OF NUCLEAR EXPLOSIONS

reliability
The predicted percentage of missiles that reach their target after being released. Each missile is assessed for reliability, weighing up the chances of every element, from motors to guidance systems, working properly. The reliability of US missiles is said to be

between 75 and 80 per cent. Soviet missiles are less reliable – between 65 and 75 per cent; or, as an American phrase has it: 'Russia's best works only as well as America's worst'.

Reliability has to be taken into account when calculating both the probability of silo kill per re-entry vehicle and the absolute numbers of missiles to have in a nuclear arsenal to ensure second-strike capability or, more likely, in the quest for a disarming first strike. At present, Soviet warheads are outmatched in number, accuracy and reliability. Only with respect to the militarily unimportant equivalent megatonnage and throw-weight is the Soviet arsenal larger than its American rival.

reprocessing nuclear fuel The extraction from spent fuel rods and casings of uranium and plutonium for further use either as they are or after they have undergone ENRICHMENT.
see also NUCLEAR FUEL CYCLE, RADIOACTIVE WASTES

retaliation A nuclear attack on an enemy that has initiated hostilities with a first strike. Other terms; second strike, retaliatory strike. This situation should never arise, according to deterrent theorists, who argue that the very possession of nuclear weapons is sufficient to dissuade an attacker from launching its nuclear weapons in the first place.

Needless to say, any state that launches a first strike attack will do so on the assumption that it will leave the enemy without sufficient forces to mount a retaliatory strike.

S-23 gun The USSR has little in the way of nuclear-capable artillery, though it is reported that they are making developments in this area. However they do have about 168 S-23s, 180 mm towed guns that have the capacity to be either conventionally armed or nuclear armed with a 1 kt nuclear shell. Its range is 30 km approximately.
see ARTILLERY, NUCLEAR

SA-5 Gammon missile The USSR has over 100 SA-5 Gammon surface-to-air missiles in service for long-range interception of enemy aircraft.
Specifications
Range: 240 km
Yield: 1 warhead, kilotonnage unknown

SALT I and II
see STRATEGIC ARMS LIMITATION TALKS

sanctuary theory Linked to the strategy of FLEXIBLE RESPONSE, the sanctuary theory assumes that if a war broke out between the superpowers, Europe would be the theatre of operations.

If tactical nuclear weapons were released it assumes that they would not be targetted on Russia because that would risk a Soviet attack on the US mainland. It is hoped that negotiations would proceed swiftly after any short-range nuclear exchanges before escalation to the use of theatre, strategic missiles or, above all, ICBMs on both sides.

The scenario of the USA and USSR untouched in a nuclear exchange appeared to weaken the ties between the USA and its European allies; it was for this reason that several of the latter called upon the USA to station ground-launched cruise missiles Pershing IIs in Europe. If ever they were used, especially against the USSR, it was argued that the USA could not expect to escape attack. The question must remain though, would the USA use such weapons to 'save' Western Europe when to do so would invite an attack on itself?
see also COUPLING, FORWARD BASED SYSTEMS

Scientists against Nuclear Arms (SANA)

A grouping of British scientists, chaired by Michael Pentz who is currently a vice-chairperson of CND. They have provided much-needed information on the effects of a nuclear attack on Britain especially with respect to CND's 'Hard Luck' counter to the Home Office's HARD ROCK civil defence exercise. They spent over a year feeding figures into a mainframe computer to calculate the effects of a 200 megaton attack on Britain for every town and village in the country. Several of its members have written books, articles and pamphlets on matters germane to nuclear war. It also publishes a newsletter.

Seabed Treaty, 1971

As with the Antarctic Treaty, the Outer-Space Treaty and the Tlatelolco Treaty, the intention of this Seabed Treaty is to prevent the introduction of international conflict and nuclear weapons into a zone as yet free of them. The treaty prohibits the emplacement of nuclear weapons or weapons of mass destruction on the seabed beyond a 12-mile coastal zone.

As far as is known the treaty has been effective, although it is hard to imagine why anyone would want to attach nuclear weapons to the seabed, given the problems of keeping the location secret and guarding the base. Both France and China refused to sign the treaty.

sea-launched cruise missile (SLCM)

The US Navy's Tomahawk (BGM-109) can be fired both from surface ships and submarines. In capability it is very similar to ground-launched and air-launched cruise missiles. Development started in the 1970s and deployment began in September 1983.

Specifications
Range: 2,500 km
Speed: 550 mph
Accuracy: CEP 30 m
Number planned: 4,068

Number deployed: 44
For Soviet SLCMs see SS-N-3, SS-N-7, SS-N-9, SS-N-12, SS-N-14, SS-N-19

second centre of decision

second centre of decision One of the arguments deployed by supporters of British or French nuclear weapons. Their argument asserts that should US resolution waver, or be perceived to do so by the USSR, the latter may yet be deterred from attacking by a nuclear deterrent in the autonomous hands of one or another European power. Also, the possession of independent sources of decision-making would make the likely reactions or responses of the Western Alliance less predictable for Soviet strategists and thus render attack more difficult.

Lord Carver has argued that any situation in which a sane British prime minister would initiate an attack on the USSR, thereby inviting the devastation of the UK is impossible to conceive. Perhaps the 'second centre' concept is seen as a goad to draw a reluctant America into an all-out war by the launching of British missiles. The British independent deterrent in fact relies on Supreme Allied Command, Europe (SACEUR) for its targeting. The 'second centre' argument sits ill with the oft-stated claim that Britain's nuclear deterrent is a 'weapon of last resort', ie a second-strike weapon; unfortunately, though, it chimes closely with the decision to purchase Trident, the accuracy of which makes it a potential first-strike weapon.

The British government claims that it can, in certain circumstances, take over complete control of Polaris or the future Trident missiles. At present all its nuclear forces are committed to NATO and are targeted by SACEUR. In reality only China and France constitute genuine second centres of decision making.

see also COUPLING, FORWARD BASED SYSTEMS

second-strike capability

second-strike capability One of the central arguments of those in favour of British and French nuclear weapons. The phrase describes the ability of a nuclear weapons state to survive a nuclear attack sufficiently to be able to launch a retaliatory attack which would inflict intolerable damage on the aggressor (see DETERRENCE, FIRST-STRIKE CAPABILITY).

The problem is that from an opponent's point of view, second-strike weapons are indistinguishable from potential first-strike weapons, especially given that NATO refuses to give a no-first-use pledge, and that such so-called second-strike 'last resort' weapons are becoming increasingly accurate, quite beyond the requirements of COUNTER-VALUE targeting. The problem with second strike doctrines is that increasingly they are discounted by both sides except in response to a small nuclear attack, in which case they take on all the aspects of a first strike or at least a damage limiting strike (this is especially true within STRATEGIC DOCTRINE (SOVIET)).

The problem that has arisen is that there is now a clear advantage to be gained in striking first with accurate MIRVed warheads. This was not the case before MIRVing, when the advantage lay with the attacked country (second strike doctrines were linked to theory of mutual assured destruction). To take a simple example in the context of ICBMs:

Suppose there were 1,000 missiles on each side (sides A and B). In the days before MIRVing, each missile would have had just one warhead. The launch by A of, say, 800 missiles cross-targeted TWO-ON-ONE would destroy a maximum of 400 of B's ICBMs. B would still have 600 missiles and could use 400 to knock out the remaining 200 ICBMs in A's arsenal provided they had not been launched before being counterattacked. B would still have 200 missiles left with which to threaten A's cities. A would have to surrender.

Now let us assume that A and B have 1,000 missiles each MIRVed with five warheads. If A launched a two-on-one first strike with 400 missiles (2,000 warheads), it could, theoretically, knock out all of B's strategic ICBM force. And A would still have 600 missiles left with which to threaten B's cities. B would have to surrender.

If we now bring back into the picture the submarine and bomber forces. B could retaliate in a second strike with these. But to do so would for certain be answered by an attack on its cities either by A's remaining ICBMs or by its SLBMs or bombers. In order to spare its cities worse destruction than the collateral damage they would have suffered as a result of A's first strike against the ICBM missile silos, B would be prudent to surrender without launching a second strike.

There is no need to spell out the implications for world stability of the strategic superiority to be gained by striking first since the advent of MIRVing technology

see MULTIPLE INDEPENDENTLY TARGETTED RE-ENTRY VEHICLE

selected attack option
see SINGLE INTEGRATED OPERATIONAL PLAN

selective employment options (SEO)
As part of its policy of FLEXIBLE RESPONSE, NATO reserves the right to attack designated targets with nuclear weapons in order to demonstrate to the enemy its determination to escalate if necessary. A tactical tightrope would have to be walked between inflicting significant damage without incurring massive retaliation. The USSR has never recognized the subtlety of NATO's flexible response or the strategic niceties of SEO. It has declared that *any* nuclear initiative from NATO – at whatever level – will be answered with massive nuclear retaliation.

see FIRST USE, NORTH ATLANTIC TREATY ORGANIZATION

seven-tenths rule
The 300-odd radioisotopes present at or created by a nuclear explosion have a HALF-LIFE that varies from a

fraction of a second to tens of thousands of years. However, tests have shown that 7 hours after an explosion the amount of radiation is roughly one tenth that of the level of radiation one hour after an explosion – the seven-tenths rule. If we multiply this period by 7 to 49 hours, the level of radioactivity will be reduced to one-hundredth of what it was initially. After $7 \times 7 \times 7$ hours (just over two weeks) it has fallen to one-thousandth of the initial level and is relatively safe, apart from the danger of ingesting it through food or drink (see also recent findings on 'intermediate fallout' in NUCLEAR WINTER). This is why two weeks is considered a long enough period for people to stay in shelters.

shelter A shelter covered by dirt or concrete in which shelter can be had against blast, heat and radioactivity providing there is filter against airborne radioactive particles. The stronger the construction the greater the level of blast it can withstand. However, if shelters are to be at all effective they have to be built deep underground, thoroughly reinforced, and equipped very differently from most civilian models on the market. There is no programme proposed to build shelters for the population in Britain or America. Things have gone slightly further in the USSR (for example the Moscow underground is equipped with blast-proof doors).

The most naive statement probably ever uttered on nuclear issues by a US cabinet member (albeit a junior one) came from the mouth of T K Jones, Deputy Under Secretary for Defense, on this subject. He said, 'Dig a hole, cover it with a couple of doors and then throw three feet of earth on top .... It's the dirt that does it ... if there are enough shovels to go around everybody's going to make it.'

see CIVIL DEFENCE, EFFECTS OF NUCLEAR EXPLOSIONS

short-range attack missile (SRAM) An air-launched missile designed to knock out enemy ground defences, the SRAM (AGM-69A) was first deployed in March 1972 (it is now being replaced by the advanced strategic air-launched missile). It is carried by B-52 bombers, each of which can carry 20 SRAMs, although the usual deployment is six to eight missiles, mounted in clusters under the wings and in a rotary dispenser in the aft bomb bay. It can also be deployed on FB-111A aircraft, which can carry up to six missiles, but which are usually equipped with two. Of the 1,140 SRAMs in service, 1,020 are deployed on B-52 bombers and 120 on FB-111As.

Specifications

Range: 160–220 km at high altitude, 56–80 km at low altitude
Yield: 1×170 or 200 kt W69 warhead
Accuracy: CEP 370 m
Speed: Mach 3.5+

short-range ballistic missile (SRBM) Land-based

ballistic missiles with a range of less than 900 km. The USSR deploys: SS-21, SS-22, SS-23, Frog 7, SS-12, SS-1 (SCUD). NATO deploys: Pershing IA, Lance, Honest John, and France deploys Pluton.

see also INTERCONTINENTAL BALLISTIC MISSILE, MEDIUM-RANGE BALLISTIC MISSILE

silo An underground emplacement in which is housed a ballistic missile and its launch mechanism. Silos are hardened against blast and heat, and sometimes radioactivity by very thick reinforced concrete and may be built to withstand 3,000 psi overpressure.

Missiles launched from silos are at present more accurate than sea-launched missiles, but they are also more vulnerable. The USSR has more land-based missiles than the US. There is something of a fixation in certain US military circles about the vulnerability of Minuteman missiles (see WINDOW OF VULNERABILITY). The whole development of the MX ICBM, for example, assumes that the USSR will attack Minuteman silos, but as former Defense Secretary Harold Brown commented, 'I think it gives them a perception that they have an advantage. I don't think it gives them a perception that they can risk a first strike nuclear attack, not on the basis of vulnerability of Minuteman alone. The reason for that is that we continue to have our submarine-launched ballistic missiles and bombers with cruise missiles that can strike back.'

see SINGLE SHOT PROBABILITY OF KILL, MISSILE ACCURACY, LETHALITY

Single Integrated Operational Plan (SIOP)

The Pentagon's most secret document, SIOP is the regularly updated list of possible targets in the Soviet Union, other Warsaw Treaty Organization countries, Cuba, Vietnam and even China and certain neutral countries. The targets can be grouped into different nuclear packages. The NATIONAL COMMAND CENTER is the 'channel of communication for the execution of the Single Integrated Operational Plan.'

SIOP was first devised in 1960, under President Eisenhower, and has been reformulated under each succeeding administration, both autonomously within the military and in response to changes in strategic doctrine. It should be mentioned here (though developed more fully under STRATEGIC DOCTRINE (AMERICAN)) that there has always been a discrepancy between public statements on deterrence theory, nuclear strategy and targeting doctrine and operational strategies. However, what is undeniable is that with the passage of time this gap is narrowing. Presidents are increasingly voicing what the military have planned for ever since the mid-fifties, namely that a nuclear war can be fought *and* won.

The most significant revision of SIOP came under the Carter Administration at the time of Presidential Directive 59. President

Carter had come to office with the intention of reducing the US nuclear arsenal to 'minimum deterrence' proportions – some 200 warheads. Perhaps frightened by the findings of the 'B team' in the CIA (which indicated that Soviet expenditure and capability was much greater than had been assumed using different measurement criteria) he quickly revised his opinion. What emerged was SIOP-5D.

This plan contained a staggering 40,000 targets. Now the obvious Soviet targets are as follows:

Civilian
cities with over 25,000 inhabitants	900	
main industrial complexes	300	
		1,200

Military
land-based missiles	1,398	
launch centres	300	
airfields for nuclear-capable planes	500	
air-defence missile sites	1,200	
submarine bases (nuclear-capable)	3	
naval fleet HQs	5	
army HQs	200	
		3,606

Total		4,806

Some of the military targets are located on the same site; on the other hand many sites would be TWO-ON-ONE cross targetted. How, though, was the figure of 40,000 arrived at? And how could they be attacked with a force of less than 10,000 warheads capable of reaching Soviet territory, especially as, for various reasons (reliability, cross targeting, lack of 100 per cent readiness, let alone any destruction through Soviet counter-attack) not all of them could by any means each take out a separate target? By looking at the breakdown of targets we can try to answer the first question; by looking at the programmes authorized by Carter we can try to answer the second.

SIOP targets are divided into four principal groups (which do not include urban centres as such, although in practise the cities would be more than touched in any attack).
1 Soviet nuclear forces:
ICBMs, IRBMs, launch facilities, launch command centres, storage sites, airfields supporting nuclear-capable aircraft, submarine bases.
2 Conventional military forces:
Barracks, supply depots, marshalling points, conventional airfields, ammunition storage points, tank and vehicle storage yards.
3 Military and political leadership:
command posts, key communications facilities.
4 Economic and industrial targets:
a) war-supporting industry;
b) industry that contributes to economic recovery.

The US President has numerous 'packages' from this list, each

associated with one of four basic attack options. These options are:
1 Major Attack Option (MAO).
2 Selected Attack Option (SAO).
3 Limited Attack Option (LAO).
4 Regional Nuclear Option (RNO).

There are two other categories especially worth mentioning: one allows for a pre-emptive attack on the USSR; the other is a launch-on-warning attack.

Certain targets – population centres and C³I facilities – are labelled 'withhold', supposedly so that negotiations could take place between Washington and Moscow, under the threat that the cities could be attacked if the USSR was not 'flexible'. However, it is widely supposed that the purpose of deploying Pershing II is to destroy Soviet C³I facilities at an early stage in a nuclear exchange. If true this posture would seem to preclude the possibility of maintaining continuous contact with the Soviet Command for negotiating purposes. As mentioned earlier, there are several thousand targets located outside the Soviet Union.

SIOP-5D continued a trend towards targeting political HQs (2,000 of them in the USSR alone were targeted in 1980) and C³I facilities. As many of these are located in cities (supposedly 'withheld' in the first attacks) it is questionable, to say the least, whether the Soviet leadership (such of it that survives) will be able to detect the subtle difference between the military-political targeting of 'limited packages' and an all-out attack. This they are meant to be able to do, so they can respond 'rationally', ie without taking full COUNTERVALUE retaliatory measures.

In order to redress the shortage of warheads compared with SIOP's targeting requirements, President Carter set in train measures that the Reagan Administration has seized on: the programmes for MX, Cruise missiles, Trident II D-5 and Pershing II.

SIOP-5D coincided with the adoption by Carter of the so-called countervailing strategy. This declared, inter alia, that the US military must be capable of 'enduring' a prolonged nuclear war. From this there was but a short step to take to a declaration that the object of a nuclear war was for the USA to 'prevail'. The Reagan administration has taken it.

Single shot probability of kill (SSP$_k$)

Defined as the percentage likelihood that a single shot from a missile (ie just one of its warheads if it is MIRVed) will hit and destroy its target. The formula for calculating it is:

$SSP_k = 1 - e^{-z}$

where e = approx 2.72

$z = K \times r/2H^{\frac{2}{3}}(0.19H^{-1} - 0.23H^{-\frac{1}{2}} + 0.068)^{\frac{2}{3}}$

r = reliability expressed as a decimal

H = hardness of the target expressed in psi overpressure capability

$$K = Y^{2/3}/CEP^2$$

Y = warhead yield in megatons

CEP = accuracy in nautical miles

The SSP_k of a Titan II is 18 per cent; of a Minuteman III, 44 per cent; of a Trident I C4, is 4 per cent. On the Soviet side, SSP_k for an SS-11 Mod 3 is only 4 per cent, but of the SS-18, Mod 3 it is 76 per cent as it is also for the SS-19 Mod 2. For the SLBM SS-N-18 Mod 2 it is only 1 per cent. (These figures assume H = 3,000 psi.)

The new generation of US missiles are of a different order and have very high SSP_k percentages. For example Trident submarine-launched ballistic missiles:

Trident I C4 (improved)	64 per cent
Trident II D5 (8 MIRV mode)	78 per cent
Trident II D5 (14 MIRV)	74 per cent
Trident II D5 (17 MIRV, 75 kt)	78 per cent

small intercontinental ballistic missile (SICBM) The
basing problems of the MX missile and the perceived vulnerability of fixed-base ICBMs, such as Minuteman III, have prompted US strategic planners to consider a new ICBM system of greater flexibility and survivability. Thousands of missiles (some estimates suggest 3,300+) would be dispersed throughout the western USA. Some would be emplaced in silos hardened to 8,000 psi overpressure, or mobilized on transporter-erector-launchers (TEL) as are ground-launched cruise missiles, or launched from helicopters or aircraft.

Three small intercontinental missile programmes have been investigated (Midgetman, SICBM and Pershing III), each comparatively light (1,000 lbs throw-weight compared to 2,400 lbs for Minuteman III or 8,300 lbs for Titan II ICBMs), accurate and dispersible. Each missile would carry one warhead in the 300–500 kt range. President Reagan's Commission on Strategic Forces' report of April 1983 envisioned an 'early 1990s' deployment of SICBM as an augmentation to, rather than a replacement of, the MX.

soft targets The term embraces COUNTERFORCE targets which
have not been hardened against blast and which, therefore, do not require great accuracy to destroy. Examples: ports, marshalling yards, depots, airfields, camps. The term can also be applied to COUNTERVALUE targets.

see also HARD TARGETS

sound surveillance systems (SOSUS) Devices for locating
and tracking submarines. This is a complicated business because of the properties of sound in water: it travels further and faster than in the air, but also bends, scatters and bounces off objects such as the seabed or coast lines.

The principal US sensing system is SOSUS which was laid down in the 1960s. It consists of passive sensing devices fixed to continental shelves. Information from these 'hydrophones' is sent through underwater cables (which are vulnerable to being severed by Soviet boats equipped for the purpose) to shore stations.

The most important sonar chains are located between Greenland and Scotland, between the northern tip of Norway and Bear Island; in the Azores to monitor traffic in and out of the Straits of Gibraltar; parallel to the Kamchatka Peninsula in the northern Pacific, and the most important station of all, Brawdy in St David's Bay, South Wales.

SOSUS can locate a submarine to within 60 miles and can work in conjunction with anti-submarine warfare (ASW) planes and ships. Two other systems are being deployed or developed: the surveillance towed array sensor system (SURTASS) which is towed behind slow-moving boats (18 are planned), and communicate to shore by satellite. The second is the rapidly deployable sensor system (RDSS), consisting of buoys with passive sensors, which can be dropped anywhere during a period of crisis.

South Africa On 22 September 1979 a US Vela satellite recorded signals compatible with the explosion of a three-to-four kiloton device in the South Atlantic in an area where the South African Navy was known to be operating. It is possible that South Africa is collaborating with Israel in the development of tactical nuclear warheads for delivery by nuclear-capable artillery. This is borne out by the knowledge that South Africa possesses 40 155 mm towed howitzers and 50 M-109 155 mm self-propelled howitzers (which have been delivered to the UK by the USA in a nuclear-capable version). It was also reported in 1982 that a US subsidiary in South Africa, Space Research Corporation, had developed a self-propelled 155 mm howitzer, the G-6, capable of 60 mph.

South Africa also possesses Gabriel missiles fitted to fast-attack naval boats and its airforce includes 5 Canberra bombers, 6 Buccaneers and 27 Mirage IIIs, all of them nuclear capable.

South Africa maintains close links with Israel – already nuclear capable – and with Argentina, South Korea and Taiwan, which are all developing a military nuclear capability.

space detection and tracking system (SADATs)
see NORTH AMERICAN AEROSPACE DEFENSE COMMAND

'Square Leg' The code-name given to the British leg of the NATO exercise 'Crusader 80' held in 1980. It assumed an attack with 125 warheads totalling around 200 megatons with 68 ground bursts and 59 air bursts.

In the first wave it was posited that US installations at Alconbury, Lakenheath, Mildenhall, Upper Heyford, Fairford, Burton Wood, Ditton Priors, Boscombe Down, Greenham Common and Molesworth were all hit, along with Leicester, Derby, Nottingham, Newcastle and Salford. Three hours later a second strike was posited which hit, among others, Birmingham, Coventry, Liverpool, Cardiff, Swansea, Bradford, Sheffield, Glasgow, Edinburgh and Aberdeen. Central London was not hit but most of London was nevertheless destroyed, with an estimated 1.1 million deaths and 2.5 million injured in the metropolitan area with 24,000 hospital beds. Lastly, 'Square Leg' realistically assumed that the nuclear reactors at Dounray and Dungeness and the nuclear reprocessing plant at Windscale (now Sellafield) were all vapourized by direct hits.

see CIVIL DEFENCE, EFFECTS OF NUCLEAR EXPLOSION

SS-1 Scud missile Scud is the NATO name for the Soviet SS-1 group of battlefield support missiles. There are two main models currently in service – Scud A and B. The latter missile is also widely deployed within the Warsaw Pact forces. There is also a Scud C in development, which has a longer range than Scud B but is not as accurate.

Scud is a mobile system, the missiles being transported and launched from eight-wheeled vehicles. The launcher vehicles have the capacity to be reloaded in the field, and the launch preparation time is in the region of one hour. Standard Scud B missiles can be equipped with either a conventional high explosive warhead or a nuclear warhead of about 1 kt. They have a range of between 160 km and 270 km and use inertial navigation.

SS-4 Sandal missile There has been a marked reduction in the number of SS-4 missiles deployed by the Soviet Union as they are slowly phased out and replaced by the considerably more accurate and more modern SS-20s. The SS-4 was first introduced as long ago as 1959 (it was the planned deployment of SS-4 missiles in Cuba in 1962 that triggered the Cuban missile crisis) and is now viewed by the Soviets as being unacceptably limited in range (2,000 km approximately) and, more crucially, accuracy (CEP: 2,300 m). Each missile carries 1×1 mt warhead and, being of the old-style liquid fuelled type, is time-consuming in launch preparation. According to *Military Balance 1983–84,* 223 of the SS-4s are still in service.

SS-5 Skean missile Like the SS-4, the SS-5 intermediate-range ballistic missile is being gradually phased out by the USSR as part of its updating programme and replaced by the much more accurate and less vulnerable SS-20. The SS-5 was first deployed in 1961 and suffers from the dual problem of slow launch speeds due to liquid-fuelling, and inaccuracy (its CEP is 1,100 m approximately). Only 16 SS-5s are still deployed and it is expected that it will be withdrawn completely in the near future.

Specifications
Range: 4,100 km
Yield: 1 × 1 mt warhead

SS-11 Sego missile

This is the oldest ICBM in the USSR's nuclear inventory, being deployed originally in 1966. Like all the old Soviet ICBMs it is liquid-fuelled and so takes some considerable time to prepare for launching. It is also relatively inaccurate when compared to more modern missiles, with a CEP of approximately 1,400 m. These two factors were obviously contributory in the Soviet decision to gradually withdraw the SS-11s and replace them with the much more accurate and sophisticated SS-19s.

Approximately 500 SS-11s are still in service, some 210 of which are equipped with a single 1 mt warhead. The remainder have three warheads, each of 100–300 kt in a MIRV'd system. The SS-11 silos are being modified to house the newer SS-17s and SS-19s.

SS-12 Scaleboard missile

In the 1960s, Soviet policy was to increase the number of land-based tactical nuclear weapons to bring it on a par with the USA. In the 1970s the emphasis changed to updating the nuclear weapons systems by withdrawing obsolete missiles and replacing them with improved models. The SS-12 is a case in point. Although 120 SS-12s are still deployed, 70 of which are targeted on Europe, they are being replaced by the far more lethal SS-22 missiles, the USSR's answer to the USA's Pershing II.

SS-13 Savage missile

This is thought to be an unsuccessful replacement for the Soviet SS-11 missile. It is big, but inaccurate. Only 60 were ever deployed and the number still in service is not known.

Specifications
Range: 4,400–10,000 km
Yield: 1 × 750 kt
Accuracy: CEP 2,000 m

SS-17 missile

This, the first of the three modern missile systems (the SS-18 and SS-19 being the other two), was introduced by the USSR in an effort to upgrade its nuclear arsenal. It is the least accurate of the new ICBMs, but it does have the capacity for 'cold launch' (the main rocket motors delay firing until after the missile has left the silo). In theory, this implies that the silo can be reloaded, although such a procedure would take a few days before a further launch could commence – thus avoiding violation of the SALT II provision which prohibits a rapid re-loading capability for ICBM launchers.

The missiles are deployed in converted SS-11 silos and the majority of those in service are equipped with MIRVs, and what is described as a 'few' in *Military Balance, 1983/84* are fitted with a massive 6 mt warhead. Their range is up to 11,000 km with a CEP in the region of 450 m.

SS-18 missile This is the largest ICBM in the Soviet inventory, and the largest intercontinental ballistic missile in the world, being at least twice the size of the scheduled US MX missile. Like the SS-17, the SS-18 is cold-launched. It is considered to be one of the most accurate of the Soviet ICBMs (together with the SS-19) and has a range of up to 12,000 km. 'These massive and accurate weapons could be used either to attack very large targets such as major conurbations, or else heavily protected facilities like major command headquarters.' (Dr Paul Rogers, *Guide to Nuclear Weapons*, 1982/83).

The missile, of which 308 were in service in 1983, can be equipped with four different warhead systems, and a fifth option is proposed for 1985:

Mode 1	1 × 20 mt (CEP: 450 m)
Mode 2	8–10 × 900 kt, MIRV (CEP: 450 m)
Mode 3	1 × 20 mt (CEP: 350 m)
Mode 4	10 × 500 kt, MIRV (CEP: 300)
Mode 5	(?10 × 750 kt, MIRV (CEP: ?250 m)

SS-19 missile The Soviet SS-19 is similar in size to the US MX ICBM and is the most recent addition to the Soviet arsenal. Although it is one of the most accurate of Soviet ICBMs, it is not as accurate or has the range of the US Minuteman III. However, the SS-19, as well as the SS-18, may be capable of taking out hardened missile silos. This formidable ICBM is destined to replace the SS-11s and SS-13s and will be housed in modified SS-11 silos.

Specifications

	Mode 2	Mode 3
Range (km)	10,000	10,000
Yield	1 × 5 mt	6 × 550 kt MIRV
Accuracy: CEP (m)	300	300

SS-19 mode 1 is no longer in service. Of those deployed, the majority (approximately 330) are MIRV'd.

SS-20 missile 'While not the 'wonder weapon' some commentators claim it to be, the SS-20 undoubtedly represents an order-of-magnitude improvement in the Soviet capability to destroy time-urgent and semi-hard targets.' (*The SIPRI Yearbook*, 1982)

A key element in the USSR's policy of replacing obsolete missiles was the introduction of the SS-20 – an intermediate-range ballistic missile (range 5,000 km) – in 1977. The missile's main advantage over the SS-4 and SS-5 is its survivability. The SS-20 is mobile, conveyed on a tracked launch vehicle, and can be launched from pre-prepared launch pads at fixed sites. It is solid-fuelled so the time required for launch preparation is reduced to about one hour – a great improvement on the old SS-4s and SS-5s, but still no match for the US's Pershing IA.

The SS-20 is equipped with 3 × 150 kt warheads (each warhead about 12 times the explosive power of the Hiroshima bomb) which can be directed to separate targets. It has a CEP of about 400 m. Although probably the most advanced of the ballistic missiles in the Soviet arsenal, the SS-20 is outclassed in terms of speed of launch and, more importantly, in terms of accuracy by ground-launched cruise and Pershing II missiles.

According to the US Department of Defense, there are about 350 SS-20s now deployed. Two-thirds of these are aimed at targets in Western Europe. The remainder are targeted on China.

The existence of the SS-20 missiles was given by NATO as the justification for the deployment of Cruise and Pershing IIs in Europe. In President Reagan's much publicized ZERO OPTION of 1981, it was proposed that deployment of Cruise and Pershing IIs in Europe would be cancelled if the Soviet Union agreed to dismantle all its SS-4, SS-5 and SS-20 missiles. The proposal was rejected by Moscow. Early in 1983 Andropov put forward an alternative suggestion: a reduction in the SS-20 force to 162 missiles in return for no Cruise or Pershing II missiles. This proposal was rejected by NATO.

SS-21 missile Since 1978 the USSR has been deploying land-based tactical SS-21 missiles to supersede their outdated Frog 7. According to *Military Balance, 1983/84*, 62 SS-21s are now in service, armed with nuclear or conventional warheads.
Specifications
Range: 120 km
Yield: nuclear warhead size unknown
Accuracy: CEP 300 m

SS-22 missile This USSR land-based tactical nuclear missile is currently being deployed (the first ones came into service in 1979) as a replacement for the ageing SS-12s. About 100 of these missiles – a counterpart to the US's Pershing II – are now in service with the Soviet Army.

In May 1984 the Soviet Union deployed approximately 40 SS-22s in East Germany and Czechoslovakia (the missiles had previously been situated only in garrisons in the Soviet Union) – a move which brought them within striking distance of Britain. The deployment of the SS-22s in Eastern Europe was said to be in retaliation for the deployment of US Cruise missiles in Western Europe.
Specifications
Range: 900 km (a little less than Pershing II)
Yield: 1 × 500 kt warhead (twice the yield of Pershing II)
CEP: 300 m (ten times *less* accurate than Pershing II, which has a CEP of 30 m)

SSBS S-3 missile A French medium-range, solid-fuelled ballistic missile (SSBS stands for Sol-Sol-Balistique-Strategique) with a nuclear warhead. It is the successor to the SSBS S-2 which formed the core of the land-based French *force de frappe* from the early 1970s. Considered the second generation of SSBS weapons, the S-3 is stored and launched in underground silos (the S-2 silos have been converted for the new missile). The launch areas are scattered and hardened against attack. The missile carries one 1 mt nuclear warhead, and has a range of about 3,500 km. Eighteen are known to be deployed at present.

see FRANCE AS A NUCLEAR POWER, PLATEAU D'ALBION

SS-CX-4 missile The USSR is in the process of testing a number of new cruise missiles, including this ground-launched version, which is believed to be the Soviet answer to the planned deployment of US cruise missiles. The missile's range is estimated to be in the region of 3,000 km, thus exceeding the range of the US cruise (2,400 km). It is mobile, transported on a wheeled tractor-trailer with four missiles to each transporter. Nothing is yet known about the warhead yield or its potential accuracy.

SS-N-3 Shaddock missile This is the oldest of the short-range sea-launched cruise missiles used by the Soviet Navy (range: 450 km) and can be armed conventionally or with a 350 kt nuclear warhead. It is deployed on attack submarines, though it is currently being phased out in favour of the more modern SS-N-12 SLBM. Some 360 are still in service.

SS-N-6 Sawfly This, the most numerous of the Soviet sea-launched ballistic missiles, with approximately 384 currently in service, is mainly on *Yankee*-class submarines. East submarine is equipped with 16 missiles.

The SS-N-6 has one of the shortest ranges (3,000 km) of all the Soviet SLBMs, and certainly much shorter than any US or British SLBM. This means that in order to hit US inland targets, the submarine would have to take station too close to US controlled waters to be safe. It carries a 1 mt warhead in two modes, and 2×200 kt in a third. The CEP is 900–1,400 m, depending on the mode.

SS-N-7 Siren missile A Soviet sea-launched cruise missile of very short range – a mere 45 km – equipped with either a conventional warhead or a nuclear warhead of 200 kt yield. It is deployed on attack submarines.

SS-N-8 missile First deployed in 1972, there are now approximately 290 SS-N-8 SLBMs attached to the Soviet Navy's *Delta*-class fleet. With a range of about 9,000 km, the missile is capable of hitting most targets in the USA from launch sites in Soviet waters, therefore making the carrying-submarines far less vulnerable than those armed with SS-N-6 missiles.

Specifications

	Mode 1	Mode 2
Range (km)	7,800	9,100
Yield	1 × 1 mt	1 × 800 kt
CEP (m)	1,300	900

SS-N-9 missile
A short-range Soviet sea-launched cruise missile (range 280 km), the SS-N-9 carries either a conventional warhead, or a 200 kt nuclear warhead. It is deployed on attack submarines, hydrofoils and corvettes.

SS-N-12 Sandbox missile
This Soviet sea-launched cruise missile was introduced in 1980. It has the longest range of all the SLCMs in the Russian arsenal – 1,000 km. It can deliver either a conventional warhead or a nuclear warhead of 350 kt yield. About 80 of the missiles are carried on E-11-class submarines and the two *Kiev*-class carriers, and is being used to replace the SS-N-3 missiles.

SS-N-14 Silex missile
Like the SS-N-7, this Soviet sea-launched cruise missile has a very short range – approximately 55 km – and delivers a nuclear warhead in the 1 kt range. About 288 are deployed on frigates and cruisers.

SS-N-18 missile
Of the Soviet *Delta*-class submarines, 14 are equipped with the SS-N-18 missile, 16 missiles to each boat. These sea-launched ballistic missiles are similar in many respects to the SS-N-8s, except that they have a far more advanced guidance system.

Specifications

	Mode 1	Mode 2	Mode 3
Range (km)	6,500	8,000	6,500
Yield	3 × 200 kt(?) MIRV	1 × 450 kt	7 × 200 kt MIRV
Accuracy: CEP (m)	1,400	600	600

SS-N-19 missile
This, the most modern of the Soviet short-range sea-launched cruise missiles, is deployed on *Kirov*-class cruisers and *Oscar*-class submarines, both having provision for launching 20 missiles. Its principal role seems to be as an anti-ship weapon, and it has a range of about 500 km and is probably equipped with inertial navigation. It is dual-capable.

SS-NX-17 missile
This Soviet missile is still in the experimental stages – designated by the X rating – and is at present on trial in one of the *Yankee*-class submarines. It may have been planned as a solid-

fuelled successor to the SS-N-8, but indications so far are that it has been an experimental failure.

SS-NX-20 missile A submarine-launched ballistic missile deployed on the newly introduced Soviet *Typhoon*-class submarines (the largest missile-carrying submarines in the world). It is solid-fuelled with a range of about 8,000 km. It is the latest SLBM to join the Soviet arsenal and is thought to have a vastly superior rating in terms of accuracy and payload than earlier SLBMs: evidence is that each missile will carry somewhere between 6 and 10 warheads in a MIRV'd system. It is believed that the missile will become fully operational in the late 1980s.

SS-NX-21 missile A sea-launched cruise missile currently under development in the USSR. No details about the missile are available yet.

SS-NX-23 missile This is believed to be the replacement for the USSR's long-serving and highly successful SS-1 Scud series of surface-to-air missiles. Only just becoming operational, the SS-X-23 is expected to have an improved range (up to 500 km) and accuracy. It is also thought that the reaction and re-fire times have been improved. The warhead yield is unknown as yet.

Standing Consultative Commission Set up between the USA and USSR in 1972 to consider any problems arising from SALT I and 'to promote its objectives'. It meets under alternating chairmen not less than twice yearly, usually in Geneva. The Commission has indeed proved to be a quiet yet effective forum for monitoring the terms of the three treaties which came out of the SALT talks.

'Star Wars' weapons A fanciful term to describe direct energy weapons situated in space which could destroy enemy missiles soon after they had been launched. Alternatively they could attack satellites. Curiously, their development (but not their deployment) is permitted under the terms of the ANTI-BALLISTIC MISSILE TREATY, part of SALT I. If ever the USA had the intention of deploying such weapons they would have to exercise the provisions for terminating their adherence to the treaty, and such an action would paralyse all further arms control negotiations. It would also raise the spectre of the USA's ability to intercept all Soviet bombers and missiles while the USSR was unable to defend itself against a US nuclear attack. In other words, such weapons would move the US decisively towards a disarming first-strike capability – the Holy Grail of nuclear strategists. Either the US may be tempted to use, or threaten to use, such strength in order to make major political demands upon the Soviet leadership, or the latter might be forced to mobilize their nuclear forces before such weapons were put into place.

The weapons
1 Killer laser powered by chemicals can concentrate vast amounts of energy over huge distances, and at the point of impact the energy applied surpasses that of a nuclear explosion. Developers hope to be capable of putting a killer laser into space by the end of the 1980s. Before this they have to develop a chemical laser with a four-metre diameter beam, suitable for use in space, a low-power tracking laser which finds the target and aims the main beam, and a huge mirror to steer the laser.
2 The X-ray laser. Many beams are aimed towards separate targets. Once on target a nuclear explosion takes place, the energy of which pulses through the laser beams, destroying all the targets in one fell swoop. (The laser would also be destroyed).
3 Proton and neutron rays which can be compared to a lightning bolt. However, they are not very accurate (though extremely powerful) because their direction is affected by the earth's magnetic field. To counter this a neutral particle beam is being developed called White Horse.

It is true that the USSR is doing research in this field and may mount a show-case laser flight before the end of the 1980s, but it is doubtful if anything could be produced for some time to come which would have the capacity to knock down US missiles or satellites.

'Stealth bomber'
see ADVANCED TECHNOLOGY BOMBER

stellar inertial guidance
see MISSILE ACCURACY

Stockholm International Peace Research Institute (SIPRI)
Established in 1966 to 'conduct scientific research on questions of conflict and co-operation of importance for international peace and security, with the aims of contributing to the understanding of the conditions for peaceful solutions of international conflict and for a stable peace.'

Its primary publication is the *Yearbook* which has appeared annually since 1968. The *Yearbook*'s remit is much wider than the only comparable publication, *The Military Balance,* published by the International Institute for Strategic Studies, namely 'to provide an overview of the whole field of development and armament technology, in military expenditure, in the arms trade, and in the attempts to halt or to reverse the process. It sets out each year to provide studies of the main armament and disarmament issues of the time.'

SIPRI and *Military Balance* often come to quite different

conclusions where they cover the same ground. However, SIPRI has a commitment to objectivity evidenced by its funding by the Swedish Parliament and the fact that its staff, governing board and scientific council are international in character.

SIPRI also publishes a number of specialist titles on particular aspects of research. Its address is SIPRI, Bergshamra, S-171 73 Solna, Sweden.

Strategic Air Command (SAC)
see COMMAND, CONTROL, COMMUNICATIONS AND INTELLIGENCE

Strategic Arms Limitation Talks (SALT I and II)

SALT I
The talks began in 1969. In October 1972 Brezhnev and Nixon signed three treaties which codified their results up to that date, known collectively as SALT I. These were:

1 Basic Principles of Relations between the USA and the USSR.
2 The Anti-Ballistic Missile Treaty, which restricted the signatory states to two such systems each; one for the protection of Washington and Moscow, the other to protect one missile launching site apiece.
3 The Interim Agreement and Protocol on Strategic Offensive Missiles. This set limits to the numbers of missile launchers and delivery systems deployable by the two states.

The ABM treaty achieved rather little at the time as neither side wished to expend vast sums on such dubious projects anyway, especially once it was realized that to explode incoming nuclear missiles over home territory would have catastrophic results, if only because of the electromagnetic pulse (EMP) effect. If President Reagan's STAR WARS ballistic missile defence (BMD) system proceeds, it will definitely breach the terms of this treaty. The significance of the Treaty has increased as both sides expand researches into BMD systems (see especially NORAD). It was renewed in October 1982.

The second 'interim' treaty was to last only five years until the signing of a more comprehensive SALT II agreement leading, perhaps, to arms reductions. At the time the USA had an advantage both in numbers of warheads and in the R&D into MIRVing. 'In retrospect, the weak effort to ban MIRVs was a key aspect of SALT ... the leading lost opportunity of the negotiations' (Gerard Smith, chief US negotiator at SALT I in *Double Talk*, New York, 1980, p. 154.)

The lack of effective US negotiating initiatives on MIRVing was no accident, and the way in which the final treaty slotted in with US strategic thinking and US plans to augment its strategic arsenal has been explained by Henry Kissinger in his briefing to the American Congress: 'during the 1960s the US had ... made the strategic decision to terminate its building programs in major offensive systems and to rely instead on qualitative improvements. By 1965, therefore, we had no active or planned programs .... The Soviet Union, on the other hand, had dynamic and accelerated deployment programs in both land-based and sea-based missiles.'

Between SALT I and SALT II the number of strategic weapons launchers on each side may not have escalated, but the number of warheads and their combined explosive force grew: for the USA from approximately 6,300 to 9,000 warheads; for the USSR from approximately 2,300 to 5,000.

The Heath government in Britain did not attempt to participate in the talks; quite the reverse. In answer to a parliamentary question Edward Heath asserted that Britain's Polaris missile was *not* definable as strategic.

Politically, the results of SALT I were (a) to imply that a new era in arms negotiation had opened and that the world was a much safer place as a result, and (b) to intensify the distance between the two superpowers and other state and inter-state bodies, ie the treaties were purely bilateral and not the result of UN or even NATO–WTO initiatives.

SALT II

Negotiations began with the Ford–Brezhnev meeting in Vladivostok in November 1974 and ended with Brezhnev and Carter signing a treaty in Vienna in June 1979. It covers a wider scope than SALT I but its stipulations are so mild as to allow for unfettered development in almost all instances. The terms restrict each country to:

● 2,400 strategic delivery vehicles (including heavy bombers) initially, to be reduced to 2,250 by the end of 1981 (1979 figures: USA 2,283; USSR 2,504);

● of these, only 1,320 can be MIRVed missiles or bombers carrying cruise missiles (1979 figures: USA 1,049; USSR 752);

● of the 1,320, 1,200 can be MIRVed strategic missiles; the remainder bombers, the number of which can be increased if the MIRVed missiles are similarly reduced;

● not more than 820 of the 1,200 MIRVed missiles can be ICBMs.

The US Congress refused to ratify SALT II as American perceptions of relations with the USSR had swung decisively away from detente. But the peripheral impact of its terms on arms limitation, even had it been adopted, is shown by President Carter's statement in 1979 that 'the MX missile; the Trident submarine and its missiles; air-, ground-, and sea-launched cruise missiles; cruise missile carrier aircraft; and a new penetrating bomber. These would be permitted.' (Speech published in US State Department publication, *Current Policy,* no 57, March 1979.)

Strategic Arms Reduction Talks (START)

see ARMS CONTROL AND ARMS LIMITATION

strategic doctrine (American)

Massive retaliation

American strategy was guided by the concept of 'massive retaliation' until the early 1960s when the USSR introduced its own intercontinental ballistic missiles and the US mainland became a potential target. The concept was described by David Alan Rosenberg, 'Document One', *International Security*, 6 (3) 1982, pp. 3–38:

> It was estimated that SAC (Strategic Air Command) could lay down an attack of 600–750 bombs by approaching Russia from many directions .... It would require about two hours from this moment until the bombs had been dropped by using the Bomb-as-you-go system .... The final impression was that virtually all of Russia would be nothing but a smoking, radiating ruin.

McNamara's 'Flexible Counterforce' strategy

In June 1962, Robert McNamara, Secretary of Defense in the Kennedy Administration, announced a new strategy:

> Basic military strategy in a possible nuclear war should be approached in much the same way that more conventional military operations have been regarded in the past. That is to say, principal military objectives should be the destruction of the enemy's military forces, not his civilian population.

The SINGLE INTEGRATED OPERATIONAL PLAN (SIOP) set to work at once to identify possible targets. By 1965 it had designated 10,000. These included missile silos, bomber airfields, C³I centres, conventional military bases and depots as well as key logistical support systems.

Mutual Assured Destruction (MAD)

Hardly had McNamara announced the previous position than he grew perturbed at Strategic Air Command's enthusiasm for a FIRST-STRIKE capability. In 1964 he announced that the most important mission of US strategic forces was 'to deter deliberate nuclear attack upon the USA and its allies by maintaining a highly reliable ability to inflict an unacceptable degree of damage upon an aggressor ... even after absorbing a surprise first strike'.

This doctrine became known as Mutual Assured Destruction or MAD, for neither side would dare to launch a first attack if they knew they faced obliteration from a retaliatory attack. As to what level of destruction was necessary to deter the USSR from striking first, McNamara's view was 'the destruction of one-fifth to one-fourth of the Soviet population plus one-half to two-thirds of its industrial capacity'. This required in his estimation, bombs with a destructive force of 400 megatons. If this doctrine had been fully adopted it would have led to a freezing of research and development of nuclear weapons, but this did not happen.

Limited strategic options

Eventually the usefulness of the MAD strategy was called into question by President Nixon as giving the President the choice between suicide or surrender. James Schlesinger, as Richard Nixon's Secretary of Defense, spelt out the new doctrine of 'limited strategic options' – 'Deterrence must operate across the entire spectrum of possible contingencies. We cannot afford gaps in its coverage that might invite probes and tests.' (Testimony to the Senate Armed Forces Committee, 5 February 1974). The SIOP targeting plan was again updated and expanded; first use of nuclear weapons became a US and then a NATO declared option.

Countervailing strategy

This was unveiled by President Carter in his 1980 Presidential Directive 59 (PD59) which called for 'the capacity for flexible, controlled retaliation against a full range of targets for any attack at any level'. His original enthusiasm for minimum deterrence with a nuclear force of some 200 warheads had now gone. Countervailing strategy is designed to ensure that the USA cannot lose at any level of a limited nuclear war as well as being able to escalate it in a controlled way. Deterrence had come to mean limiting nuclear war, rather than preventing it.

American strategy in Europe

The defence of Western Europe presents the USA and its West European NATO allies with painful dilemmas:

1 The allies feel they require US nuclear weapons to protect them against the USSR.

2 The US, subscribing to the theory of limited nuclear war, agrees with the allies and deploys ground-launched cruise missiles and Pershing IIs in addition to about 7,000 tactical nuclear weapons on West European soil. These the USA describes as 'theatre' as opposed to strategic weapons in the hope that the USSR will, in the event of those weapons being used, respect the difference and not attack the USA directly.

3 To act as a credible deterrent these weapons must be usable in certain conditions.

4 However, even a controlled, 'limited' European war would utterly destroy large amounts of the areas defended.

5 Therefore any rational defence policy of a European nation must ensure the weapons are never used.

6 But if this is done they will cease to be credible – the bluff will be exposed.

7 The USA is put into a quandary. By placing US nuclear weapons in Europe under US control it has to be committed to using them while, at the same time, creating the idea in the USA that no European nuclear exchange will escalate to the homeland. The USA will remain a sanctuary (see SANCTUARY THEORY). However, in diplomatic

contacts with the USSR it must convince the Soviets that it is prepared to fight a nuclear war in Europe.

8   The European NATO countries seek to extract from the USA a guarantee that it will defend them if necessary by attacking the USSR. Yet this is the one guarantee the USA cannot give – fearing strategic retaliation. On the other hand, a purely European theatre nuclear war which excludes the superpowers from direct attack is unacceptable to the Europeans.

9   The dilemma is intensified by the USSR's unequivocal declaration that the US's concept of a limited war will not be recognized and that *any* theatre exchange will be escalated to a strategic level. It insists that any such attack from whatever quarter (ie even if it came from theatre-designated missiles based in Europe) would be regarded as a strategic attack and would be met with a massive nuclear response on the US mainland.

10   The strategies of flexible response and controlled escalation allow for any aggression to be met, matched and then escalated in a controlled way through a series of 'rungs' on the 'ladder of escalation'. At each stage the threat of more escalation is used as a way of deterring the enemy. A major problem with these doctrines is that they rely on the other side understanding and agreeing to adopt the rules of limited nuclear war.

11   Thus in Europe, too, 'deterrence' stands for two different concepts: (a) the prevention of the outbreak of nuclear war (b) the limiting of it should it break out. The concept of flexible response, together with countervailing strategy and limited strategic options, all have one thing in common: to make the threat of nuclear war more credible by developing weapons, strategies and C^3I systems which can be used.

12   NATO's unwillingness to forgo first use of nuclear weapons ensures that any conventional war will be more likely to acquire nuclear proportions.

see STRATEGIC DOCTRINE (SOVIET)

strategic doctrine (Soviet)   Soviet strategic doctrine is different in almost every respect from Western doctrine. It is largely the product of military thinking, insisting that, while nuclear weapons have clearly changed the character of the war, they have not altered its essence. For the USSR, war means the extension of the fight against the politics of imperialism. So, although Soviet strategy faces many problems in terms of missiles, air defence, anti-submarine warfare and even conventional warfare technology, as a doctrine, it does not lack internal coherence.

Limited war does not make sense to Soviet strategists, not only for technical reasons or because of a lack of faith in the viability of 'crisis management' in the event of a nuclear exchange, but because they believe that the essence and scope of war is determined by its political goals. Thus if, as they believe, US aims are unlimited, namely to achieve escalation dominance over the USSR in order to dictate terms which would affect the very nature of the Soviet Union, it follows that war operations cannot remain limited until those goals are achieved or the US suffers major reverses – whatever the intentions of the US military.

It is possible, however, that the USSR is beginning to consider the possibility of limited nuclear confrontations in non-vital theatres, eg the Middle East (see ISRAEL AS A NUCLEAR POWER). Europe is unlikely to be included in this thinking; as Brezhnev commented, 'If a nuclear war breaks out in Europe or elsewhere, it will necessarily and unavoidably be universal.'

Soviet strategists have never subscribed to mutual assured destruction (MAD), believing that the US military posture went beyond 'deterrence by punishment' towards an increased COUNTER-FORCE capability. They maintain that they had no option but to follow suit to avoid the USSR being pushed into a hostage position by the US.

The USSR's strategy for the use of nuclear weapons is clear-cut. If they received information that a nuclear attack was under way, they would immediately launch a massive retaliatory nuclear strike. Their aim would be to knock out as many enemy nuclear missiles as possible. But it would go further than this: US C³I facilities, troop concentrations and military logistical soft targets would also be hit, to weaken the ability of the USA to continue a war; economic targets would be hit to undermine the USA, both in terms of their capacity to conduct the war and to recover from it afterwards.

Swift action is constantly stressed in this the most vital part of the war: 'the launching of the first massed nuclear attack acquires decisive importance for achieving the objectives of the war'. And, under pressure from a perceived US supremacy in highly accurate counterforce weapons, one cannot rule out from Soviet thinking an anticipatory strike, despite the pledge not to be the first to use nuclear weapons.

What is certain is that Soviet strategy rules out absorbing an initial strike before launching a Soviet retaliatory strike. The memory of the first phase of the German onslaught in World War II is still too fresh, and the devastation of Soviet territory in that war has ensured that future strategies imply taking the war into enemy territory as soon as possible. Also, as yet, the USSR does not possess missiles of sufficient accuracy in adequate numbers to be able to rely on having an effective second-strike capability.

The USSR maintains that, in the face of the development of the US MX, Trident II D-5, air-launched cruise missiles in growing numbers, ground-launched cruise missiles, Pershing II, the B-1 bomber, the 'Stealth' bomber and advances in anti-submarine warfare, it has no choice but to pursue a vast modernization programme of its own in every field, but perhaps especially in air defence against cruise and bombers, and in ballistic missile defence.

Thus Soviet strategists envisage global nuclear war, what has been called the 'strategic disruptive strike', at an early stage in any war begun by a nuclear attack. They regard the Western notion of a 'warning shot' as 'the height of strategic foolishness', achieving no military advantage and providing the USSR with every incentive to hit back while it still has the strategic missiles to do so.

Soviet strategists have few illusions that the territories of the two sides would be anything but devastated after an exchange of such magnitude. However, they persevere in the belief that both sides will still have a warfighting capability, including tactical nuclear weapons. It is at this point that their 'combined arms' strategy comes into play: a predominantly conventional military force would advance across probably contaminated territory to destroy the enemy's military forces in what could be a protracted war.

strategic triad This describes the three arms of intercontinental-range nuclear weapons: submarine-launched ballistic missiles, bombers and intercontinental ballistic missiles.

stockpile, nuclear The most graphic illustration of the size of the world nuclear stockpile as at 1983 is by Jim Garrison and Pyare Shivpuri, *The Russian Threat,* p. 6:

> All the gunpowder that has been used in wars since it was invented could be carried in a train 50 miles long, if the freight cars were forty feet long and carried fifty tons each. Our [the world's] nuclear stockpile now stands at 16 billion tons of TNT equivalent. We would need a train 2,424,242 miles long. Such a train would encircle the earth at the equator over 97 times or cover the distance to the moon and back five times. If we could compress our nuclear stockpiles into bombs of the size dropped onto Hiroshima and exploded one bomb every day it would take us 4,600 years to get rid of them all.

The USA and USSR have between them approximately 50,000 nuclear warheads representing an explosive potential of some 20,000 megatons – the equivalent of 1,333,333 Hiroshimas.

SU-7 Fitter A strike aircraft Originally deployed in 1959, this is the oldest member of the Soviet strike force. About 150 are still in service.

SU-17 Fitter D/H strike aircraft Deployed in 1974, the SU-17 Fitter D/H has a much shorter combat radius than its contemporary in the Soviet strike force, the SU-24 Fencer – a mere 900 km. However, it has a superior weapons payload. Approximately 650 are in service.

SU-24 Fencer strike aircraft
One of the most sophisticated aircraft in the Soviet strike force, the SU-24 Fencer is the closest rival to the similar Western swing-wing penetration fighter-bombers. It has terrain-hugging radar and laser-assisted range finder linked to the on-board weapons computer, as well as an inertial navigation system and 'head-up' display of terrain and weapons sighting. According to *Military Balance,* approximately 800 are in service.
Specifications
Speed: Mach 2.3
Weapons payload: 3,624 kg
Combat radius: 2,000 km

submarine-launched ballistic missile (SLBM)
Long-range missiles launched from submerged submarines. They represent the most mobile and least vulnerable form of missile basing.

	number deployed	range km	accuracy CEP, m	yield
USA				
Poseidon C-3	304	4,600	450	6-14 × 50 kt MIRV
Trident C-4	264	7,400	450	8 × 100 kt MIRV
UK				
Polaris A-3	64	4,600	900	3 × 200 kt MIRV (Chevaline improvement will double the warheads)
France				
MSBS M-20	80	3,000	na	1 × 1 mt
USSR				
SS-N-5	48	1,400	2,800	1 × 1 mt
SS-N-6	384	2,400–3,000	900–1,400	2 × 200 kt & 1 × 1 mt
SS-N-8	292	7,800–9,000	900	1 × 800 kt
SS-N-17	12	3,900	1,500	1 × mt
SS-N-18	224	6,500–8,000	600	1 × 450 kt & 7 × 200 kt MIRV
SS-NX-20 (? operational)	20	8,300	na	6–9 MIRV

(SUBROC) anti-submarine rocket
A US rocket-propelled nuclear depth charge in the 1–5 kt range is fired from the torpedo tubes of an attack submarine. The rocket leaves the water and then re-enters to destroy an enemy submarine. It is planned that by 1989–90 SUBROC will be replaced by a new anti-submarine stand-off weapon (ASWSOW) currently being developed. However, there are approximately 400 SUBROCs deployed on 73 US submarines.
see ASROC

Super Etendard strike aircraft
Thirty-six of these French strike aircraft are based on the carriers *Clemenceau* and *Foch*. They have a combat radius of 1,000 km, speeds of up to Mach 1.0 and a

weapons payload of 7,248 kg which includes a 15 kt gravity nuclear bomb.

Supreme Allied Command, Europe (SACEUR) In

peacetime SACEUR is responsible for NATO'S European Sector, excluding UK, Iceland, France and Portugal. In wartime SACEUR would control all land, sea and air operations, including the air defence of Britain. Its commander-in-chief is always a US officer; its HQ is at Mons, Belgium.

SACEUR has at its immediate disposal some 6,000 tactical nuclear weapons including Lance and Pershing IAs, 400 MIRVed warheads belonging to the Poseidon fleet based at Holy Loch (which, though counted in the SALT II negotiations as strategic weapons are, in fact, under SACEUR's control and would be more likely to be used in theatre operations, 66 divisions or their equivalents and 3,500 tactical aircraft in around 200 airfields.

All British nuclear forces are committed to NATO and fall under SACEUR's command. These include not only Polaris A-3 missiles, but many tactical weapons – artillery as well as missiles – gravity bombs and depth charges, and the bombers, fighter planes and helicopters to deliver them. The targeting for Polaris is wholly integrated into SACEUR, the targeting plan for which is developed by the Nuclear Activities Branch at Supreme HQ for Allied Powers in Europe (SHAPE). The plan is divided in two parts: (a) for the selective use of tactical weapons and (b) for general response. In the latter eventuality, SACEUR's forces would be used in parallel with US strategic arsenals targeted by the SINGLE INTEGRATED OPERA-TIONAL PLAN (SIOP). The decision to purchase Trident is to be seen less as an addition to the British 'nuclear deterrent' as to NATO's European forces. Lastly, SACEUR controls the ground-launched cruise missiles and Pershing IIs in or arriving in Europe.

surveillance towed array sensor (SURTASS)
see SOUND SURVEILLANCE SYSTEM

survivability low frequency communication system
see COMMAND, CONTROL, COMMUNICATIONS AND INTELLIGENCE

target data inventory
see NATIONAL STRATEGIC TARGET LIST

terrain contour matching (TERCOM) A guidance system at present fitted to cruise missiles, TERCOM correlates the terrain being overflown with an on-board pre-programmed computer map. TERCOM is used in conjunction with, and as a continual update of, the missile's INERTIAL GUIDANCE system.

TERCOM's radar altimeter and computer measure height

variations during flight and accordingly adjust the inertial guidance. Thus, instead of the missile becoming increasingly less accurate during the course of its flight – as it inevitably would if it had to rely on inertial guidance alone – it becomes increasingly accurate and, at the point of impact, can be within 30 m of its target.

Obviously, the pre-programmed maps are of vital importance and the main reference point during the flight. They are established by satellite surveillance, the Defense Mapping Agency and the Defense Intelligence Agency working with the manufacturer. Targeting is the responsibility of Supreme Allied Command Europe (SACEUR). It has been suggested that over 100 million references have to be built into a TERCOM map, at a cost of н1 billion for the whole cruise programme (J C Toomay, 'Technical Characteristics', in *Cruise Missiles: Technology, Strategy, Politics,* ed. Richard K Betts, Brookings Institute, 1981).

theatre nuclear weapons The term covers nuclear weapons with a range of less than 5,500 km and is usually divided into short-, medium- and long-range weapons. The first are also known as tactical or battlefield weapons and extend in range to 200km. The second, also known as intermediate-range weapons can travel between 200 and somewhat over 1,000 km. The third category (up to 5,500 km) are also referred to as Eurostrategic weapons. For the USSR, medium-range weapons operate between 1,000 and 5,500 km.

Nuclear-capable aircraft complicate matters:
a because of their re-fuelling capacity which enlarges their range;
b because of the assortment of nuclear weaponry they can carry – tactical, anti-submarine warfare weapons, medium range missiles and gravity bombs amongst them;
c because it is difficult to know whether an aircraft is already nuclear-capable or whether it could easily be transformed into a nuclear-capable version. Also, dependent on its armoury, the same aircraft can sometimes fulfil different combat missions (interceptor/strike/bomber);
d because if it is based on an aircraft carrier, an aircraft's range from its home port is limitless.

Another problem with theatre weapons is rooted in the geopolitics of Europe. A 'theatre' nuclear weapon launched from the West can hit Moscow and much of the USSR but a Soviet theatre weapon is genuinely that, although it could reach Alaska from the Soviet Far East.

As for the distinctions between short-, medium- and long-range, while they serve some military purposes when assigning tasks, they also serve to prevent agreement on arms control. They are yet three more analytical categories to be added to such items as numbers deployed, megatonnage, accuracy, reloadability, reliability, MIRVing, MARVing, speed, and location. Any skilful negotiator intent on avoiding an agreement can easily find an opposing missile of a particular type or range or yield which is more numerous than the equivalent missile on his or her own side.

The classic example is the deployment of Soviet SS-20s which, being land-based, MIRVed and supposedly accurate, provided the excuse for deploying Cruise and Pershing II in Europe. However, as Denis Healey has pointed out, the USSR had land-based missile superiority in Europe for 20 years and no one noticed. By focussing on land-based Eurostrategic missiles and discerning a gap between the two sides, the real balance in Europe, which has to include tactical weapons, aircraft, US Poseidon submarines and, above all, the French and British submarine fleets, slips from public view.

thermonuclear weapons A nuclear weapon which derives most of its explosive force from the fusion of deuterium and tritium to produce helium, the release of one neutron and a vast amount of energy. The temperature required for a fusion reaction is so great that a small fission explosion is needed to trigger it. The 'thermo' element of a thermonuclear bomb represents the fission-produced heat, while the 'nuclear' element refers to the fusion reaction.

Thermonuclear bombs are much more powerful than fission (atomic) bombs because it is possible to pack large quantities of lithium deuteride into a casing without it becoming critical and exploding prematurely.

Three-Mile Island accident
see HARRISBERG ACCIDENT

Threshold Test Ban Treaty, 1974 The USA and the USSR agreed to prohibit any underground nuclear weapons tests having a yield exceeding 150 kt, thus establishing a nuclear 'threshold'. The treaty also contained a protocol concerning the exchange of technical data between the two countries, such as the geographical boundaries and geology of each one's testing areas. (This information is useful in verifying test yields.) This was the first time any agreement had been reached about releasing information directly related to the countries' individual nuclear weapons programmes. The treaty does not, however, do anything to halt the development and construction of nuclear weapons.

throw-weight The 'useful' parts of a ballistic missile – re-entry vehicles carrying the warhead, post-boost vehicle carrying the re-entry vehicles, penetration aids to deflect or destroy anti-ballistic defences – as distinct from the main propulsion system.

time-sensitive/time-urgent targets If a first strike is to be successfully disabling, all the targeted enemy silos, with their missiles and C³I centres, must be destroyed before retaliatory missiles can be launched. Speed and accuracy are therefore paramount.

A strike against C³I (decapitation strike) hits at the nerve centres of retaliatory capability. C³I centres are therefore extremely time-sensitive and the Soviet military's appreciation of this is demonstrated by their expressed anxiety about Pershing II missiles which, within 12 minutes of launch in West Germany, could strike targets in the USSR with great accuracy (CEP 30 m). The only defence against such a threat is, as the USSR has declared, to launch-on-warning, ie to fire retaliatory missiles before they can be caught in the silos – as soon as *any* warning of a Pershing II attack (perhaps unconfirmed) is received.

It is currently being debated whether or not cruise missiles have any value against Soviet time-sensitive targets, as they travel comparatively slowly (550 mph). Their main function may be to destroy Soviet re-loads in those silos or mobile launchers that survive the first attack.
see MISSILE ACCURACY, COUNTER MILITARY POTENTIAL, SINGLE-SHOT PROBABILITY OF KILL

Titan II ICBM The largest, least accurate and oldest of the US's ICBMs, Titan's are deployed at air force bases at Little Rock, Arkansas, McConnell, Kansas, and Davis-Monthan, Arizona. Titan IIs became operational as long ago as June 1963, and 45 are still in service. With its single, massive warhead it provides the most destructive soft target capability (ie against cities and industrial centres). In October 1982 the Titans began to be retired – a process that should be completed when the first 40 MX ICBMs are deployed in 1986.
Specifications
Range: 15,000 km
Yield: 1×9 mt W53 warhead
Accuracy: 1,300 m
Speed: 15,000 mph

top-table theory An argument for the retention of British nuclear weapons. By such possession, it is argued, the UK still has world-wide political influence (not least vis-à-vis a much more economically powerful Germany within the EEC) and is entitled to sit at top-level arms negotiations and other matters of world importance. Without the nuclear force Britain would be reduced to a second- or third-rate power and would cede to France the dominant military presence in Western Europe.

A certain very convoluted version of the top-table theory has it that Britain must maintain a nuclear strike force in order to be able to argue among the other nuclear powers for nuclear disarmament or at least for arms reductions. In practice, however, British representatives have never so argued and have often not even been at the 'top table' (eg SALT I and II, INF talks, START talks).

Tornado aircraft The Panavia Tornado multi-role combat aircraft has been developed by a British–Italian–German consortium. Two versions, the strike (GR1) and the interceptor (F2), are being acquired by Britain as the most expensive aircraft system since World War II (£11.3 billion). The strike version is nuclear-capable with variable yields up to 500 kt per aircraft.

Britain plans to acquire 220 GR1s (to replace 48 Vulcans and 28 Buccaneers) during the 1980s, and 165 F2s. The current production rate is 40 per year. They will be based in the UK and West Germany. There are 36 Tornados already in service with the Italian air force, and 30 with the West German air force.

Qualitatively the Tornado represents a major advance. It is equipped with a terrain-following navigation system and all-weather operation. An advanced navigation/attack system allows for accurate single-pass attacks on targets. The combat radius of 1,280 km will be enhanced by aerial refuelling.

transporter-erector-launcher (TEL) A wheeled vehicle designed to carry a ballistic or cruise missile from its base to a firing site, raise it into position and fire it. The TEL for the recently deployed US ground-launched cruise missile is a heavy vehicle – 17 m long and 35.5 tonnes. Its four missiles, once sited, are loaded through armoured rear doors, raised to 45° and fired from aluminium canisters.

Treaty of Tlatelolco, 1967 Many of the Latin American countries had been sufficiently alarmed by the Cuban missile crisis in 1962 to propose that a treaty be drawn up to establish Latin America as a nuclear free zone. The basic obligations of this treaty are contained in its first article:

1 The Contracting Parties hereby undertake to use exclusively for peaceful purposes the nuclear material and facilities which are under their jurisdiction, and to prohibit and prevent in their respective territories:

(a) The testing, use, manufacture, production or acquisition by any means whatsoever of any nuclear weapons, by the Parties themselves, directly or indirectly, on behalf of anyone else or in any other way, and

(b) The receipt, storage, installation, deployment and any form of possession of nuclear weapons, directly or indirectly, by the Parties themselves, by anyone on their behalf or in any other way.

2 The Contracting Parties also undertake to refrain from engaging in, encouraging or authorizing directly or indirectly, or in any way participating in the testing, use, manufacture, production, possession or control of any nuclear weapon.

The 'Contracting Parties' included the Latin American countries themselves, and all those non-Latin American states that had possessions in the nuclear free zone (UK, Netherlands, USA and

167

France) and the nuclear-weapons states (of which, China, France, USSR, UK and USA have signed).

So far, Cuba has refused to sign the treaty, and the three most powerful countries in Latin America – Brazil, Argentina and Chile – have shown some degree of ambiguity in their commitment to it. There was some evidence that Britain had violated the treaty's terms during the 1982 Falklands war by sending over forces equipped with nuclear weapons, although this was denied by the British government.

Tlatelolco is the suburb of Mexico City where the representatives of the participating countries met to sign the treaty on 14 February 1967.

Trident submarine Designated as Ohio class, the Trident is the newest and largest of the USA's nuclear ballistic missile launchers. There are three currently in service, each carrying 24 Trident I C-4 missiles (8×100 kt MIRV'd warheads per missile). By December 1990 12 Trident submarines will be in service with the US Navy. The ninth submarine onwards will be armed with the Trident II D-5 (range: 12,000 km, 10–15 warheads – each 150–600 kt – per missile, CEP approximately 50 m) and the first eight boats will then be refitted with D-5s.

British Trident

In March 1982 the UK Goverment decided to replace its ageing Polaris system by the mid-1990s with Trident submarines armed with Trident II D-5 missiles. Such a move would mean that Britain's SLBM count will increase, theoretically, from a present figure of 192 (assuming Chevaline improvements to Polaris are completed) to 1,440. The *Defence Committee report on the Defence Estimates, 1984*, puts the cost of Trident at £9.4 billion. The first of Britain's Trident submarines is expected to enter service in 1992.

Trident I C4 missile A submarine-launched ballistic missile which will be fitted to the first eight *Ohio*-class Trident submarines. Three such vessels are now in service (*Ohio, Michigan, Florida*). It is a three-stage, solid-fuelled MIRV'd 8–14 warheads. Although the range of Trident I C4 is greater than Poseidon C3 (4,600–7,400 km) it is equally accurate (450 m). Its main targets would be military and industrial centres as well as cities. In October 1979 a programme was started to fit Trident Is into 12 Poseidon submarines, at a cost of $200 million per vessel. It will be replaced by Trident II D5 in the late 1980s.

Specifications
Range: 7,400 km
Accuracy: CEP 450 m
Yield: 8–14×100 kt MIRV'd warheads
Number deployed: 264

Trident II D5 The most advanced submarine-launched ballistic missile being developed by the USA, the Trident II D5 will be fitted to Trident submarines in late 1988. In 1982 Britain elected to buy the missile and submarine system as a replacement for POLARIS.

The missile grew out of an investigation into the problems of accurate targeting during battle, and the improved accuracy by comparison with Poseidon C3 (CEP 450 m) and Trident I C4 (CEP 450 m) is dramatic. Whereas Poseidon and Trident I were seen as countervalue or soft target weapons (cities, dockyards, industrial complexes) a CEP of 133 m for Trident II makes it a counterforce or hard target weapon (missile silos, C^3I centres) for any such target anywhere in the USSR. In addition to improved accuracy, the plan is to increase the number of high-yield warheads carried by each missile to $9–10 \times 475–600$ kt. It will also be capable of carrying 15×150 kt MIRV'd warheads.

It is planned to deploy 914 missiles for 20 submarines, and according to the US Department of Defense 'will nearly double the capability of each Trident submarine'.

Specifications
Range: 7,400–11,000 km
Accuracy: CEP 133 m
Yield: $9–10 \times 475–600$ kt MIRV
15×150 kt MIRV

Tritium A hydrogen isotope the nucleus of which has two neutrons and one proton. It is produced by neutron irradiation of lithium in fission reactors. There are large reserves of lithium as a future source of tritium. At present it is a component of a hydrogen bomb where it combines with deuterium in a fusion reaction which releases one neutron and an enormous amount of energy. If fusion reactors ever become workable energy sources, tritium would be used as part of the fuel.

Tu-16 Badger bomber The mainstay of the USSR's theatre bomber force, the Tu-16 is now being replaced by the Tu-22 Backfire bombers. Of the 440 aircraft still in operation, some 220 are based on carriers of the Soviet Navy. It carries short-range cruise missiles such as the AS-2 Kipper and the more modern, AS-6 Kingfish.

Specifications
Speed: Mach 0.8
Weapons payload: 9,060 kg
Combat radius: 2,000 km

Tu-22 Blinder bomber About 165 Tu-22s are currently deployed, either from land bases or from carriers. It is capable of carrying either a gravity nuclear bomb, or a single short-range air-launched cruise missile.

Specifications
Speed: Mach 1.5
Weapons payload: 5,436 kg
Combat radius: 1,200 km

Tu-22 M/26 Backfire bomber

A Soviet swing-wing aircraft for use primarily in the European theatre although, theoretically, it is possible for the Tu-22 to reach the USA with in-flight re-fuelling. It is likely that the USSR will concentrate on promoting its strategic/theatre versatility to match the US B-52, B1-B and FB-111A by arming it with long-range, air-launched cruise missiles. The aircraft can carry a range of free-fall bombs as well as the AS-4 and AS-6 short-range cruise missiles.

Specifications
Speed: Mach 2.5
Weapons payload: 7,927 kg
Combat radius: 3,000 km

Tu-95 Bear bomber

Both Tu-95 and the Mya-4 Bison are old Soviet long-range bombers; about 100 are still operational. They have a range of up to 12,800 km and about two-thirds of the total complement are equipped with nuclear missiles. The remainder carry 3×1 mt gravity bombs.

'Two-on-one' cross-targeting

The practice of targeting two warheads from different missiles onto the same target to increase the probability of kill. The equation for two-on-one cross targeting probability of kill (CTP_k) is:

$$CTP_k = 1 - (1 - P_{kl}t)^2$$

where $P_{kl} = SSP_k$ assuming that r (reliability) has now risen to 100 per cent. For the formula for SSP_k see SINGLE-SHOT PROBABILITY OF KILL. Cross-targeting does not involve more than two warheads because of the fear that the electromagnetic pulse generated by the first explosion would destroy any further incoming warheads.

typhoon-class submarines

The Typhoon-class submarine is the largest Soviet strategic nuclear submarine. The first was launched in 1980 and it is reported that a second is currently undergoing sea-trials. It is believed to carry some 20 ballistic missiles, each missile probably equipped with 12 warheads (total: 240). Approximately 170 m long, the Typhoon is 30 per cent bigger than the biggest US submarine. However, the USA's Ohio-class Trident submarines carry 24 Trident I C-4 missiles, each capable of carrying up to 14 MIRV'd re-entry vehicles (warheads) – total 336 warheads – and with the introduction of Trident II D5 missiles could carry up to 408. The Typhoon's missile range is in the region of 8,000 km, making it capable of hitting most targets in the United States from Soviet waters.

unilateralism The word is often misconstrued by the general public and distorted by its opponents. Many unilateralists would argue that the term be dropped altogether in favour of *independent* or *national* or *unconditional* measures for nuclear disarmament.

The international context

In many ways the unilateral position and the multilateral stance are meshed together. After all, no multilateralist approach can succeed if the will to take even limited steps to halt the arms race is not there.

Charles Osgood of Illinois University, in his seminal book *An Alternative to War or Surrender* (1962) devised a model called 'Graduated Reciprocation in Tension Reduction (GRIT)' which he counterposed to the arms race. The rules Osgood outlined are as follows:

1 Unilateral moves must not reduce one side's missiles to the point that it could not deliver an unacceptable second strike. Missile levels should be reduced on both sides to that of 'minimum deterrence' (see EQUIVALENT MEGATONNAGE); the retention or not of these final missiles would be discussed at bilateral talks.

2 The moves should not cripple the capacity for defence by conventional means.

3 Moves should be graduated in risk according to response. Reciprocation might take time but the first move should be substantial in order to achieve credibility.

4 Moves can be diverse in nature and location (eg cultural or economic, not just military).

5 Moves should be publicly announced before they take place and should be identified as tension-reducing measures.

6 Moves must be unambiguous and open to verification.

7 Moves should continue despite disagreements in other areas.

Britain

There is a wide variety of positions held by unilateralists in Britain, many of them overlapping. The list below refers to some of the differing goals pursued, as opposed to any tactical or limited demands which might be made in order to achieve them; obviously what might appear as a reasonable goal to one person might be viewed as a limited demand in pursuance of a more radical goal to another. It is not an exhaustive list but it highlights the major areas of concern as far as the unilateralists are concerned:

1 To rid a nuclear-weapons state of nuclear weapons and any foreign bases on its soil or in its territorial waters, whether or not this is reciprocated by a potential enemy.

2 To extricate Britain from NATO for as long as the latter is nuclear armed.

3 To remove Britain from NATO for as long as the latter retains a possible first-use policy on nuclear arms.

4 For Britain to stay in NATO, but to fight for it to adopt a no-first-

use policy as an initial step towards nuclear disarmament, and for Britain to leave the alliance if these objectives are not realized.

5   To argue for the dissolution of both NATO and the Warsaw Treaty Organization (WTO) as a way of ridding Europe of the blocs that divide it and to organize around the goal of a nuclear-free Europe 'from Portugal to Poland'.

6   To remove all US forces and command structures from Britain.

7   To remove all NATO forces and command structures from Britain.

8   To abandon all British nuclear weapons, but to stay in NATO and to retain certain US nuclear bases as a guarantee against possible Soviet nuclear blackmail and until US–USSR talks had achieved GND or at least removed nuclear weapons from Europe.

9   To persuade the British Government to adopt a policy of non-nuclear defence with non-aggressive but sophisticated conventional weapons.

10   To oppose all military procurements of whatever kind.

11   To ban the export of all arms.

12   To urge for the closure of nuclear power generating, reprocessing and enrichment plants.

13   To work for the closing down of some aspects of the nuclear power programme.

United Nations Special Session on Disarmament (UNSSD)

The first such session took place between 23 May and 1 July 1978 amid growing concern over rising nuclear stockpiles, new weapons technology and a worsening of the political climate between East and West. The final document was passed by consensus, but little was done by governments to carry out its proposals. The British Government was suitably laconic: 'The Declaration suffers from a lack of balance through insufficient emphasis on measures to limit conventional weapons and on the need to prevent the spread of nuclear weapons.'

The Declaration said, inter alia, 'The achievement of nuclear disarmament will require urgent negotiation of agreements at appropriate stages and with adequate measures of verification satisfactory to the States concerned for:

a   cessation of the qualitative improvement and development of nuclear-weapons systems;

b   cessation of the production of all types of nuclear weapons and their means of delivery, and the production of fissionable material for weapons purposes.'

All in all the first Special Session laid down the foundations for a viable international disarmament strategy. It fired the hopes of peace movements and millions of others throughout the world.

The second Special Session, however, was a dismal failure. It met at a time of great tension between the superpowers in July 1982 with several 'hot' wars in progress throughout the world. Moreover, it was poorly prepared – high hopes that the nuclear powers could be prevailed upon to change course during the sessions should have given way to concrete measures of a limited but definite kind, such as the cessation of all tests or the outlawing of chemical weapons. In the event neither the more grandiose nor the limited steps took place.

The Session did allow many heads of state to put forward their position, and although little that was new surfaced, the USSR took the opportunity to pledge a unilateral commitment not to be the first to use nuclear weapons (see FIRST USE).

The Stockholm International Peace Research Institute (SIPRI) summed up the mood thus: 'Insofar as the function of the Special Session was to provide some stimulus to arms control or disarmament negotiations, it must be counted a failure. The Special Session had some effect in bringing home to the public a recognition of the total inadequacy of the current attempts to move towards measures of arms control or disarmament in any of the forums in which these matters are now being discussed.'

uranium A radioactive chemical element – the heaviest naturally occurring element – of the actinide series. U-238 (92 protons and 146 neutrons) is its most common isotope, making up 99.27 per cent of mined uranium; U-235 (92 protons and 143 neutrons) makes up 0.72 per cent, and U-234 just 0.006 per cent of natural uranium. U-238 has a HALF-LIFE of 4,510,000,000 years and is used for dating the age of the earth by measuring the amount of lead in uranium-containing rocks – for lead is uranium's ultimate decay product.

In 1938 Otto Hahn and Fritz Strassmann discovered nuclear fission in uranium bombarded with slow neutrons. The following year Enrico Fermi postulated that neutrons might be amongst the fission products and could continue the fission in a chain reaction. Leo Szilard, Herbert Anderson and Jean-Fredéric Joliot-Curie confirmed this in 1939. The first self-sustaining chain reaction took place in Chicago in 1942 – and the rest is history (see ATOM BOMB, MANHATTAN PROJECT).

Fission occurs with slow neutrons in U-235, the only naturally occurring fissile material. For bomb production either U-238 must be enriched to produce sufficient quantities of U-235 for weapon-grade material, or U-238 is induced to absorb slow-moving neutrons in a nuclear reactor and allowed to decay into fissile plutonium-239.

Natural uranium, in the form of uranium-dioxide pellets, is used in Magnox and heavy-water reactors. Other reactors require enrichment of the U-238 to increase the percentage of U-235 present to whatever proportion is suitable for the process. Weapon-grade uranium requires enrichment to 70 per cent U-235, at the least.

One pound of uranium can yield as much energy as 1,340 tons of coal.

uranium supply controls The first controls on uranium supply were set up in wartime between Britain the USA and Canada, known as the Combined Development Trust. They agreed to buy up all stocks of uranium. The Acheson Lilienthal plan envisaged the internationalization of all uranium mines but this was scotched by the appointment of Baruch to present the plan to the UN: he would have none of it. Even before ATOMS FOR PEACE was launched there were fears about proliferation of the bomb. This led to the formation of the Western Suppliers Group in 1954 bringing together the USA, UK, Canada, South Africa, France, Belgium (because of the Congo, which before the war had been the world's largest supplier of uranium), Australia, where there were known deposits, and Portugal, because of its African empire.

During the 1950s there were extensive explorations to prevent a feared uranium shortfall. But in the following decade many mines were closed down in Canada, South Africa and Australia. The US had a huge stockpile and its missile programme was geared to smaller warheads, while the nuclear power programmes had not yet grown sufficiently to take up the slack in demand. By 1967 the US was selling natural uranium at $6 a pound and an embargo was placed on uranium imports to the US. By 1971 the price had fallen to $4.50 a pound – less than the cost of extracting the metal from the ground.

The US Atomic Energy Commission began selling off its stock of 50,000 tons, using a ploy only possible because of its monopoly on the enrichment process. This left France with huge reserves of uranium and a falling price at a time when the French were trying to build up capability right through the uranium fuel cycle. The French found allies in other countries with extensive interests in uranium mining and formed a defensive cartel designed in the first instance to minimize their losses rather than to expand their profits. The participants were France, Canada, South Africa and the Rio Tinto Zinc Company, which, with about one-fifth of the Western world's known reserves, was treated as a sovereign state. They estimated that demand until 1977 would run to 26,000 tons while production could be as much as 100,000.

In addition there were very rich deposits of uranium discovered in Australia and at Rabbit Lake in Canada. The latter, however, was owned by Gulf Oil. Both Gulf and Australia knew of the secret cartel and forced their way into it in May 1972, thus forming the Club of Five.

They set themselves a floor price of $6.25 a pound. Each of the five would in turn be given the chance to be the first bidder for any new contract; a 'runner-up' was designated and was required to put in a phoney bid for the contract above the floor price. It was agreed that higher prices would be quoted to any 'middlemen'. This was an oblique reference to Westinghouse which had made a practice of guaranteeing fixed-price supplies of uranium as a sweetener to encourage purchases of its nuclear reactors. Westinghouse was playing the futures market, and when, by October 1975, the price it had to pay for uranium had exceeded the $20 per pound for which it was selling the mineral, the corporation reneged on its contracts. The owners of the firm's reactors put in a suit for $2 billion damages. Westinghouse in turn sued the Club of Five for $6 billion in the most expensive law suit of all time.

However, the rivalry between the USA and other countries over the price of uranium, and between different corporations over the sale of reactors was put in the shade in 1974 by the explosion of the Indian nuclear device. Canada urged the reconvening of the old Western Suppliers Group, this time to exert controls on the supply of reactor technology as well as to monitor uranium sales – at the time the International Atomic Energy Agency which was dominated by a block of developing nations, had decided not to require Non-Proliferation Treaty safeguards on technology.

In autumn 1974 representatives met at the US embassy in London from the USA, USSR, Britain, France, Canada, Germany, and Japan. They drew up what became known as the 'trigger list' of sensitive technology which was to be restricted from export unless safeguarded. Another seven nations were asked to join, and the following year the London Club or the London Suppliers Club was given official existence.

Canada and the USA wanted far more rigorous controls than the other countries in the Club. Canada wanted no material, whether uranium or equipment, to be exported to a country which possessed any unsafeguarded equipment of any kind. Essentially this meant countries that had not signed the Non-Proliferation Treaty and included India, Israel and South Africa. The other countries could not agree to this but Canada and the USA observed it anyway.

The USA went further, seeking a ban on the export of all reprocessing and enrichment plants. At the time this affected a massive German sale to Brazil and large French sales to South Korea, Taiwan, Pakistan and Iraq. The Germans refused to pull out of their Brazilian contract but agreed not to make any further sales elsewhere. South Korea was prevailed upon to cancel its order; Taiwan dismantled its plant and Pakistan did not get its reprocessing facilities. The Israelis dealt with the Iraqi plant in less diplomatic fashion.

However, the INTERNATIONAL ATOMIC ENERGY AGENCY was not able to impose effective 'critical time' controls on the Germans or the Japanese; and President Carter's attempt to ban the production of reprocessing plants and fast-breeder reactors was strongly resisted not only by the French and British but also by the large US corporations. The idea was abandoned.

'use them or lose them' The phrase used to describe the situation now emerging as COUNTERFORCE targeting becomes ever more accurate, as the numbers of counterforce-capable weapons increases on both sides. At the moment the USA probably has a lead in technology and, with the introduction of Cruise, Pershing II, Trident II D-5 and MX Peacekeeper, in numbers as well. If, by the end of the 1980s the USA has a disarming first-strike capability, the Soviet Union could be faced with an agonising choice: either to launch a pre-emptive first strike against the USA to try to destroy as many missiles, bombers and submarines as possible and hope to survive the consequences in some shape or form (ie 'use them'), or to sit tight in the knowledge that should the USA decide to launch a first strike it could destroy the USSR's entire nuclear force rendering it utterly defenceless (ie 'lose them'). Even the threat of such an attack could only induce abject surrender – unless the USSR fired first.

'Use them or lose them' sums up in one graphic phrase the way that political thinking, aggressive Cold-War ideology, technical innovation and hard-nosed strategic doctrines have combined together to render obsolete the comparatively cosy certainties of mutual assured destruction which, in its 'balance of terror', probably did help to keep the peace for a short time.

vertical launch system (VLA)

A magazine-load system for the US Navy from which ASROC, ASW Standoff weapons, Harpoon and Tomahawk missiles can be launched. The system allows for a higher number of missiles to be fired than the present rail and box launchers. It also enables the missiles to be targeted against ships, aircraft and submarines simultaneously. There will be 61 missiles to each magazine and the system is being fitted to a wide range of vessels, including submarines.

Warsaw Treaty Organization (Warsaw Pact; WTO)

Formed on 14 May 1955, the signatories of the Treaty of Mutual Assistance included the USSR, Albania, Bulgaria, Czechoslovakia, the German Democratic Republic, Hungary, Poland and Romania. Albania left it in 1968. Members are committed to the collective defence of European territory. It combines with a system of bi-lateral treaties.

The WTO is headed by the Political Consultative Committee made up of party leaders, heads of government, and foreign and defence ministers, the chief of the Soviet armed forces and the chief of staff of the WTO Joint High Command (JHC). The Permanent Commission is in Moscow. A Council of Foreign Ministers advises on foreign policy matters, and a Council of Defence Ministers meets to supervise the JHC.

The JHC is headed by a Soviet marshal and all important posts are in Soviet hands. Each country assigns a senior general to the JHC and a senior Soviet general is in turn assigned to the defence HQs of each member state (except Romania). The JHC controls all Soviet forces in

Eastern Europe and Western USSR and forces of member countries are controlled by it in wartime.

There are three WTO Commands:

1 Soviet Forces Group, Germany (HQ at Zossen-Wünsdorf, near Berlin);

2 Northern Forces Group (HQ at Milovice, near Prague);

3 Southern Forces Group (HQ near Budapest).

Figures for WTO forces are difficult to come by and even more difficult to evaluate, but it is generally assumed that its troops are less well trained and equipped than their NATO adversaries. Furthermore, they include more non-battlefield personnel than are included in NATO head counts so that the numbers of troops on either side is more even than a cursory glance at the totals would lead one to suppose, especially if one were to count only the number of divisions on either side, for WTO divisions are smaller than those of NATO.

Soviet tanks, though nearly 2.5:1 greater in number than NATO's, are often old and even when new are often technologically inferior and less reliable than NATO's.

It is clear that a proportion of Soviet and other WTO forces in Europe are used less to confront NATO forces than to subdue the local population or at least to remind it of who is in charge. The WTO is an instrument of Soviet power within Eastern Europe. It enables the USSR to keep a very close watch on and supervise the training of the other armies within the Pact. An example of this training is that only Romania (which has no Soviet troops within its borders) has developed and trained its armed forces for mass guerrilla and operations along the lines of the Yugoslav partisans. The Polish and Czech armies have no such training.

It cannot be assumed that in a war all non-Soviet troops would be reliable. It is no accident that while the USSR possesses tactical nuclear weapons they are kept on Soviet territory.

Figures for 1978 for tactical aircraft reveal that (a) NATO had a preponderance of fighter/ground attack aircraft (2,028:1,725) (b) the WTO had a preponderance of interceptors – a massive one (3,025:655). Both sides would argue that their preponderance is in defensive weapons; NATO assumes a massive WTO tank attack which could be blunted by its ground-attack aircraft; the WTO assumes massive aerial attacks from NATO forces unwilling even to try to pierce its ground defences, and interceptors are the best hope of blunting that attack. Both are right; nevertheless, it has to be said that interceptors are purely defensive while ground-attack planes can go on the offensive.

The nuclear balance is dealt with elsewhere. With all these provisos, below is a comparison of selected NATO and WTO forces in Europe

Available within 3 days in Germany

Arms Category	NATO	Ratio	WTO
main battle tanks	7,000	1:2.5	17,500
artillery pieces	2,700	1:2.8	7,500
anti-tank guided weapons launchers	4,000	3.3:1	1,200
fixed wing combat aircraft	1,150	1:2.3	2,700
armed helicopters	400	2.6:1	150
military manpower	780,000	1:1.2	950,000
divisions	32	1:1.5	47

Available within 30 days in Germany

main battle tanks	10,000	1:3	30,000
artillery pieces	4,000	1:4.2	17,000
anti-tank guided weapons launchers	4,600	3.1:1	1,500
fixed wing combat aircraft	3,500	1:2	7,000
armed helicopters	800	1.3:1	600
military manpower	1,900,000	1:1.2	2,200,000
divisions	60	1:2	120

source: E Dinter and P Griffith, *Not Over by Christmas: NATO's Central Front on World War III,* Anthony Bird/Hippocrene, 1983, p. 44

Publicly expressed fears of a massive conventional attack from the East are usually discounted in private or in the serious media. This is not only because there seems no good reason for such an attack but also because it would most signally fail. Military theory usually assumes that a ratio of three-to-one is necessary for an attacker to achieve success *ceteris paribus*.

The nuclear weapons assigned to WTO forces by the USSR are:

a 137 Scud B/C short-range ballistic missiles;

b 198 FROG 3/5/7 short-range ballistic missiles.

In addition 115 Su-7 Fitter and 35 Su-20 Fitter strike aircraft are deployed with the Czech and Polish air forces (Source, *Military Balance 1983/84*)

'window of vulnerability' A phrase of the 1970s meant to describe the US fear that the Soviet ICBM force was large enough and accurate enough to destroy the entire US ICBM force, thus leaving the US with only the less strategically useful weapons deployed in submarines and on bombers. With only a soft target option, the US President would have to decide whether to commit these last-resort weapons in the knowledge that the USSR might still have sufficient weapons to answer in kind.

The entire 'window of vulnerability' idea rests on a WORST-CASE ANALYSIS that the USSR, unlike the USA, would use its ICBMs in a pre-emptive first strike knowing that its own cities and industrial centres could be devastated by a retaliatory strike. Nevertheless, the concept served a useful purpose for those advocating a return to vigorous nuclear build-ups after the 'quiet' years of the 1960s. It helped create a climate of opinion in the US which made it possible to fund the MX ICBM.

weapon-grade material Material of suitable purity, quantity and fissability to be employed in the construction of a nuclear weapon. In practice that means either uranium-238 enriched to contain high percentages of U-233 or U-235, or plutonium-239 which is produced by all nuclear reactors, especially fast breeders, and which can be extracted from waste material in reprocessing plants.

Western Suppliers Club

see URANIUM SUPPLY CONTROLS

worst-case analysis An enemy's capability is more or less known; his intentions can only be guessed at. Worst-case analysis assumes the very worst intentions of the enemy, estimates what he is capable of with his known nuclear strength and plans counter-strategy and investment programmes in new missiles, accordingly. Intentions are in effect collapsed into and become identical with capability.

Worst-case analysis applies to the enemy the same dictum that von Clausewitz applied to war in general in the celebrated passage from *On War* on 'friction': 'The military machine – the army and everything related to it – is basically very simple and therefore seems easy to manage .... In fact, it is different, and every fault and exaggeration of the theory is instantly exposed in war.' It is unfortunate that Clausewitz's exposition has been ignored except by those military men, such as Lord Mountbatten, who came or have come to see the futility of nuclear weapons.

Worst-case analysis of the enemy is an ideological exercise; it is radically different from 'knowing the enemy' which has been the touchstone for military success in the past.

Worst-case analysis ought to be applied to the grand strategic doctrines of flexible response, countervailing strategy and limited nuclear options. Lord Mountbatten fought in both world wars and summoned up all his eloquence to warn of the future: 'In warfare the unexpected is the rule and no one can anticipate what an opponent's reaction will be to the unexpected .... But that was all conventional war and, horrible as it was, we all felt we had a "fighting" chance of survival. In the event of a nuclear war there will be no chances, there will be no survivors – all will be obliterated .... I repeat in all sincerity as a military man I can see no use for any nuclear weapons which would not end in escalation, with consequences that no one can conceive.'

Worst-case analysis is especially dangerous when it reads into Soviet deployment practices and armed force (including nuclear) categories intentions derived from Western strategic manuals. For the Soviet Union has radically different strategic concepts from the West and the result can only lead to confusion – see STRATEGIC DOCTRINE (SOVIET). Undoubtedly the USSR leadership also practises worst-case analysis – far too high a price was paid for ignoring the ample warnings that Hitler would invade them, ever to be caught again. As

Yakov Lomko, Deputy Chairman of the Soviet Union of Journalists, said in 1982, 'There are no Soviet military bases around the United States, but there are 2,000 hostile bases around our country. That is why we have to play with black figures.'

yield The amount of nuclear explosive energy released and expressed as the equivalent of the energy produced by a given number of tons of TNT.

see KILOTON, MEGATON, THROW-WEIGHT, STOCKPILE, NUCLEAR

zero option The position first advanced by Chancellor Helmut Schmidt and later, on 25 November 1981 by President Reagan: the USA would cancel the proposed deployment of 464 GLCMs and 108 Pershing II missiles in Europe if the USSR would dismantle all 600 SS-4, SS-5 and SS-20 missiles already in position regardless of their location (ie including those missiles pointing East against China).

When Chancellor Schmidt put forward the proposal, US Secretary of State Haig called the idea preposterous. The US had every intention of deploying its missiles according to the 1979 NATO agenda. True the 'twin-track' NATO decision also called for simultaneous negotiations with the USSR. However, the USA insisted within NATO that each 'track' – military implementation and disarmament diplomacy – be handled by a separate NATO committee and that each be chaired by a Reagan official. As one US official commented, 'We have a deployment schedule which is not related to disarmament talks.'

In fact there was never any chance that the USSR could or would accept the zero option. If they had, they would, at the Eurostrategic level, have been left with just 30 (maximum) SS-N-5 SLBMs missiles (identified as targeted on Europe by SALT) which are old and inaccurate, to face 64 British Polaris A-3 missiles, 18 French SSBS S-3 missiles, 80 French MSBS M-20 missiles and 400 Poseidon C-3 missiles in submarines based at Holy Loch and under the command of SACEUR.

The zero option proposal was nevertheless a stunning propaganda coup. It is the very clearest example of the negotiating practice of isolating one component of weapon in order to show a disparity to one's own disadvantage. It quite overlooked the fact that the USSR is a European power while the USA is not. It left submarines and aircraft and tactical weapons on both sides out of account in trying to assess what the European balance was. Some might say that the option was bound to fail and that was its raison d'être. The way was thus open for the deployment of GLCMs and Pershing IIs in Europe, the first time US missiles had been stationed there since the withdrawal of Mace missiles 15 years earlier.

Abbreviations

AAM	air-to-air missile
AB	airburst
ABM	anti-ballistic missile
ACDA	Arms Control and Disarmament Agency
ACHDF	Air Command Home Defence Forces
ACM	Advanced Cruise missile
ADM	atomic demolition munition
AEA	Atomic Energy Authority
AEC	Atomic Energy Commission
AERE	Atomic Energy Research Establishment
AEW	airborne early warning
AFAP	artillery-fired atomic projectile
AfP	Atoms for Peace
AGM	air-to-ground missile
AGR	advanced gas-cooled reactor
ALBM	air-launched ballistic missile
ALCM	air-launched cruise missile
ASALM	advanced strategic air-launched missile
ASAT	anti-satellite
ASBM	air-to-surface ballistic missile
ASC	American Security Council
ASM	air-to-surface missile
ASROC	anti-submarine rocket
ASW	anti-submarine warfare
ATB	advanced technology bomber (Stealth)
AUR	all-up round
AWACS	airborne warning and control system
AWDREY	atomic weapons detection, recognition, and estimation of yield
AWRE	Atomic Weapons Research Establishment
BIT	built-in test
BMD	ballistic missile defence
BMEWS	ballistic missile early warning system
BWR	boiling water reactor
C^{3}I	command, control, communication and intelligence
CCD	Conference of the Committee on Disarmament
CD	Committee on Disarmament
CDS	command disable system
CEP	circular error probable

Abbreviations

CINCUSEUR	Commander in Chief, US Forces, Europe
CM	Cruise missile
CMP	counter military potential
CND	Campaign for Nuclear Disarmament
CPS	Coalition for Peace through Strength
CSCE	Conference on Security and Cooperation in Europe
CTB	comprehensive test ban
DDRE	Directorate of Defense Research and Engineering (US)
DGZ	desired ground zero
DMA	Defense Mapping Agency (US)
DP	deep basing
DSMAC	digital scene matching area correlation
ECM	electronic counter-measures
ELINT	electronic intelligence
EMt	equivalent megatonnage
EMP	electromagnetic pulse
END	European Nuclear Disarmament
ENDC	Eighteen Nation Disarmament Committee
ER-RB	enhanced radiation-reduced blast
ERW	enhanced radiation weapon
FBR	fast-breeder reactor
FBS	forward based systems
FOBS	fractional orbital bombardment system
FOST	Force Océanique Stratégique
FROD	functionally related observable differences
GAMA	GLCM alert and maintenance area
GAO	General Accounting Office (US Congress)
GB	ground burst
GCI	ground-controlled intercept
GLCM	ground-launched cruise missile
GZ	ground zero
HLG	High Level Group (NATO)
IAEA	International Atomic Energy Agency
ICBM	intercontinental ballistic missile
IISS	International Institute of Strategic Studies
INF	intermediate-range nuclear force
IOC	initial operational capability
IRBM	intermediate-range ballistic missile
ISMA	International Satellite Monitoring Agency

JANE	Journalists Against Nuclear Extermination
JCMPO	Joint Cruise Missile Project Office
kt	kiloton
LCC	launch control centre
LNO	limited nuclear options
LNW	limited nuclear war
LORAN	long-range navigation
LOW	launch-on-warning
LRTNF	long-range theatre nuclear force
LRTNW	long-range theatre nuclear weapons
LTA	launch-through attack
LWR	light water reactor
MAD	mutual assured destruction
MAPW	Medical Association for Prevention of War
MARV	manoeuvring re-entry vehicle
MBFR	mutual and balanced force reductions
MCANW	Medical Campaign Against Nuclear War
MIRV	multiple independently retargetable re-entry vehicle
MLF	multi-lateral force
MRASM	Medium-range air-to-surface missile
MRBM	medium-range ballistic missile
MRL	multiple rocket launchers
MRTNF	medium-range theatre nuclear force
MRV	multiple re-entry vehicle
Mt	megaton
M-X	missile experimental
NATO	North Atlantic Treaty Organization
NFZ	nuclear free zone
NND	non-nuclear defence
NOP	nuclear operations plans
NORAD	North American Aerospace Defense Command
NPG	Nuclear Planning Group (NATO)
NPT	Non-Proliferation Treaty
NVDA	non-violent direct action
OPANAL	Agency for the Prohibition of Nuclear Weapons in Latin America
PAL	permissive action link
PBV	post-boost vehicle
PGW	precision guided weapon
PLS	pre-launch survivability

Abbreviations

PNET	Peaceful Nuclear Explosions Treaty
PTBT	Partial Test Ban Treaty
PTP	probability to penetrate
QRA	quick reaction alert
RW	radiological weapon
RV	re-entry vehicle
SAC	Strategic Air Command (USAF)
SACEUR	Supreme Allied Command, Europe (NATO)
SALT	Strategic Arms Limitation Talks
SAM	surface-to-air missile
SANA	Scientists against Nuclear Arms
SCC	Standing Consultative Commission
SCG	Special Consultative Group (NATO)
SEO	selective employment options
SHAPE	Supreme Headquarters Allied Powers, Europe (NATO)
SICBM	small intercontinental ballistic missile
SIOP	single integrated operational plan
SIPRI	Stockholm International Peace Research Institute
SLBM	submarine-launched ballistic missile
SLCM	sea-launched cruise missile
SOSUS	sound surveillance system
SRAM	short-range attack missile
SRBM	short-range ballistic missile
SRDB	Scientific Research and Development Branch (of UK Home Office)
SSBN	nuclear-powered ballistic missile submarine
SSPK	single shot probability of kill
SSM	surface-to-surface missile
SSN	nuclear-powered attack submarine
START	Strategic Arms Reductions Talks
SUBROC	submarine rocket
TAC	Tactical Air Command
TEL	transporter-erector-launcher
TERCOM	terrain contour matching
TNF	theatre nuclear forces
TNW	theatre nuclear war
TTBT	Threshold Test Ban Treaty
UNA	United Nations Association
UNSSD	United Nations Special Session on Disarmament
USAF	United States Air Force

VLS	vertical launch system
WDC	World Disarmament Campaign
WTO	Warsaw Treaty Organization

Bibliography

Adams, R and Cullen, S (eds), *The Final Epidemic: Physicians and Scientists on Nuclear War*. University of Chicago Press, 1981

Aldridge, R C, *The Counterforce Syndrome: A Guide to US Nuclear Weapons and Strategic Doctrine*. Institute of Policy Studies, Washington, 1981

Aldridge, R C, *First Strike: The Pentagon's Strategy for Nuclear War*. Pluto Press, London, 1983

Arkin, W M, *Research Guide to Current Military and Strategic Affairs*. Institute for Policy Studies, Washington, 1981

Barnaby F and Thomas, G P (eds), *The Nuclear Arms Race: Control and Catastrophe*. Francis Pinter, London 1982

Baylis, J and Segal, G (eds), *Soviet Strategy*. Croom Helm, London, 1981

Campaign for Nuclear Disarmament, *Sanity* (monthly journal)

Campbell, C, *War Facts Now*. Fontana, London, 1982

Campbell, D, *War Plan UK*. Paladin, London, 1983

Chalmers, M, *The Cost of Britain's Defence*. Peace Studies Papers, No. 10, Bradford School of Peace Studies. Housmans, London, 1982

Chomsky, N, *Towards a New Cold War*. Sinclaire Browne, London, 1982

Clarke, M and Mowlam, M (eds), *Debate on Disarmament*. Routledge & Kegan Paul, London, 1982

Cochran, T B, Arkin, W M, and Hoenig, M, *US Nuclear Forces and Capabilities*, Vol. 1. Ballinger, Cambridge, Mass., 1984

Cox, J, *Overkill*. Penguin, Harmondsworth, 1981

Crabbe, D and McBride, R, *The World Energy Book*. Kogan Page, London, 1978

Crossley, G, *Civil Defence in Britain*. Peace Studies Papers, No. 7, Bradford School of Peace Studies. Housmans, London, 1982

Crossley, G, 'Unilateral Initiatives: A Route to Safer International Relations' (unnpublished paper). Bradford School of Peace Studies

Curtis, R and Hogan, E, *Nuclear Lessons*. Turnstone Press, Wellingborough, 1980

Dando, M and Rogers, P. *The Death of Deterrence*. CND Publications, London, 1984

European Nuclear Disarmament, *END* (bi-monthly journal)

Freedman, L, *The Evolution of Nuclear Strategy*. Macmillan, London, 1981

Garrison, J and Shivpuri, P, *The Russian Threat: Its Myths and Realities*. Gateway Books, London, 1983

Goodwin, P, *Nuclear War: The Facts*. Macmillan, London, 1982

Greene, O, *Europe's Folly: The Facts and Arguments about Cruise*. CND Publications, London, 1983

Halliday, F, *The Making of the Second Cold War*. Verso, London, 1983

Holloway, D, *The Soviet Union and the Arms Race*. Yale University Press, 1983

Independent Commission on Disarmament and Security Issues, *Common Security: A Programme for Disarmament*. Pan, London, 1982

International Institute for Strategic Studies (IISS), *The Military Balance, 1983–84*. IISS, London, 1983

Jungk, R, *The Nuclear State*. John Calder, London, 1979

Kaldor, M, *The Baroque Arsenal*. Andre Deutsch, London, 1982

Kaplan, F, *The Wizards of Armageddon*. Simon & Schuster, New York, 1983

Kelly, A, *Not by Numbers Alone*. Peace Studies Papers, No. 11, Bradford School of Peace Studies. Housmans, London, 1984

Lee, C, *The Final Decade*. Sphere, London, 1983

McMahon, J, *British Nuclear Weapons: For and Against*. Junction Books, London, 1981

Minnion, J and Bolsover, P (eds), *The CND Story*. Allison & Busby, London, 1983

Morgan, P M, *Deterrence: A Conceptual Analysis*. Sage, London, 1977

Myrdal, A, *The Game of Disarmament: How the US and Russia Run the Arms Race*. Manchester University Press, 1977

NATO, *The North Atlantic Treaty Organization: Facts and Figures*. NATO Information Service, Brussels, 1981

Neild, R, *How to Make Up Your Mind about the Bomb*. Andre Deutsch, London, 1981

Neuman, H J, *Nuclear Forces in Europe: A Handbook for the Debate*. International Institute for Strategic Studies, London, 1984

Openshaw, S, Steadman, P, and Greene, O, *Doomsday: Britain after Nuclear Attack*. Blackwell, Oxford, 1983

Pringle, P and Spigelman, J, *The Nuclear Barons*. Sphere, London, 1983

Pringle, P and Arkin, W. *SIOP: Nuclear War from the Inside*. Sphere, London, 1983

Prins, G (Ed.), *Defended to Death*. Penguin, Harmondsworth, 1983

Rogers, P, *Guide to Nuclear Weapons, 1983–84*. University of Bradford School of Peace Studies, 1984

Rogers, P, Dando, M and van den Dungen, P, *As Lambs to the Slaughter: The Facts about Nuclear War*. Arrow Books, London, 1981

Schear, J (ed.), *Nuclear Weapons Proliferation and Nuclear Risk*. Gower, London, 1983

Stephenson, M and Hearn, R, *The Nuclear Casebook*. Muller, London, 1983

Stockholm International Peace Research Institute (SIPRI), *The Arms Race and Arms Control, 1983*. Taylor & Francis, London, 1983

Stockholm International Peace Research Institute (SIPRI), *Theatre*

Bibliography

    Nuclear Weapons: European Perspectives. Taylor & Francis, London, 1978

Stockholm International Peace Research Institute (SIPRI), *Yearbook of World Armaments and Disarmament, 1983–84*. SIPRI, Stockholm, 1984

Thompson, E P and Smith, D (eds), *Protest and Survive*. Penguin, Harmondsworth, 1980

United Nations, *Nuclear Weapons Report of the UN Secretary-General*. Frances Pinter, London, 1981

Webber, P, Wilkinson, G and Rubin, B, *Crisis over Cruise*. Penguin, Harmondsworth, 1983

White, A, *Symbols of War: Pershing II and Cruise Missiles in Europe*. Merlin Press, London, 1983

Wilson, A, *The Disarmer's Handbook of Military Technology and Organization*. Penguin, Harmondsworth, 1983

Zuckerman, S, *Nuclear Illusion and Reality*. Collins, London, 1982